T0373758

The Political Economy of AIDS

Edited by Merrill Singer

Hispanic Health Council
Hartford, Connecticut

Critical Approaches in the Health Social Sciences Series
Series Editor: **Ray Elling**

Routledge
Taylor & Francis Group

LONDON AND NEW YORK

First published 1998 by Baywood Publishing Company

2 Park Square, Milton Park, Abingdon, Oxfordshire OX14 4RN
52 Vanderbilt Avenue, New York, NY 10017

Routledge is an imprint of the Taylor & Francis Group, an informa business

Copyright © 1998 Taylor & Francis

Library of Congress Catalog Number: 97-6399

Library of Congress Cataloging-in-Publication Data

The political economy of AIDS / edited by Merrill Singer.
     p. cm. - - (Critical approaches in the health social sciences series)
   Includes bibliographical references and index.
   ISBN 0-89503-177-9 (cloth)
   1. AIDS (Disease)- -Economic aspects. 2. AIDS (Disease)- -Political aspects. I. Singer, Merrill. II. Series.
RA644.A25P64   1998
362.1'969792- -DC21   97-6399
                                                CIP

ISBN 13: 978-0-89503-177-8 (hbk)
ISBN 13: 978-0-415-78398-9 (pbk)

DEDICATION

For Jacob and Elyse in hope that the world they grow up in
conquers AIDS and the social inequalities
that promote such epidemics.

Contents

Preface

At the 1989 annual meeting of the American Anthropological Association held in Washington, D.C., I organized and chaired a symposium entitled "The Politics of AIDS" with the intention of drawing greater attention to social structural factors that have contributed to the development and character of the AIDS epidemic. Some of the papers from that session were published together in 1994 in the journal *Social Science and Medicine*. In 1993, Stephen Koester and Robert Carlson organized a session entitled "The Political Economy of HIV Risk" at the annual meeting of the Society for Applied Anthropology in San Antonio, Texas, in which I served as a discussant. The idea for this volume grew out of the latter session. Bringing together the research of a number of leading health social scientists, this volume emphasizes the social nature of disease, including AIDS. While generally there is lip service paid to the fact that all diseases have a social dimension (e.g., as the name implies, sexually transmitted diseases do not spread in the absence of human sexual relations), focused analysis on the exact ways in which social inequality, discrimination, exploitation, poverty, the denial of dignity, structurally imposed limited life options, and similar expressions of oppressive social relationships produce AIDS risk, limit access to AIDS health and social services, or similarly contribute to the spread of the epidemic and its impact on human lives is much less common. For the most part, well into the second decade of the pandemic, little has been done to address the structural causes of AIDS. Individual-level (one-on-one or small group) AIDS prevention education and counseling, by contrast, has consumed the bulk of AIDS prevention funding. The chapters in this volume attempt to overcome the limitations in existing AIDS research, prevention, and discourse by focusing their analytic attention on the roles of political economy in diverse settings and populations in spreading AIDS or blocking access to resources among people who are already infected. The goal is nothing less than achieving a paradigm shift in our understanding of AIDS. Conceiving of AIDS as a disease of oppression and social inequality leads to fundamentally different approaches to prevention and service delivery than those that currently are in place.

Merrill Singer

SECTION I

Understanding Epidemics in Political Economic Context

CHAPTER 1

Forging a Political Economy of AIDS

Merrill Singer

EPIDEMICS IN SOCIAL CONTEXT

Epidemics, and the social ways in which people respond to them, provide a window on the nature of human societies. Briggs' description of nineteenth-century cholera as "a disease of society in the most profound sense" applies as well to many other epidemics, including the contemporary global AIDS pandemic [1, p. 77]. One of the "lessons of history" from past epidemics like cholera or the Black Death of the fourteenth century is the frequent pattern of "victimizing and stigmatizing of helpless members of minority groups and the indifference of public officials callous to human suffering" [3, p. 2]. With specific reference to the cholera epidemic, Briggs notes:

> Whenever cholera threatened European countries, it quickened social appre-
> hensions. Wherever it appeared, it tested the efficiency and resilience of local
> administrative structures. It exposed relentlessly political, social, and moral
> shortcomings. It prompted rumors, suspicions, and, at times, violent social
> conflicts [1, p. 77].

Similarly, the Black Death, the name given to the devastating epidemic of the bubonic plague that killed as much as one-third of the total population of Europe between the years 1346-1350, led to the persecution of Jewish people who were blamed for spreading the disease by their Christian neighbors. This chilling episode in European disease history began in 1340 in the town of Chillon on Lake Geneva. Hard hit by the rat-borne pestilence, officials there brought criminal charges against a group of Jewish citizens accusing them of poisoning local wells.

3

Tortured into false confessions, the Jews were found guilty and punished. Similar actions became commonplace throughout the region. In Balse, for example, a law was passed binding city officials

> to burn the Jews, and to forbid persons of that community from entering their city, for the space of two hundred years. Upon this, all the Jews of Balse, whose number could not have been inconsiderable, were enclosed in a wooden building, constructed for the purpose, and burnt together with it, upon the mere outcry of the people, without sentence or trial, which indeed would have availed them nothing [4, p. 41].

Elsewhere in Germany, the Brotherhood of Flagellants (also known as the Brethren of the Cross), a militant religious sect brought into being by the social disruptions caused by the plague, violently attacked Jewish communities and drove people from their homes. Ironically, although the Flagellants came into existence with the purpose of expressing repentance for their own sins and extracting similar confession from others as a means of winning God's forgiveness and averting the plague's deadly toll, their processions from town to town "undoubtedly promoted the spreading of the plague" [4, p. 40].

These descriptions affirm the realization that the character of epidemics are shaped as much by social as they are biological factors [5]. The AIDS epidemic is no different. Writing of AIDS in Africa, for example, Stein notes:

> HIV infection spreads along trade routes and in the path of wars and their concomitant geographic and social dislocations. Tourism also spreads the infection. Migration of men and women in the labor force, because it divides families, makes a large contribution to the spread of HIV in many regions of Africa [6, p. 5].

As this account suggests, among the range of social factors that shape the direction, extent, and character of an epidemic, *the structure of social relations that grow out of the system of economic production* may have particular importance. This realization draws our attention to the role of political economy in understanding epidemics, including AIDS.

POLITICAL ECONOMY AND
THE SOCIAL SCIENCE OF HEALTH

Despite the frequency with which the term political economy is used in the social sciences these days, it is not certain that a clear understanding of the term exists. In part, this confusion may be rooted in the fact that the most common meanings attached to the term have changed over time. Eric Wolf, in his seminal political economic study entitled *Europe and the People Without History,* examined the nature this sociolinguistic change and its underlying causes. As Wolf emphasizes, the field of political economy predates and was parent to contemporary social sciences like sociology, anthropology, economics, and political science [7, pp. 7-8]. Until the middle of the nineteenth century, political economy referred to study of " 'the wealth of nations,' the production and distribution of wealth within and between political entities and the classes composing them." But events at mid-century led the global field of political economy to fragment and "inquiry into the nature and varieties of humankind split into separate (and unequal) specialties and disciplines" [7, p. 7].

The key events in question, namely the rise to dominance of the capitalist mode of production and of a set of opposed social classes brought into existence by it, disrupted the unity not only of social inquiry but the cohesiveness of society as well. By mid-century, the specter of revolution hung in the air and eventually found expression in the armed clashes of a looming class war. In the midst of mounting turmoil, the question of the nature of social solidarity and social order were raised as burning issues of scholarly research. The field of sociology branched off from political economy with the expressed mission of delving into the structure of social relations and social institutions. The new disciple came to define its problem as understanding the character of the bonds and associated cohesion-generating beliefs and customs that tie individuals together to form families, small groups, institutions, and societies. Quickly the early sociologists came to view ties among individuals and the development of community as the casual engine driving the functioning and unity of society. In this way, the issues of concern to political economy, including how ties among individuals are shaped by the relations among classes in the production of national and international wealth, were submerged.

While sociology focused its attention on the grand industrial societies brought into existence by the rise of capitalism, anthropology, its sister discipline, developed as the study of the small scale, non-Western societies situated in the interstitial spaces between and within industrial centers. Under the methodological banner of direct observation in natural settings, anthropologists came to concentrate their investigative lens on the subtle details and unique social and cultural configurations of individual cases, while ignoring the sweeping processes and broader social relations that transcend micro-populations historically tying them to each other and to developments in capitalist production.

A similar narrowing of focus and jettisoning of a macro-perspective gave birth to the fields of economics and political science. These disciplines were formed by defining economics and politics as separate narrow domains of social action and value expression. Economics became the study of the role of demand in the creation of markets, independent of the actual social contexts in which production occurs, markets arise, or demand is generated, while political science became a study of government decision-making, policy formation, and political culture, with little consideration of either the exercise of power for self-interested objectives or the interrelationship of politics and economics. In political science, concern with understanding class conflict gave way to a pluralistic view of society characterized by a "multiplicity of cross-cutting conflicts and alliances" in which antagonisms "are well contained within the fabric of the institutional order" [8, p. 32]. In sum, Wolf argues, all of the contemporary social sciences, each of which now has developed its own approach to (and subdiscipline concerned with) health issues, "owe their existence to a common rebellion against political economy, their parent discipline" [7, p. 19].

As this account reveals, the academic social science disciplines are better understood as the "reified products of sociopolitical processes" [9, p. 28] rather than, as they are sometimes presented, natural outgrowths of normal intellectual interest in distinct arenas of human social life. With disciplinary fragmentation, the topics of concern to political economy and their implications for health and well-being were marginalized as issues of little interest to any of the emergent academic disciplines. For example, in reviewing the approaches taken by the health social sciences in analyzing the determinants of illness beliefs within a community, Elling notes that:

> Much of the work on this question . . . has reflected the cultural concerns of anthropologists—the cross-cultural study of health and illness conceptions and behaviors. Recently, those who worked from this perspective have begun to realize that social structural forces—the very establishment of modern facilities, or the support by the government of one traditional medical group or another—bring about changes in health orientations and behaviors. But these changing perspectives often remain at a microcosmic level—the structural changes going on in the immediate area of a village one is studying and the concomitant changes in health and illness beliefs, values, attitudes, and behaviors. Or [as in much medical sociology], if a broader perspective is adopted, including national political forces, these may be treated as relatively free-standing or capricious aspects of some leader or party, without clear recognition of the intertwining of political and economic forces often extending into and stemming from an extranational world capitalist political economy [10, pp. 1-2].

Similarly, within the Weberian tradition, much of the work conducted in medical sociology has taken an interactionist approach and "concentrated on the immediate social relationships between individuals and groups in the medical context," while paying "relatively little attention to the political and economic structure of the medical care systems, or to its relationship with the wider society" [11, p. 15].

THE ORIGIN AND SURVIVAL OF
THE POLITICAL ECONOMY OF HEALTH

Despite the general turn away from unified macro-analysis in the social sciences, the desire to forge a global understanding of the impact on health of the intertwinement of the production of wealth and the exercise of power in a world of antagonistic social classes never completely disappeared. Indisputably, the key figure in sustaining a general commitment to addressing these issues was Karl Marx, and it is for this reason that today political economy is seen as a progressive perspective while during the last century its adherents ranged across the political spectrum. No doubt Marx's attention to social classes and their conflicted interests in specific historic content, indeed his elevation of class conflict as the key concept of social analysis and the key force in historical process, contributed in no small way to the urgency with which the nascent social sciences abandoned the concerns of political economy and developed their own socially acceptable arenas of narrow specialization, including confined approaches to questions of health and illness. Beyond Marx, modern political economy has been significantly influenced by the work of a variety of theorists, including Antonio Gramsci on the nature of hegemony, E. P. Thompson on culture as a material product, Immanuel Wallerstein on the evolution and structure of the capitalist world system, and Andre Gunner Frank on dependency relations in underdeveloped countries. All of these workers were themselves deeply influenced by Marx and sought to extend ideas inherent in his analyses.

Specific concern within the development of a political economic approach to health issues can be traced, on the one hand, to Marx's closest colleague, Frederick Engels, and to the latter's study of the deplorable state of the working class of Manchester and, on the other, to Rudolf Virchow's examination (which was influenced by Engels' work) of structural factors in a typhus epidemic in East Prussia, both of which occurred in the 1840s. Engels' seminal study, published under the title, *The Condition of the Working Class in England,* examined the etiology of illness and early death in the working class in terms of an oppressive structure of class relations produced by industrial capitalism and its accompanying social and physical environments. Work on this volume was presaged by a smaller study Engels completed at the age of nineteen of the textile factory area of the lower Rhineland where he was born. Entitled "Letters from the Wuppertal," the earlier study was published in 1839 in the newspaper *Telegraph für Deutschland.* In this work, Engels described the life of factory workers and the difficult conditions under which they were compelled to live and work by rich factory owners. Engels linked these deplorable conditions to the poor state of health of factory workers, including rampant tuberculosis and venereal disease as well as to the ill effects of great quantities of cheap alcohol being imported into the Rhineland from Prussia. Three years after completing this study, Engels left Germany for Manchester at his father's behest. At the time, England was in a recession and Engels' found "everywhere crowds of unemployed still standing at street corners, and many factories . . . still standing idle" [Engels, quoted in 12, p. 91]. During the twenty-one months he lived in Manchester, ostensibly overseeing his father's interest in a local factory, Engels undertook his groundbreaking study of health and social conditions. While rarely given the recognition it deserves as a seminal work, this study constitutes one of the earliest ethnographies in the health social sciences. In a section of *The Condition of the Working Class in England* that is addressed to the "Working-classes of Great Britain," Engels described his research methods in terms that would be familiar to contemporary medical anthropologists:

> ... I have studied the various official and non-official documents as far as I was able to get hold of them—[but] I have not been satisfied with this, I wanted more than a mere *abstract* knowledge of my subject, I wanted to see you in your own homes, to observe you in your every-day life, to chat with you on your condition and grievances, to witness your struggles against the social and political power of your oppressors [13, p. 323].

Mary Burns, an illiterate Irish factory worker, served as Engels' key informant (and lover) and she willing led him through the back allies and hidden social recesses of the working class sections of her town. Through her expert entree, Engels came to know Manchester on intimate terms.

These experiences allowed Engels to write a graphic account of the emiseration of the working poor, complete with full descriptions of the close association between particular conditions and specific health problems. Thus, he noted that overcrowding, poor ventilation, and open fires depleted the air of oxygen and led to chronic lung afflictions like tuberculosis, as well as "mental and physical lassitude and low vitality" [13, p. 127]. Stagnant sewers and polluted water contributed to continual epidemics of typhus and other diseases. Readily available alcohol and opiates such as laudanum contributed to a range of health and social problems among adults while respiratory diseases, poor quality food, and dangerous living conditions insured a high mortality rate among young children. Overall, Engels directly linked the poor health of the working class of Manchester to social relations of production and to their position in a class structured and oppressive society.

> ... when society places hundreds of proletarians in such a position that they inevitably meet a too early and an unnatural death, one which is quite as much a death by violence as that by the sword or the bullet; when it deprives thousands of the necessaries of life, places them under conditions in which they *cannot* live—forces them, through the strong arm of the law, to remain in such conditions until that death ensues which is the inevitable conse-quence ... its deed is murder just as surely as the deed of the single individual [13, p. 126].

This unambiguously political economic explanation of the etiology of disease had a direct impact on Virchow, the founder of cell biology. Early in his career, as a clinical pathologist at Charité Hospital, Virchow became interested in the underlying social causes of epidemics. When a typhus outbreak swept through the Upper Silesia region, a deeply impoverished section of East Prussia with a primarily Polish-speaking minority population, Virchow convinced his hospital supervisors to support an epidemiological study that could make recommenda-tions to avert future epidemics. Arriving in Upper Silesia, Virchow found that thousands were dying, not just of disease but also from the effects of an ongoing famine.

In his subsequent writings, Virchow emphasized political economic factors in accounting for the ultimate causes of the epidemic, including unemployment, the failure of the government to provide food during a famine, the poor state of housing, and the intense overcrowding in the region. He wrote, "It is rather certain that hunger and typhus are not produced apart from each other but that the latter has spread so extensively only through hunger" [quoted in 14, p. 84]. Virchow also discussed the iatrogenic aspects of the epidemic, commenting in several letters to his father about the failures of physicians for not taking care of the poor because of a "love of money" and reluctance "to put bills aside," as well as noting the damaging effects of the linguistic differences between Prussian doctors and their Polish-speaking patients [quoted in 14, p. 84]. He called for the creation of a public health service to respond to medical emergencies, as well as for improved employment opportunities, better housing, the creation of agricultural cooperatives, a more progressive system of taxation, linguistic training for physicians, and autonomy in local decision making. Virchow looked to medicine to provide only a limited number of solutions, believing that social prevention, especially improving the material conditions of people's lives, was the best approach. He argued that, "The improvement of medicine would eventually prolong human life, but improvement of social conditions could achieve this result even more rapidly and successfully" [14, p. 88]. Later Virchow founded a popular medical journal, *Die Medizinische Reform (Medical Reform)*, in which he printed his famous dictum: "Medicine is a social science, and politics is nothing more than medicine in larger scale" [quoted in 15, p. 31].

Through the work of Engels and Virchow, the foundation was set for the development of a political economy of health. This approach, however, did not receive a generally positive response from the managers of the emergent health care system of the nineteenth century. Instead the dominant approach to health, an orientation that was supported by the wealthiest social classes, came to view social conditions

> as natural phenomena, governed by natural, biological, and harmonious laws. Disease was explained as caused by an agent—the bacteria—always present in the diseased body. Within that theoretical construct, causality was defined as an association of the observable phenomena, with the subject for investigation being the micro-agent under the microscope. In focusing on the micro level, the macro social conditions were conveniently put aside [16, p. 527].

This approach not only came to dominate biomedicine, but through the influence of biomedicine, had a profound effect on the various social sciences of health as they emerged from their respective disciplines over time.

The ideas of Engels and Virchow, however, were kept alive by a number of individuals who recognized the limitations of the biomedical model. A particularly important figure in this regard was Henry Sigerst, whose work had an important influence on the development of social medicine and public health. A critic of what Stark has aptly called biomedicine's "undersocialized . . . views of disease" [17, p. 432], Sigerist migrated to the United States from Europe and brought with him the ideas of Marx, Engels, and Virchow. These found a responsive audience among health workers who daily saw the health consequences of social inequality as well as the immediate effects of a highly stratified health care system.

As Baer suggests, the political economy of health "is a subject which has been dropped and rediscovered several times since the mid-19th century" [18, p. 2]. The period after the 1930s began one of the several periods of lapsed attention to which Baer refers. This was an era during which biomedicine had fully "turned away from a broader social understanding of health and disease" [19, p. 13] as part of a conservative response to the exploration of the social origins of disease initiated by Engels and Virchow. Notes Brown:

> It became clear to increasing numbers of physicians that the complete profes-
> sionalization of medicine could come only when they developed an ideology
> and a practice that was consistent with the ideas and interests of social and
> politically dominant groups in society. . . . The medical profession discovered
> an ideology that was compatible with the world view of, and politically and
> economically useful to, the capitalist class and the emerging managerial and
> professional stratum [20, p. 71].

The social sciences followed suit and did not return to a significant focus on the political economy of health until the 1970s.

In 1971, Sander Kelman published a political economic analysis of U.S. medicine from its origin as a cottage industry of independent practitioners to its development as a complex corporate and state system [21]. Kelman's study helped to open the door to what has become a growing number of analyses of health-related issues from the political-economic perspective. Especially at first these new studies were conducted by medical sociologists but by the 1980s a critical medical anthropology had emerged as well [19, 22]. Also of considerable significance during this period was the work of a set of radical health activists, such as those associated with the Health Policy Advisory Center and the Medical Committee for Human Rights.

Several individuals have come to make particularly notable contributions to political economy of health studies in recent years, especially Vicente Navarro, Howard Waitzkin, Ray Elling, and Lesley Doyal. Central among these is Vicente Navarro, a physician and international political activist with considerable train- ing in the social sciences whose work "has played an instrumental role in the development of the political economy of health" [22, p. 130]. Navarro's contribu- tions include analyses of the political economy of health and health care both in the underdeveloped and the developed world, critiques of alternative theoretical approaches that fall short of a thorough going political-economic approach, and evaluations of various health policies in terms of the relations among opposed social classes. Also he has produced extensive case studies of health care in Great Britain, Sweden, Chile, and, prior to its collapse, the Soviet Union. In addition, he serves as editor of the *International Journal of Health Services,* a primary source for political economy of health analyses. Howard Waitzkin, who is also a physician, as well as a medical sociologist, has been both an important political economy of health researcher and community health activist. He has written extensively on the impact of capitalism on health and health care and on the micropolitics of doctor-patient relations. His careful analyses of medical encounters have shown that

> Patients experience [social problems like economic insecurity] ... as personal trouble that they express, directly or in passing, during conversations with doctors. The structure of medical discourse tends to marginalize such troubles. . . . Management of contextual difficulties takes place in several ways: through subtle ideologic messages that reinforce adherence to mainstream expectation, through the absence of criticism of context or exploration of collective action, through professional surveillance that enhances social control, and through therapeutic actions that provide personal gratification, reifying contextual conditions and encouraging consent [23, p. 259].

Ray Elling, a health sociologist, has focused on transnational comparison of alternative health systems using a case study approach, the impact of workers' movements on health, and the generation of illness within the context of capitalist production. Elling also has played an important role in bridging disciplinary lines and forging working relations with critical health social scientists from other fields. Leslie Doyal authored one of the first book-length analyses of health care from a political-economic perspective. Her study of the British medicine and the National Health Service in the context of British capitalism in the volume *The Political Economy of Health* had a significant impact on the field. In this volume, she demonstrated that

> health politics and medical care systems in capitalist countries ... represent the outcome at any particular moment of the struggle between ... conflicting forces. They are not the rational policies of a benevolent state ensuring healthy lives and scientific medicine for all its people, but nor are they the manipulative policies of an all-seeing state controlling every aspect of the daily lives of its members [11, p. 45].

This commitment to careful exploration of the nature and—at any point in time— impact of class conflict on health and health care has helped to set the agenda for research and understanding in the political economy of health. Other important contributors to the development of this perspective include Ruth and Victor Sidel, Ronald Frankenberg, Sally Guttmacher, Richard Brown, John McKinlay, Soheir Morsy, Peter Kong-ming New, Hans Baer, as well as several of the contributors to this volume.

Given the dominant perspectives within the social sciences, individuals who have attempted to promote political economy often have been marginalized within their respective disciplines. As Navarro argues, even the terms of political-economic discourse have been tainted.

> Concepts and terms such as class struggle, capitalism, and imperialism are frequently considered to be rhetorical and dismissed by the dominant functionalist and positivist schools. They are usually written between quotation marks, as if to alert the reader that they are subject to suspicion. Marxists contributing to social science journals are very frequently encouraged to rewrite their articles using more "understandable" and "less value-laden terms" more attune to prevalent sociological thought [24, pp. 7-8].

Despite discrimination, a strong tradition of political economy of health has survived and the literature associated with this perspective has grown considerably during the 1980s and 1990s. Adherents see this approach as offering a much needed "corrective for the disciplinary fragmentation of social science that obscures the relationship among economic systems, political power, and ideologies" [9, p. 27].

DOMINANT APPROACHES TO THE AIDS EPIDEMIC

In light of the political-economic critique of the narrowness of conventional social science of health approaches, it is important to consider the dominant understandings of AIDS and the approaches to stopping the epidemic that have emerged since the beginning of the pandemic. In the Western world, standard prevention efforts have been targeted to a set of constructed epidemiological categories linked to particular routes of known HIV transmission, most notably homosexual/bisexual sexual men, injection drug users, and sex partners of injection drug users. Often these constructed categories have been treated as if they label naturally occurring social groups that share cohesive patterns of behavior, common sociocultural identities, and unified attitudes and values. Variation within these broad exposure categories has not been a primary concern of prevention efforts. However, actual studies of individuals grouped into each of the major epidemiological categories has revealed considerable variation [25]. For example, a comparison of injection drug users in Miami, Florida, and Hartford, Connecticut, found substantial regional differences in sociodemographic characteristics, drug use patterns, and needle-related HIV risk patterns [26]. This study, conducted before Connecticut changed its needle possession and prescription laws in 1992 and a needle exchange program was implemented in Hartford in 1993, found that Hartford injection drug users (IDUs) were more likely to report lending and borrowing needles than Miami IDUs. This pattern existed for both males and females. While about 52 percent of Miami IDU respondents reported never borrowing needles, this figure was only 44 percent in Hartford, and Hartford IDUs also were more likely to borrow needles more than half the time that they injected drugs than their counterparts in Miami. IDUs in Miami were found to be much more likely to report that they obtain their needles legally, obtain new needles before "shooting up," and use needles only once than were the Hartford IDUs. Limited access to new needles in Hartford at the time appears to have contributed to a greater tendency to borrow needles. Other studies have found that even among IDUs of the same self-reported ethnicity, substantial variation exists across geographic areas [27]. Similarly, in their study of a random sample of persons with diagnosed AIDS in New Jersey, Glick Schiller et al. found a wide range of sociodemographic characteristics, cultural norms, and behavior patterns that cut across transmission group categories [28].

> Those with a history of drug use had been poorer pre-AIDS than gay men, but there was significant internal variation within each of the 'risk groups.' Prior to diagnosis, 32% of the intravenous drug users fell into the lowest income category, earning less than $10,000, while only 15% of gay men earned less than $10,000. Thirty-three percent of the gay men and the same proportion of intravenous drug users were in the middle income group of $10,000-$20,000. Half of the gay men (52%) and a little more than one-third of the intravenous drug users (35%) had incomes from $30,000 to $50,000 prior to diagnosis [28, p. 1342].

Cross group variation of similar extent also was found in education, occupation, employment history, residential stability, homelessness, family involvement, and relationship status. What was not found was a group of injection drug users with a homogeneous subculture or lifestyle. Cultural boundaries did not neatly separate gays and IDUs into two distinct groups, nor is it likely that such boundaries exist between the people living with AIDS in the New Jersey study and their neighbors who are not infected (except to the degree that it is created by social ostracism).

Moreover, the exposure categories that guide contemporary AIDS prevention often are not culturally meaningful to targeted populations. Being in a sexual relationship with an IDU, for example, does not create a common identity nor does it produce shared behavioral traits. Some such people are wives or husbands, others are lovers, others are passing acquaintances or customers. However, creation of the epidemiological category "sexual partner of an IDU" allows the perception to continue that only certain people, people who are marginal to mainstream society, are at risk for AIDS. At the same time, it provides a rationale for treating people with AIDS as dangers to rather than part of society. As Glick Schiller et al. observe,

> Not only have spousal matings often been removed from a 'family' context and thus defamiliarized, but there have been virtually no descriptions of the relations between members of these risk groups and their families of origin. Mothers, fathers, sisters, brothers, grandmothers, aunts, uncles, cousins and children have seldom appeared in the literature unless the topic is children

who have contracted AIDS at birth from their mother. To place individuals outside the bound of the family is to place them outside the human family, to dehumanize them, to turn actor into object [28, p. 1341].

Additionally, AIDS prevention has been dominated by a set of psychological models of human motivation and behavioral change, including the Theory of Reasoned Action, the Health Belief Model, Self-Efficacy Theory, and the Stages of Change Model [29]. These approaches have tended to focus attention at the individual level, treating the targets of intervention as if they were independent beings and not members of families, peer groups, communities, and the broader society. Prevention emphasis has been placed on cognitive and motivational variables including how individuals interpret behavioral information, how they value that information, how capable they feel about using the information, and how prepared and committed they are to personal change, rather than on social and structural influences on individual behavior. As Auerbach, Wypijewska, and Brodie indicate in their review of the dominant psychological models:

> By the mid-1980s, most models of behavioral performance [utilized in AIDS work] included an amalgam of variables from health beliefs models and social cognitive learning theory. This amalgamated theory tends to assume that individuals who formulate an intention to behave in a particular way and have the skills and self-efficacy beliefs to do so are likely to carry out the intended behavior [30, p. 84].

This overemphasis on "rational factors and cognitive process that shape the isolated individual's decision-making . . . have obscured the social and relational factors involved in behavior . . ." [30, p. 88].

The literature on injection drug users is especially noteworthy in this regard [31]. One consequence of the failure to understand this population in social context has been the false insight that needle "sharing" is a ritual act of social bonding among a group of individuals who otherwise would be cut off from supportive community involvement. In this social psychologistic understanding, injection drug users are seen as treating needle sharing as a symbolic act of group intensification (much like breaking bread together in a religious community) that helps to forge and maintain otherwise unobtainable supportive social ties. This act has been depicted as being of special importance to injection drug users because they are believed to inhabit a dangerous and atomistic netherworld largely devoid of trust or true caring. Ethnographic research, however, has determined that the transfer of "dirty" needles from one drug injector to another, which is known to be a major route of HIV transmission, is in fact a socially undesired necessity caused by structurally imposed needle scarcity [32], a condition produced by the societal creation and enforcement of needle prescription and drug paraphernalia laws [33]. While injection drug users generally do not like to "share" needles (except, perhaps, between individuals like partners, relatives, or close friends, with whom they otherwise maintain a close, multi-stranded personal relationship), lack of access to new needles forces them to buy, rent, or borrow used (and potentially infected) needles. Participation in this behavior persists despite awareness of HIV risk because of a lack of alternatives for many drug addicted individuals (including the alternative of ceasing drug use because of the numerous structural, sociocultural, and practical barriers encountered when they attempt to enter into drug treatment) [34]. The bleaching of used needles, which has been aggressively promoted as a strategy for eliminating the virus from infected surfaces, has been found to be far less than a foolproof prevention method [35]. In addition, because of the cost of drugs and the inability of many drug injectors to raise sufficient money to cover the cost of their addiction, pooling of resources to make a drug buy is common practice. Joint ownership of purchased drugs leads to multiple opportunities for the transmission of HIV through the "indirect" sharing of drug paraphernalia (e.g., dipping needles into a common drug cooker, stirring drugs in the cooker with the plunger from one of the participant's needles, or squirting drugs from one needle to another). These risky behaviors are not best understood in terms of isolated individual motives, but in terms of group coping strategies developed to contend with the impress of broader social forces that structure the context of drug injection, including laws outlawing drug use and needle access, police pressure and surveillance, lack of societal commitment to adequate drug treatment, the limited set of life course options for the poor, and the ready availability of illicit mood altering drugs in a society in which

> Physicians and the pharmacological industry have combined to hold out the promise of putting an end to personal distress through chemistry. Drug manufacturers seeking new markets and bigger profits urge everyone to feel better fast ("relief is only a swallow away"), and attempt to persuade physicians and the public that *unpleasant human feelings are abnormal*—an "illness" that should be corrected with drugs [36, p. 118, emphasis in original].

These circumstances suggest the need for breaking through the "prison" of reigning epidemiological risk exposure categories and individual level prevention models by focusing "on the way in which 'risky' social behavior is shaped by external social and economic context" [28, p. 1340]. Developing approaches for this breakthrough to a political economy of AIDS is the primary goal of this volume.

AIDS AS A GLOBAL PANDEMIC

This goal gains importance with each passing day as the devastating toll of the global AIDS pandemic continues to mount. Although exact figures are impossible to develop, the World Health Organization (WHO) estimated that by the end of 1994 more than fifteen million adults and children worldwide had been infected with the Human Immunodeficiency Virus and about one-fifth, three million, had developed full-blown AIDS. Of those diagnosed with AIDS, 90 percent have died. WHO projects that the number of people with HIV infection will jump to thirty-eight million while the number of AIDS cases will climb to twelve million by the end of the century. Unprotected sexual intercourse remains the primary route of infection, accounting for three-quarters of all cases. Although the disease was first discovered among gay men in 1981, heterosexual transmission continues to be the predominant mode worldwide, with women constituting five out of every eleven new adult cases. Approximately one million infants have been infected through mother-to-child transmission [37, 38]. Mann et al. note that globally there are three primary features of the continuing pandemic.

> 1) No country or community within a country has halted spread of the virus once infections have begun locally; consequently the major impacts of the pandemic are yet to come. 2) HIV is spreading—sometimes at a very rapid pace—to new communities or subgroups that were previously untouched by the pandemic; HIV has demonstrated its ability to cross all borders be they social, cultural, linguistic, geographic, economic, or political. 3) The global pandemic is a composite of a complex of local epidemics; the spread of HIV may be different from one locale to another depending on the profile of risk behaviors, social conditions, and social networks locally, and the virus is spread at different rates (sometimes dramatically so) among the various subgroups in most local settings [38].

The largest number of cases (over 50%) are still in sub-Saharan Africa, where it is believed that more than one million people have been infected. While during the early years of the pandemic most African cases were located in the central and eastern sections of the continent, an area that came to be known as the "AIDS epidemic belt," HIV is now spreading rapidly to the south, north, and west. While there are some heavily infected rural areas (e.g., Rakai district, Uganda; Kagera district, Tanzania), infection is comparatively higher in the cities than in the countryside. It is estimated that one in every fifty Africans is infected and that one million new infections occurs every year throughout the continent [39]. In Nigeria, for example, sexually transmitted disease (STD) patients had HIV prevalence rates of 22 percent by 1992, while 6 percent of pregnant women were infected. Nigeria is estimated now to have over half a million HIV-infected people. In Botswana, a study of antenatal clinics in Francistown found that 34 percent of pregnant women tested positive for HIV. In Abidjan, Cote d'Ivoire as high as 10 to 15 percent of the adult population had HIV-1 (the major viral type worldwide), HIV-2 (a type of HIV found primarily in West Africa), or both by 1990 [37]. In the south, in Lesotho, Romero-Daza reports rapid increases in the number of reported cases especially in the capital city where about one-fifth of the population is concentrated [40]. Testing of young adults, fifteen to twenty-five years of age, in KwaZulu/Natal, South Africa found no HIV infection in 1985 but by 1992 the infection rate was 2.5 percent [41]. In the north, there have been significant increases in the number of blood donors who test positive in Khartoum, while infection rates of 40 percent have been reported among prostitutes in southern Sudan [37]. All of these studies suggest a continued spread of HIV in Africa, especially in areas and to subgroups that were less affected by the first wave of the pandemic.

Outside of Africa, the pandemic has intensified most dramatically in Asia, an area that during the early years was seen as a very low infection region [37, 38]. In Thailand, in 1990 there were over 50,000 people with HIV disease. Two years later, this number had climbed to 450,000, almost a tenfold increase. Among STD clinic patients infection rates rose from 8.8 to 13.2 percent in the northern part of the country and from 4.4 to 7.1 percent in the central area between 1990 and 1991. Among injection drug users rates of infection have stabilized at 35 percent. India also has experienced an explosion in HIV infection. In Bombay, HIV prevalence among STD patients leaped from 4.3 percent in 1989-90 to 32.1 percent in 1991. Similar (and in some studies, even larger) increases were found among women sex workers. During the same period, the rate of infection among injection drug users in the state of Manipur increased from 0 to 54 percent. In Madras, in the south of India, between 1988 and 1990 infection among pregnant women rose from 0 to 1.3 percent. Among drug injectors in Ho Chi Minh City, rates of infection rose from 2.4 to 34.8 percent between 1992 and 1994 [42]. Other areas of Asia in which HIV has spread rapidly include Myanmar, Nepal, and Cambodia. Some AIDS workers believe there will be more HIV cases in Asia than in Africa by the end of the century.

In Latin America and the Caribbean Islands, especially the latter, HIV disease has been spreading rapidly in recent years. Some of the highest per capita AIDS rates in the world are found in the Caribbean [43]. In Haiti and Martinique rates of infection above 40 percent have been recorded among commercial sex workers. In Latin America, rates are especially high in Brazil, where WHO estimates there are a million people with HIV disease. In Mexico, Argentina, and Brazil, levels of HIV infection in homosexual men range between 20 to 35 percent. Among injection drug users in Brazil, rates have been found as high as 40 percent in Rio de Janeiro, 54 percent in São Paulo, and 57 percent in Santos [38].

In Western Europe and the United States, where the pandemic was first iden-tified among homosexual men, there has been a marked drop in HIV incidence in this population [44]. Prevalence rates among men who have sex with men in the United States range between 15 to 60 percent by location, with a median of about 39 percent. Drug users, both injectors and non-injection crack cocaine users, are the primary source of new infection, with rates varying by region from under 5 percent to over 50 percent. Rates of infection generally are higher in urban areas than rural areas (although, as evidenced by the Bellglade, Florida case, there are exceptions). Ethnicity is an important predictor of infection. Overall, whites have accounted for a decreasing proportion of reported AIDS cases, dropping from 60 percent in 1985, to 48 percent in 1992, to 45 percent in 1993 [45]. By contrast, African Americans, who comprise approximately 12 percent of the total U.S. population, accounted for 26 percent of AIDS cases by February 1989 [46]. By September 1990, this percentage had increased to 28 percent [47]. By the end of 1993, the percentage had risen again to 36 percent [48]. Once infected, African-American patients progress more quickly to full-blown AIDS and their survival time after diagnosis is shorter than for white persons with AIDS [49, 50].

These patterns also are found in other communities of color in the United States. From 1992 to 1993, there was a 111 percent increase in the incidence of AIDS (in part because of the Centers for Disease Control and Prevention's adoption of an expanded case definition to include all HIV-infected persons who have either a low CD4+ lymphocyte count or have been diagnosed with pulmonary tuber-culosis, invasive cervical cancer, or recurrent pneumonia). While the rate of increase in the white (non-Hispanic) population was 102 percent during this period, among people of color, increases were as follows: Hispanics 114 percent, African Americans (non-Hispanic) 123 percent, Asian/Pacific Islanders 123 per-cent, and American Indians/Alaska Natives 181 percent [48]. AIDS is now one of the leading causes of death for persons of color between the ages of twenty-five and forty-four years [51].

In a study of births in New York City, antibodies to HIV were found in .39 percent of white newborns compared to 2.17 percent of African American and 1.7 percent of Hispanic babies [52]. Anonymous umbilical cord HIV testing of 98 percent of all women who gave birth in 1989 in one inner-city hospital in New York City found that 3.3 percent were seropositive, with rates higher among African-American women (4.5%) than others (1.5%). The majority of the infected women (79%) denied injection drug use and appear to have been infected through heterosexual contact, an increasingly important transmission mode in the indus-trialized world [45].

France, Italy, and Spain have the largest number of AIDS cases in Western Europe, with over 60 percent of all European cases by 1992. Seroprevalence studies among pregnancy women have found infection rates of .41 percent in Paris and a similar rate in London. The gender ratio (men to women) among HIV-positive adults is 5:1 in Western Europe, significantly lower than in the United States (where the rate is 10:1, although in the Northeast it is closer to the Western European pattern).

A variety of factors, including cultural practices (e.g., sexual patterns, drug use behavior), social factors (e.g., character of the transportation and cargo transport system), epidemiological factors (e.g., timing of viral introduction, demographic structure, population mobility), and biological factors (e.g., viral strain, pre-infection health of the population, efficiency of various transmission modes) contribute to the profile of the pandemic and its constituent local epidemics. In addition, as the following three examples indicate, political economic facts play a significant role as well. Writing of Southern Africa, Baldo and Cabral argue:

The most important historical structural processes concerning HIV in Southern Africa are the LIW [Low Intensity Wars] and the disruption of the economy, particularly the rural economy. Various population groups are forced into continuous movements, including displacement flight from the war affected areas, regular armies and groups of bandits, rural populations moving to towns (joining the poverty and marginality circle including prostitution and street children) and rural populations moving near army barracks for trading [53, p. 40].

In this instance, the now-failed effort by South Africa to maintain its apartheid system of labor and social control and its geopolitical regional dominance by promoting low intensity wars of destabilization against its neighboring countries produced social conditions that contributed significantly to the opportunities for human infection. Ironically, at the same time, the South African "right wing . . . seized on the threat of an epidemic in the black community to focus its racial prejudices and fears into a call for renewed segregation, accompanied by a belief in some quarters that the epidemic might solve the country's political and demographic problems [by decimating the African population of the country]" [54, pp. 122-123]. Other, yet related, political-economic factors also have been identified. With reference to Zaire, Schoepf comments:

Disease epidemics generally erupt in times of crisis, and AIDS is no exception. Zaire, like most other sub-Saharan nations and much of the Third World, is in the throes of economic turmoil. Propelled by declining terms of trade and burdensome debt service, the contradictions of distorted neocolonial economies with rapid class formation have created what appears to be a permanent, deepening crisis. . . . In Zaire, as elsewhere in the region, economic crisis and the structure of employment inherited from the colonial period shape the current configuration, contributing to the feminization of poverty and consequently to the spread of AIDS (e.g., through prostitution or multiple partner sexual relationships associated with smuggling networks developed to contend with the worsening economic conditions) [55, p. 267].

Finally, in the United States, where it has been widely publicized among drug users that injecting drugs in a shooting gallery is especially risky for HIV transmission (because it is the site where drug injection equipment, including syringes, drug cookers, needle rinse water, and cotton drug filters, get passed around and re-used by various people), has not eliminated shooting gallery use in many locales. While generally recognizing that HIV risk is involved, drug injectors also are aware that shooting galleries confer definite benefits. These include: access to syringes, access to water, protection from police surveillance, help in case of a drug overdose, access to drugs, and access to people with whom the cost of a drug purchase can be shared. Shooting gallery use (and the HIV risk it generates), in other words, has evolved as a kind of coping behavior adopted in response to the efforts of society to punish drug users and to make it difficult for them to gain access to drugs and drug paraphernalia. As Grove emphasizes, Western society has adopted "a paradigm of condemnation as its primary way of understanding illicit drug use . . ." [56, p. 1]. Shooting gallery use, in short, is best understood as a social response to adversity as it is structured within society. Historically, however, federal and state drug laws were adopted less because of the negative health effects of drug use, or because of the rising rate of drug addiction in the United States, than because of international geopolitics (e.g., the desire to counter British profit-making on drug sales in China) and internal racism (i.e., fears about rebelliousness among subordinated ethnic minorities under the influence of drugs) [57, 58]. Moreover, Waterson, following Herbert Gans' classic analysis of the social functions of poverty, argues more broadly that street drug addicts, while widely condemned, nonetheless perform useful functions for capitalist society, including serving as a source of cheap, easily expendable labor and, more importantly, as scapegoats blamable for various ills of society (e.g., crime) [59]. In this capacity, drug users inadvertently help to deflect popular attention away from the underlying structural sources of social problems thereby helping to protect those who most benefit from society as constituted.

As these examples show, while the human immunodeficiency virus has a biological existence independent of social factors, its role and importance as a source of morbidity and mortality among humans cannot be understood in isolation from political economy.

TOWARD A POLITICAL ECONOMY OF AIDS

The effort to develop a political-economic understanding of AIDS is still in its early stages [60]. Already, however, a number of key insights have been achieved, and some alternative perspectives have emerged. Political-economic analysis in the Third World has focused attention on AIDS as a disease of development and underdevelopment [61] and on the intersection between global political economy, on the one hand, and on local culture and action, on the other [62]. With reference to Brazil, for example, Parker presents the following analysis of AIDS as a disease of development and underdevelopment:

> The political economy of debt and dependence has produced a series of severe economic crises, resulting in a deeply rooted and apparently long-term recession by the late 1980s and early 1990s. Perhaps most important, twenty years of authoritarian military rule between 1964 and 1984, followed by a gradual return to democratic government in the mid-to-late 1980s, have largely undermined the legitimacy of many political institutions. Together, these developments have resulted in the extensive deterioration of both the public health and social welfare systems, limiting Brazilian society's capacity to address its many already existing health problems. . . . It is within this context that the HIV/AIDS epidemic began to take shape in Brazil in the early 1980s, and the ways in which this epidemic has developed, as well as the ways in which

Brazilian society has responded to it over the course of its first decade, have
been affected by this particular set of circumstances [63, p. 32].

Brook Schoepf has presented similar analysis of the spread of AIDS in Zaire [64].
In addition, she has argued that there is a need to understand "how the macro-level
political economy affects sociocultural dynamics at the micro-level—including
the spread of disease and the social response to epidemics" [65, p. 280]. Moreover,
she maintains, it is critical to study the "countercurrents of resistance to dominant
ideologies and structures. . . . Using a methodological framework linking political
economy and culture, studies of response to the AIDS pandemic can illustrate
interrelationships between social structures and human agency" [65, 280].
Schoepf and others also have called attention to the importance of gender identity,
gender relations, and gender inequality as important factors in the spread of AIDS
globally [66, 67].

In the developed world, political-economic analysis of AIDS has examined the
epidemic in terms of unequal class, gender, sexual orientation, and ethnic/racial
social relationships. In addition to social inequality and the role of culture, key
concepts have included power, hegemony, and the political economy of risk.
Quam, for example, has analyzed the impact of widening class disparities of
wealth produced by the "Reagan revolution" on the rapid spread of AIDS among
the urban poor, especially people of color [68]. Several studies have shown that
AIDS spreads most easily along several "vectors of disadvantage" [69] disproportionately striking those already bearing heavy burdens of unemployment,
racial discrimination, neighborhood decay, inadequate housing and homelessness,
street violence, poor sanitation, hunger and malnutrition, inadequate medical care,
policy-maker indifference or outright hostility, and "high levels of stress caused
by all of these adverse conditions" [68, p. 150]. Indeed, oppressed minority
populations do not face AIDS as a single epidemic, but rather as part of a
"synergism of plagues" [70]. AIDS in these communities is not an isolated threat,
but is an integral part of a far broader "syndemic" of intertwined diseases and
noxious social conditions [50]. Similarly, analysis of the role of political economy
in drug use among the poor [59, 71], the creation of urban gay sexual identity
and gay-centered communities following the Second World War, and the subsequent spread of AIDS in these communities [72, 73], as well as of the
ways "women's subordination influences their risk status and experience of
HIV/AIDS" [74, p. 45; 65; 67] have been central themes in the development of a
political economy of AIDS in developed nations. These studies have begun to
show that high rates of infection among gay men, African Americans, and Latinos
(including, disproportionately, gay African Americans and Latinos), and women
(especially those who are African American and Latina) reflect the fact that
people "have been rendered vulnerable to AIDS through *social processes* [like]
economic, political, and cultural forces that . . . shape the dynamics of AIDS
transmission" [66, p. 23].

Finally, central to the work that already has been done in the development of a political economy of AIDS is a strong emphasis on practice. The objective of most political-economic research has not merely been to understand the spread of AIDS and people's responses to it, rather, the full agenda of this approach includes a driving concern with the development of useful knowledge and a commitment to collaboration with people living with AIDS and at high vulnerability to AIDS in the development of effective and sensitive programs of prevention, support, and advocacy [75, 76].

Interestingly, one of the most significant challenges to the political-economic approach to AIDS has come from an adherent of the perspective. While acknowledging the contribution of studies like those cited above and those included in this collection, Robert Carlson [77] questions some of the basic assumptions (e.g., conflict theory, praxis theory) of the political economy of AIDS perspective. Labeling most such work "political economy as context," he asserts that "[b]laming the political-economic context or, by implication, powerful institutions and classes, entails the assumption that the means of significantly reducing—or perhaps eliminating—HIV transmission are within the capacity of the system *as it is currently constituted*" [77, pp. 266-267, emphasis in original]. More broadly, Carlson seeks to debunk the alleged political-economic notion that there are distinct groups with and without power in society, a phenomenon, following Gregory Bateson's systems theory approach, that he refers to as "the myth of power." He also critiques the existence within the political-economic perspective of a supposed determinist philosophy that assumes that the outcomes of intervention can be predicted and controlled, as well as the presumption that political action ultimately is a productive approach for achieving meaningful and lasting social change. Instead Carlson argues that it is time to move beyond political-economic strategies to those that emphasize complementarity among social groups rather than confrontation.

As the studies in this volume suggest, it is not evident that Carlson's assertions accurately fit the field he is critiquing. Much of his argument falters because of his failure to directly address the political-economic concepts, derived from Gramsci, of hegemony and counterhegemony. As Glick Schiller notes, these terms give "us the language with which to investigate the manner in which dominant classes or sectors of society use culture to obtain consent from subordinated populations. . . . Hegemonic processes are the means by which subordinated populations participate in cultural constructions that contribute to their continuing subordination" [31, p. 248]. In other words, dominant ideas in society tend to reflect the political and economic interests of the dominant groups, and these ideas are repeated in various ways (e.g., in songs, sayings, jokes, speeches, prayers, advertisements, texts, medical proscriptions) throughout the key institutions of society (e.g., schools, churches, hospitals, the media) and are embraced and defended across social strata. A critical characteristic of these ideas is their redundancy. As Wolf notes, "The development of an overall hegemonic pattern or 'design for living' is not so much the victory of a collective cognitive logic or aesthetic impulse as the development of redundancy—the continuous repetition, in diverse instrumental domains, of the same basic propositions regarding the nature of constructed reality" [7, p. 388]. In American society, an emphasis on individualization and individual responsibility are exemplary of such hegemonic propositions, examples that have real and important implications for the way people have viewed and responded to AIDS. In this sense, there is a clear recognition already within political economy that those with greater and lesser control over the institutions and formal and informal mechanisms of power and social decision-making are part and parcel of a common system. But systems need not exist in complementarity, rather, and this is especially true of social systems, until significantly challenged from within or without they generally exist in a state of balanced contestation and opposition across social strata. Thus, as the political economy of AIDS literature argues, "the politics of AIDS—from the beginning— have not been one-sided. The AIDS text is multivocal, and includes not only the voice of authority but also the [counterhegemonic] voice of resistance" [60, p. 1323]. In other words, as confirmed by several of the chapters in this volume, the simplistic understanding of power that Carlson ascribes to the political economy of AIDS literature is a straw man, easily knocked down because it has no actual substance. Political economy, to use Wolf's term, views any existing "design for living" as the changing product of an ongoing compromise between socially opposed and continuously contending forces (e.g., classes, genders, ethnic groups, sexual orientation groups) rather than the imposition of the powerful upon the powerless or a mystical achievement of human complementarity across social groups.

This said, Carlson's argument that in the capitalist world system "people . . . participate in high-risk relationships or practices to fulfill specific goals and to create reality in relationship to values and needs that are in part stimulated through capitalist marketing of the symbol" [77, p. 274] is an important reminder of a common theme in the political economy of health literature, namely the importance of examining unforeseen negative health consequences of hegemonic processes [e.g., 78]. Carlson illustrates this point with reference to crack cocaine use in the United States, a behavior that has played a significant role in the sexual transmission of HIV among the inner-city poor. He notes that "it is often in contexts where individuals face a great disjunction between media-reinforced expectations for success and the ability to participate in such expectations through the purchase and consumption of commodities that HIV infection occurs" [77, p. 271]. In the case of crack, its primary appeal, he argues, lies in the cultural association of the drug with power and success. Possessing and using crack, and distributing it to others in exchange for money, sexual favors, or other commodities and services, allows those denied access to accomplishment and mastery in mainstream society the opportunity to realize hegemonic capitalist values through alternative means. As Liebow noted, "on the streetcorner, public fictions support a system of values which, together with the value system of society at large, make for a world of ambivalence, contradiction and paradox, where failures are rationalized into phantom successes and weaknesses magically transformed into strengths" [79, p. 214]. The contradictions of capitalism, however, are not only those of commodity distribution or symbolic mediation but also of labor. Based on intensive ethnographic work in the East Harlem sector of New York City, Bourgeois notes that young people turn to selling crack after failing to fulfill "their early childhood dreams of finding stable, well-paid legal work" [74, p. 114]. He notes,

> Highly motivated, ambitious inner-city youths have been attracted to the rapidly expanding, multibillion-dollar drug economy during the 1980s and 1990s precisely because they believe in Horatio Alger's version of the American Dream [74, p. 326].

The drug trade, in fact, is one of the few equal opportunity avenues of employment for these youth that pays more than minimum wage.

The remainder of Carlson's critique, including his apparent disdain for confrontational social action, appears to reflect a broader postmodern, postVietnam academic attitude [80]. This sentiment was expressed early in the development of postmodernism by Lyotard, who asserted that radical efforts to change a social system usually are ill conceived because the social system thereby produced will only "end up resembling the system it was meant to replace" [81, p. 66]. However, in the communities hardest hit by AIDS, the scholarly formulation of erudite and obscure pronouncements about the futility of struggle are recognized for what they are: expressions of ruling class hegemony. As Quam observes, the residents of poor communities commonly "have a better grasp on the big picture than do many researchers . . ." [68, p. 150]. Following Gorz [82], by contrast, the political economy of health literature differentiates three alternative approaches to change:

- "system-correcting praxis"—labels the conscious implementation of minor material improvements in the lives of subordinate groups that avoid any alteration of the basic structure of social relations in a society. The "Say No to Drugs" campaign, which discourages drug use but does not address the social conditions that lead to the use of mood altering substances, is an example of this type of social change;
- "system-challenging praxis"—refers to changes that reveal and challenge the social inequalities of society. Much of the advocacy work done around gaining rapid access to AIDS medicines, to clinical trials, and to both information about AIDS and the social construction of AIDS discourse are examples of system-challenging praxis.
- "structural transformation"—refers to significant, enduring changes in the structure of relationships in society, in the distribution of power, and in control over productive and reproductive means [83].

As this formulation suggests, meaningful and significant social change is possible even short of total systemic transformation. The Civil Rights Movement, for example, or the AIDS Movement, have produced far reaching improvements in the lives poor people and those in need of health and social services. These gains were achieved through direct challenge and confrontation, as well as through the creation of relationships among diverse social elements, and they reveal, contrary to Carlson's assertions, that the means of significantly reducing much suffering and ill health are within the capacity of the system. They also reveal that it is only an accurate assignment of blame (i.e., cause) and associated confrontational social action that push inherently conservative social systems to change.

Each in their own way, the chapters that comprise this book address the issues discussed above. The authors of these chapters include some of the leading figures in the social science of AIDS research. The book is divided into four sections. The two chapters in Section I, including this chapter, are concerned with locating the AIDS pandemic in political-economic and sociocultural context. In the chapter that follows this Introduction, Shirley Lindenbaum, of the City University of New York, draws on her well-known research on the kuru epidemic in Papua New Guinea and existing studies of the bubonic plague in India at the turn of the century to clarify the social dimensions of the AIDS epidemic and of epidemics generally. Her goal is to push contemporary AIDS discourse toward a better understanding of the political and economic conditions that give rise to epidemics and their social interpretation. The fragmented and conflicted views of AIDS to be found in diverse corners of our society, she argues, reflect the class divided and socially fragmented character of the society that produced them.

Section II contains three chapters that examine the intersection of race, class, and ethnicity in the U.S. inner-city AIDS crisis. These themes are of particular importance because of the notably high rates of AIDS among inner-city populations, especially Latinos and African-Americans. Chapter 3, authored by the editor of this volume, employs a case study approach in which the focus is on the life of a single individual with HIV/AIDS, in this instance a Puerto Rican man living in Hartford, Connecticut. Like many other members of oppressed ethnic minority communities, this individual became infected with AIDS through injection drug use. The objective of the chapter is to simultaneously put a human face on the grim statistics that mark the toll of AIDS on communities of color and to show how even the life experience of a single PLWA (person living with AIDS) is shaped by political economy. Biography and political economy, in short, are not fundamentally opposed levels of analysis or understanding. Rather, they are tied together like the enlarged and shrunken images found at either end of a telescope.

The next chapter focuses on African-American women. The author, E. J. Sobo, is a member of the anthropology department at the University of Durham in Durham, England. Based on her field research in Cleveland, Sobo addresses a fundamental question: why do people engage in AIDS risk behavior? In the case of her study population, she argues that several social values (e.g., about the nature of a good relationship) that have their origin in industrial capitalism are of such fundamental importance to people's image of themselves that they can lead to denial of the actual character of interpersonal relations and the risks they can create in a sexually transmitted epidemic.

Sam Friedman, the lead author of Chapter 5, is an internationally known AIDS and drug abuse researcher. Along with colleagues from the National Development and Research Institutes, Inc. (NDRI) in New York City, Friedman explores that issue of double discrimination, namely: if ethnic subordination leads to higher levels of HIV infection, what happens to people who are subject to multiple forms of subordination? The target population for the research reported by Friedman et al. is Black Latino drug injectors (primarily Puerto Ricans) living in New York City. Multiple subordination, they conclude, is a particularly risky status that warrants concentrated social action.

Section III moves from the topics of risk and primary prevention to the political economy of accessing health care and social support. Chapter 7, which also is authored by researchers from NDRI, addresses the problem of injection drug user access to drug abuse treatment and HIV testing. This discussion is especially timely because of the fundamental transformation now going on in the U.S. health care system around managed care and health care coverage. The authors, lead by Russell Rockwell, argue that access to HIV-related services is shaped by ethnic inequalities and homelessness, both of which, in turn, are strongly influenced by structural shifts in the U.S. political economy.

Following a related theme, the second chapter in this section, authored by Anthony Lemelle and Charlene Harrington, questions the moral climate of care giving for people with AIDS in the United States. Responsibility for AIDS in the United States, as Senator Thurman has done publicly on numerous occasions, often is placed on the infected individual. This strategic laying of blame shields the wider society and the social inequalities it maintains from view and from ultimate responsibility for creating social conditions that foster the epidemic. The goal of this chapter is to examine the role of federal government policy and insurance industry maneuvering within a capitalist political economy in producing discrimination against people infected with HIV.

The final section of the volume moves beyond the boundaries of AIDS in the United States to look at AIDS in two other areas of the world, Africa and Southeast Asia, that, like North America, have extremely high rates of HIV infection and AIDS. Chapter 8 by Meredeth Turshen examines AIDS in Africa from a political ecological perspective. The chapter reviews the spread of AIDS in the 1980s and 1990s in light of the changing political economy of Africa, especially with reference to the financial difficulties of health care in Africa and the role of the World Bank in promoting health care privatization. As Turshen shows, the program of the World Bank to resolve the debt crisis in Africa failed to examine the actual distribution of health care services and the impact privatization of medical care would have on public health care for the poor. The end result, she argues, has been a needless worsening of the AIDS epidemic.

Chapter 9 also focuses on Africa, indeed, on a part of Africa, the south, where the human immunodeficiency virus presently is raging out of control. The special focus of this chapter by Nancy Romero-Daza and David Himmelgreen is the country of Lesotho, a national entity that is completely surrounded by and has been historically dominated by South Africa. The authors examine the interface between political economy, in particular dependency-based labor migration from Lesotho to South Africa, and a set of cultural practices and social adjustments to the South African labor migration system that creates a risky situation for rapid HIV transmission among Lesotho's impoverished population.

Patricia Symond's chapter examines HIV/AIDS among the Hmong of Northern Thailand. This chapter, which harkens back to the analysis of minority discrimination and AIDS by Friedman and co-workers in Chapter 5, argues that as an oppressed minority the Hmong are at special risk for infection. Like other authors in this volume, Symond emphasizes the important interaction between political-economic forces and local cultural practices in the spread of HIV. She provides a careful cultural presentation of traditional and changing Hmong beliefs and practices while not remaining stuck at the cultural level of explanation.

In sum, the analyses presented in this book provide concrete illustrations of the fundamental importance of understanding AIDS in terms of relevant political-economic factors in particular social settings. It must be stressed, however, that none of the chapters adopts a simple or narrow political-economic determinist framework to account for the spread of AIDS or related issues. Rather, all of the authors are keenly sensitive to the complex interplay between culture and power, that is to say, between socially meaningful (and perhaps traditional) beliefs and practices and the impress of dominant institutions and social groups. In part, attention to cultural patterns is a natural reflex for the contributors to this volume, in that the information they report generally is the product of on-the-ground fieldwork with their target population. In addition, however, all of the contributors recognize the intricacies of human behavior and the role of culturally constituted expectations, values, roles, and relationships in guiding behavior. As a result, the analyses presented in this book represent models for the emergent micro-macro approach that is strongly needed in social science of health research.

Stepping back from the individual chapters that make up this volume, it is evident that the AIDS epidemic, with its jarring mix of painful and inspiring personal stories of human suffering and resistive will, combined with a deadening and persistent cascade of faceless statistics, provides a significant challenge to public health systems, to community health workers, and to the health social sciences. It is the contention of this volume that we will fail this challenge badly if our attention remains focused on individual motivations and behaviors and ignores the wider political economy of AIDS. While individual behaviors and the biographies they produce are of considerable importance, as are the cultural frames that shape and give meanings to those behaviors and lives as they are enacted in local contexts, both the acts of individuals and content of cultural systems are generated in relation to political-economic constraints and opportunities. Powerful political-economic forces, from the apartheid policies of the old South Africa to the lending program of the World Bank, from ethnic discrimination to gender oppression, and from homophobia to neocolonialism, cause AIDS risk in certain populations, as well as produce the level and quality of help available once an AIDS diagnosis is made (if it ever is made). *Political economy, in short, constitutes not just the context but also part of the content of human social life.* Consequently, there can be no accurate analysis of AIDS in the absence of a consideration of the role of political economy. This, in brief, is the argument of this book.

REFERENCES

1. A. Briggs, Cholera and Society in the Nineteenth Century, *Past and Present: Journal of Historical Studies, 19*, pp. 76-96, 1961.
2. V. Berridge, AIDS: History and Contemporary History, in *The Time of AIDS*, G. Herdt and S. Lindenbaum (eds.), Sage, Newbury Park, pp. 41-64, 1992.
3. E. Fee and D. Fox, *AIDS: The Making of a Chronic Disease*, University of California Press, Berkeley, 1992.
4. J. Hecker, *The Epidemics of the Middle Ages*, The Sydenham Society, London, 1844.
5. R. Frankenberg, Medical Anthropology and Development: A Theoretical Perspective, *Social Science and Medicine, 14B*, pp. 197-207, 1980.
6. Z. Stein, AIDS and HIV in Southern Africa, in *Action on AIDS in Southern Africa*, Z. Stein and A. Zwi (eds.), CHISA, New York, pp. 5-7, 1990.
7. E. Wolf, *Europe and the People Without History*, University of California Press, Berkeley, 1982.
8. A. Giddens, *Sociology: A Brief But Critical Introduction*, Harcourt Brace Jovanovich, Publishers, San Diego, 1987.
9. S. Morsy, Political Economy in Medical Anthropology, in *Medical Anthropology: Contemporary Theory and Method*, T. Johnson and C. Sargent (eds.), Praeger, New York, pp. 26-36, 1990.
10. R. Elling, *Cross-National Study of Health Systems*, Transaction Books, New Brunswick, 1981.
11. L. Doyal, *The Political Economy of Health*, South End Press, Boston, 1979.
12. S. Marcus, *Engels, Manchester, and the Working Class*, W. W. Norton, Inc., New York, 1985.
13. F. Engels, *The Condition of the Working Class in England*, Granada Publishing, London, 1962.
14. H. Waitzkin, The Social Origins of Illness: A Neglected History, *International Journal of Health Services, 11*, pp. 77-103, 1981.
15. N. Scott, Medical Anthropology, in *Biennial Review of Anthropology*, B. Siegal (ed.), Stanford University Press, Stanford, pp. 30-68, 1963.
16. V. Navarro, U.S. Marxist Scholarship in the Analysis of Health and Medicine, *International Journal of Health Services, 15*, pp. 525-545, 1985.
17. E. Stark, Doctors in Spite of Themselves: The Limits of Radical Health Criticism, *International Journal of Health Services, 12*, pp. 419-457, 1982.

18. H. Baer, On the Political Economy of Health, *Medical Anthropology Newsletter, 14*:1, pp. 1-3, 13-17, 1982.
19. M. Singer and H. Baer, *Critical Medical Anthropology,* Baywood Publishing, Amityville, New York, 1995.
20. E. R. Brown, *Rockefeller Medicine Men,* University of California Press, Berkeley, 1979.
21. S. Kelman, Toward the Political Economy of Medical Care, *Inquiry, 8,* pp. 30-38, 1971.
22. H. Baer, Sociological Contributions to the Political Economy of Health: Lessons for Medical Anthropologists, *Medical Anthropology Quarterly* (O.S.), *17,* pp. 129-131, 1986.
23. H. Waitzkin, *The Politics of Medical Encounters,* Yale University Press, New Haven, 1991.
24. V. Navarro, The Labor Process and Health: A Historical Materialist Interpretation, *International Journal of Health Services, 12*:1, pp. 5-29, 1982.
25. S. Kane and T. Mason, IV Drug Users and Sex Partners: The Limits of Epidemiological Categories and the Ethnography of Risk, in *The Time of AIDS,* G. Herdt and S. Lindenbaum (eds.), Sage Publications, Newbury Park, California, pp. 199-223, 1992.
26. M. Singer, Z. Jia, J. Schensul, M. Weeks, and J. B. Page, AIDS and the IV Drug User: The Local Context in Prevention Efforts, *Medical Anthropology, 14,* pp. 285-306, 1992.
27. M. Singer and Z. Jia, AIDS and Puerto Rican Injection Drug Users in the United States, in *Handbook on Risk of AIDS: Injection Drug Users and Sexual Partners,* B. Brown and G. Beschner (eds.), Greenwood Press, Westport, Connecticut, pp. 227-255, 1993.
28. N. Glick Schiller, S. Crystal, and D. Lewellen, Risky Business: The Cultural Construction of AIDS Risk Groups, *Social Science and Medicine, 38*:10, pp. 1337-1346, 1994.
29. R. Valdiserri, *Preventing AIDS: The Design of Effective Programs,* Rutgers University Press, New Brunswick, New Jersey, 1989.
30. J. Auerbach, C. Wypijewska, and H. K. Brodie (eds.), *AIDS and Behavior: An Integrated Approach,* National Academy Press, Washington, D.C., 1994.
31. N. Glick Schiller, What's Wrong with This Picture? The Hegemonic Construction of Culture in AIDS Research in the United States, *Medical Anthropology Quarterly, 6,* pp. 237-254, 1992.
32. R. Carlson, H. Siegal, and R. Falck, Ethnography, Epidemiology, and Public Policy: Needle Use Practices and HIV Risk Reduction among Injecting Drug Users in the Midwest, in *Global AIDS Policy,* D. Feldman (ed.), Greenwood Press, Westport, Connecticut, pp. 185-214, 1994.
33. S. Koester, Copping, Running, and Paraphernalia Laws: Contextual Variables and Needle Risk Behavior among Injection Drug Users in Denver, *Human Organization, 53,* pp. 287-295, 1994.
34. M. Singer, M. Weeks, K. Varjas, and T. Newsome, Getting Some Drug Help: Barriers to Drug Treatment for Women of Color, presented at the Society for Applied Anthropology meeting, Albuquerque, New Mexico, 1995.
35. H. Haverkos and T. S. Jones, HIV, Drug-Use Paraphernalia, and Bleach, *Journal of Acquired Immune Deficiency Syndromes, 7,* pp. 741-742, 1994.
36. S. Hills, *Demystifying Social Deviance,* McGraw-Hill, New York, 1981.
37. A. Fontanet and P. Piot, State of Our Knowledge: The Epidemiology of AIDS, *Health Transition Review, 4,* pp. 11-23, 1994.

38. J. Mann, D. Tarantola, and T. Netter, *AIDS in the World*, Harvard University Press, Cambridge, Massachusetts, 1992.
39. C. Good, Traditional Healers and AIDS Management, in *AIDS in Africa: The Social and Policy Impact*, N. Miller and R. Rockwell (eds.), The Edwin Mellen Press, Lewiston, New York, pp. 97-113, 1988.
40. N. Romero-Daza, Knowledge and Beliefs about AIDS among Women in Highland Lesotho, *Human Organization, 53*, pp. 192-205, 1994.
41. E. Preston-Whyte, Gender and the Lost Generation: The Dynamics of HIV Transmission among Black South African Teenagers in KwaZulu/Natal, *Health Transition Review*, Supplement to Volume 4, pp. 241-256, 1994.
42. P. Pelia, IV Drug Use and Patterns of HIV Infection in Asia, *Alcohol and Drug Study Newsletter, 31*, pp. 4-5, 1994.
43. PAHO (Pan American Health Organization), AIDS in Latin America and the Caribbean: Current Situation, *Epidemiological Bulletin, 13*, pp. 1-8, 1992.
44. R. Anderson, AIDS: Trends, Predictions, Controversy, *Nature, 363*, pp. 393-394, 1993.
45. Department of Public Health and Addition Services, *AIDS in Connecticut, Annual Surveillance Report*, December 31, 1993.
46. E. Quimby, Anthropological Witnessing for African Americans: Power, Responsibility, and Choice in the Age of AIDS, in *The Time of AIDS*, G. Herdt and S. Lindenbaum (eds.), Sage Publications, Newbury Park, California, pp. 159-184, 1992.
47. S. Duh, *Blacks and AIDS*, Sage Publications, Newbury Park, California, 1991.
48. Centers for Disease Control and Prevention, *HIV/AIDS Surveillance Report 5* (no. 1), Provisional Data, March 29, 1994.
49. M. Weeks, M. Singer, M. Greer, J. Hunte-Marrow, and C. Haughton, AIDS Prevention and the African American Injection Drug User, *Transforming Anthropology, 4*:1-2, pp. 39-51, 1993.
50. M. Singer, AIDS and the Health Crisis of the U.S. Urban Poor: The Perspective of Critical Medical Anthropology, *Social Science and Medicine, 39*:7, pp. 931-948, 1994.
51. P. Selik, S. Chu, and J. Beuhler, HIV Deaths in Young Adults, *Journal of the American Medical Association, 269*:23, pp. 2990-2993, 1993.
52. L. Novick, D. Berns, R. Stricof, R. Stevens, K. Pass, and J. Wethers, HIV Seroprevalence in Newborns in New York State, *Journal of the American Medical Association, 261*, pp. 1745-1750, 1989.
53. M. Baldo and A. Cabral, Low Intensity Wars and Social Determination of HIV Transmission: The Search for a New Paradigm to Guide Research and Control of the HIV-AIDS Pandemic, in *Action on AIDS in Southern Africa*, Z. Stein and A. Zwi (eds.), CHISA, New York, pp. 34-45, 1990.
54. V. van der Vliet, Apartheid and the Politics of AIDS, in *Global AIDS Policy*, D. Feldman (ed.), Greenwood Press, Westport, Connecticut, pp. 107-129, 1994.
55. B. Schoepf, Women at Risk: Case Studies from Zaire, in *The Time of AIDS*, G. Herdt and S. Lindenbaum (eds.), Sage Publications, Newbury Park, California, pp. 259-286, 1992.
56. D. Grove, Real Harm Reduction: Underground Survival Strategies, *Harm Reduction Communication, 2*, 1996.
57. D. Klein, Ill and Against the Law: The Social and Medical Control of Heroin Users, *Journal of Drug Issues, 13*, pp. 31-55, 1983.
58. D. Musto, *The American Disease: Origins of Narcotics Control*, Oxford University Press, New York, 1987.
59. A. Waterston, *Street Addicts in the Political Economy*, Temple University Press, Philadelphia, 1993.

60. M. Singer, The Politics of AIDS, *Social Science and Medicine, 38*:10, pp. 1321-1324, 1994.
61. B. Schoepf, Women, AIDS and Economic Crisis in Zaire, *Canadian Journal of African Studies, 22*:3, pp. 625-644, 1988.
62. P. Farmer, *AIDS and Accusation: Haiti and the Geography of Blame,* University of California Press, Berkeley, 1992.
63. R. Parker, Political Activism, and AIDS in Brazil, in *Global AIDS Policy,* D. Feldman (ed.), Bergin and Garvey, Westport, Connecticut, pp. 28-46, 1994.
64. B. Schoepf, W. Rukarangira, C. Schoepf, E. Walu, and N. Payanzo, AIDS and Society in Central Africa: A View from Zaire, in *AIDS in Africa: Social and Policy Impact,* N. Miller and R. Rockwell (eds.), Edwin Mellen, Lewiston, New York, pp. 211-235, 1988.
65. B. Schoepf, Gender, Development, and AIDS: A Political Economy and Cultural Framework, in *Women and International Development Annual,* R. Gallin, A. Ferguson, and J. Harper (eds.), Westview Press, Boulder, Colorado, pp. 53-85, 1993.
66. P. Farmer, M. Connors, and J. Simmonds (eds.), *Women, Poverty and AIDS: Sex, Drugs, and Structural Violence,* Common Courage Press, Monroe, Maine, 1996.
67. L. Doyal, J. Naidoo, and T. Wilton, *AIDS: Setting a Feminist Agenda,* Taylor & Francis, London, 1994.
68. M. Quam, AIDS Policy and United States Political Economy, in *Global AIDS Policy,* D. Feldman (ed.), Bergin and Garvey, Westport, Connecticut, pp. 142-159, 1994.
69. M. Haan and G. Kaplan, The Contribution of Socioeconomic Position to Minority Health, in *Report of the Secretary's Task Force on Black and Minority Health,* Vol. 2, U.S. Department of Health and Human Services, Washington, D.C., pp. 67-103, 1985.
70. R. Wallace, A Synergism of Plagues: 'Planned Shrinkage,' Contagious Housing Destruction and AIDS in the Bronx, *Environmental Research, 47,* pp. 1-33, 1988.
71. M. Singer, Providing Substance Abuse Treatment to Puerto Rican Clients Living in the Continental United States, in *Substance Abuse Treatment in the Era of AIDS,* O. Amulezu-Marshall (ed.), Center for Substance Abuse Treatment, Rockville, Maryland, pp. 93-114, 1995.
72. C. Patton, *Sex and Germs: The Politics of AIDS,* South End Press, Boston, 1985.
73. P. Davies, F. Hickson, P. Weatherburn, and A. Hunt, *Sex, Gay Men and AIDS,* The Falmer Press, London, 1993.
74. P. Bourgeois, *In Search of Respect,* Cambridge University Press, Cambridge, 1995.
75. R. Bolton and M. Singer (eds.), *Rethinking AIDS Prevention: Cultural Approaches,* Gordon and Breach Science Publishers, Philadelphia, 1992.
76. J. Van Vugt (ed.), *AIDS Prevention and Services,* Bergin and Garvey, Westport, Connecticut, 1994.
77. R. Carlson, The Political Economy of AIDS among Drug Users in the United States, *American Anthropologist, 98*:2, pp. 266-278, 1996.
78. M. Singer, L. Davison, and G. Gerdes, Culture, Critical Theory, and Reproductive Illness Behavior in Haiti, *Medical Anthropology Quarterly, 2*:4, pp. 370-385, 1988.
79. E. Liebow, *Tally's Corner,* Little Brown and Company, Boston, 1967.
80. M. Singer, Postmodernism and Medical Anthropology: Words of Caution, *Medical Anthropology, 12,* pp. 289-304, 1990.
81. J.-F. Lyotard, *The Postmodern Condition,* University of Minnesota Press, Minneapolis, 1984.
82. A. Gorz, *Socialism and Revolution,* Basic Books, Garden City, New York, 1973.
83. M. Singer, Beyond the Ivory Tower: Critical Praxis in Medical Anthropology, *Medical Anthropology Quarterly, 9*:1, pp. 80-106, 1995.

CHAPTER 2

Images of Catastrophe: The Making of an Epidemic

Shirley Lindenbaum

The unexpected emergence of AIDS in the early 1980s seemed to reverse the historical trends of the twentieth century. It signaled the return of the industrialized nations to what we had assumed was a vanished world of epidemic disease [1].[1] In the United States, epidemic disease soon provided an image of catastrophe that supplanted nuclear war in terms of media attention, academic scholarship, and individual preoccupation.

For the better part of a decade, the daily press has acquainted us with the tally of local, national, and international AIDS deaths—by age, sex, ethnic groups, and region—as well as with the numbers of those suffering from HIV disease and those currently infected. We receive the staggering news that seventeen million people throughout the world are now infected with the virus, and that the major impact is yet to come [2]. By the end of the twenty-first century HIV may infect 110 million people worldwide [3]. Newspapers document the cost of treating AIDS patients and offer poignant accounts of the lives spoiled by the disease—drug users, children, Ugandan wives, hemophiliacs, heterosexuals, homosexuals, hospital workers, the famous, and the unknown. We scan the obituary pages for the open or veiled accounts of AIDS deaths in the fields of art, entertainment,

---

[1] An earlier version of this chapter was presented at the City University of New York Anthropology Colloquia in honor of Lucille Brockway, October 1992.

33

business, and the professions. Television (in contrast to Hollywood) has taken over the category of "serious storytelling,"[2] and rap musicians, everyday sociologists who deliver their messages in a musical form, have become a potent vehicle for safe-sex education, taking on the job which some feel the government should perform [5]. The shelf space occupied by AIDS literature in our local bookstores is burgeoning, and half of American adults who are single and under forty-five years of age say they have changed their sexual behavior because of the fear of getting the disorder [6]. This may be the most widely discussed disease in the history of medicine. The flurry of historical publications on the subject has recently been dubbed the "AIDS history industry" [7], and an issue of *AIDS and Society* provided information on how to gain access to AIDS literature and resources, including Internet, the international electronic superhighway [8].

Our apocalyptic view of AIDS is in some ways surprising since, due to its extreme localization in some communities and neighborhoods, most Americans still go through the day without seeing a case of AIDS. A recent poll showed that most have never knowingly encountered a person with the disease.[3] Moreover, despite its awful ravages, AIDS is not the leading cause of death either here or abroad.[4] Forty-five thousand people died of AIDS in the United States in 1991, about as many as were killed in traffic accidents. Nevertheless, by late 1988, after a slow start, AIDS was fast becoming the single largest program in the U.S. federal health bureaucracy, ascending to funding levels reached by heart disease and cancer, the nation's two leading causes of death [10].

How do we account for the fact that AIDS has elicited such a widespread and sometimes inflamed response in the United States in the absence of extensive personal experience?

To begin to answer that question, I wish to turn for a moment to another contemporary epidemic, that of kuru, a fatal neurological disease occurring in Papua New Guinea. It is often suggested that the two epidemics have much in common. Our sense of their comparability may stem from the fact that they are both slow infections, that is, diseases that become manifest some years after the precipitating incident, and are caused by viruses with unconventional properties—

---

[2] Jonathan Demme's film "Philadelphia" broke the barrier against selecting AIDS as a theme of a major American movie. By 1994, however, with the "Crisis in the Hot Zone" and "Outbreak" two Hollywood producers had turned to the more general theme of the threat of viruses escaping from medical laboratories [see 4].

[3] An October 1991 Gallup Poll reported that only 18 percent of respondents said they knew someone who had contracted the disease [see 9].

[4] In Africa, for example, malnutrition and malaria are more common than AIDS.

a so-called slow virus in the case of kuru[5] and a retrovirus in AIDS. Both epidemics sprang upon the scientific community with the allure of syndromes scarcely foreseen by medical theory, and in their terminal phases, both diseases lead to neurological involvement or dementia. They are similar also in that disease transmission can be intercepted, entirely for kuru and in most cases for AIDS, by changes in personal behavior rather than by the acts of biologists or engineers—by abandoning cannibalism in the case of kuru, and by attention to the exchange of body fluids in the case of AIDS. Both are also fatal diseases of the young.

In its opening moments (in the 1930s and 1940s), the epidemic of kuru, like AIDS, elicited wonder and indecision among the Fore, the people in Papua New Guinea afflicted by the disease, as well as among medical investigators (in the 1950s). At its peak, kuru was also the source of foreign media attention, medical research, and widespread concern among the Fore.[6] During the crisis years of the epidemic in the late 1950s and the early 1960s, the South Fore population was in fact on the brink of decline. Between 1957 and 1977 some 2,500 people in a total population of 14,000 died from kuru, most of them adult Fore women in their reproductive years. Due to the pronounced sexual bias in kuru mortality, the excess of deaths of females over males led to male-female ratios in some South Fore hamlets of 3:1, and of 2:1 for the South Fore as a whole. For several decades, from the mid 1950s to the mid 1970s, the Fore held public rallies, private investigations, and pursued different therapies in an attempt to put an end to the epidemic that they feared would lead to their extinction.

Both kuru and AIDS thus elicited an agitated public response. In the case of kuru, however, the response seems to accurately reflect the epidemic's demographic and social impact. In the case of AIDS, the relationship between personal experience and reaction is more complex.

---

[5] The infectious agent in kuru remains stable on storage at 70 degrees C. for many years, after freeze drying, and is not totally inactivated by temperatures of 85 degrees for 30 minutes. Fore cooking methods, therefore, did not destroy it. The agent is readily transmissible to laboratory primates in extremely low dilutions. A recent shift in thinking concerns the nature of the infectious agent. The inability to find any typical virus particle consisting of nucleic acid and protein, coupled with the unusual resistance of infectivity to agents that normally inactivate nucleic acids, has led Stanley Prusiner and colleagues to propose that a new type of proteinaceous infectious particle, or "prion," is involved. So-called prion diseases now include scrapie in sheep, encephalopathy of cattle ("mad cow disease"), and Creutzfeldt-Jakob disease and Gerstmann-Strauss-Scheinker syndrome in humans, a category to which kuru is also thought to belong. Just as the concept of a slow virus developed around the earlier research on kuru, these prion diseases indicate that medical research faces a new frontier, in this case at the interface of genetics, cell biology, and virology [see 11].

[6] In the 1960s the South Fore population, separated by a mountain ridge from the North, was estimated at 8000 persons in a total Fore population of 14,000. Robert Glasse and I conducted fieldwork in this region from 1961 to 1963, at the height of the epidemic, and I returned for shorter periods of study in 1970, 1991, and 1993.

EPIDEMICS AS BIOLOGICAL AND
SOCIAL EVENTS

The difference points to the fact that epidemics are not mere demographic incidents. They are also intellectual constructs, lightning rods for expressing the particular terrors that monitor the social forms and cultural values of different communities. Epidemics, like the diseases that comprise them, are both biological and socio-cultural events.

When AIDS first seized our attention in the early 1980s, a number of authors, searching for parallels, chose to write about bubonic plague, cholera, polio, yellow fever, and leprosy [1, 12], curiously skipping over the influenza pandemic that had killed more than twenty-one million people as recently as 1918-1919. Although a senior generation of living Americans must have witnessed the influenza epidemic as it swept through their communities, since one out of every four persons was stricken and 500,000 Americans died, the epidemic left little imprint in the public record. Absent from war histories, college texts, and most novels of the period, the influenza pandemic is said to have passed too rapidly to have had more than an ephemeral effect on the economy, its demographic effects apparently concealed by the war [13].[7,8] AIDS, by way of contrast, continues to make its mark in both high and popular culture. Although there are recent signs of declining interest [16], AIDS is still well represented in art, novels, magazines, street theatre, music, and in a voluminous record of scholarly research. Between 1983 and 1991 the MEDLINE database listed 200,000 AIDS-related citations.

Certain epidemics and diseases thus acquire an iconic status, fading in and out of consciousness in ways that depend on more than the facts of biology or demography [17]. Their biological and socio-cultural profiles are shaped by particular political and cultural circumstances. Individuals who provide accepted origin stories and narratives of causation and blame belong to dominant social groups with the moral authority to influence perception and interpretation. Marginal groups also generate their own counter-histories and alternate interpretations.

Although kuru and AIDS constitute the main focus for demonstrating the conjunction of interests and events that define an epidemic, the bubonic plague in India and neurosyphilis in Europe provide telling examples of the particular interplay of perception, politics, and "reality" that constitute what is regarded as a noteworthy epidemic.

---

[7] Slack notes that when a violent epidemic occurs only once, it produces a single shock, which may be quickly forgotten. This may apply to the influenza epidemics of 1557-1559 in England, and to the pandemic of 1918 [see 14].

[8] In his discussion of typhoons on Yap, David Schneider makes a similar point concerning unique catastrophes and chronic threat, the latter taking on distinct meanings that provide a focus for long-standing social anxieties, guilts, fears, and hostilities [see 15].

THE PLAGUE IN INDIA

As with AIDS, the bubonic plague was not the most destructive disease in its day, although it killed eight million people in India between 1896 and 1914. During the same period more people died of malaria and TB, and influenza killed twice as many in a four-month period between 1918 and 1919. Yet, as Chandavarkar notes, no other epidemic evoked the fear and panic generated by the Indian plague, prompting massive state intervention to control its spread, as well as fierce resistance, riots, and occasional mob attacks on Europeans and British officials [18, pp. 203-204].

The most spectacular events took place around Bombay, even though the plague proved to be far more lethal in the Punjab. Bombay was a city that had grown prodigiously in the second half of the nineteenth century, and city health officers had regularly predicted devastating epidemics of perhaps smallpox or cholera. When the plague arrived, the colonial government's primary objective was to identify and isolate the sick, remove them to hospital, and segregate their relatives into so-called "health camps." Houses were disinfected, floors dug up, and personal effects fumigated and sometimes burned. Buildings were limewashed (usually at the owner's expense) and drains and sewers flushed daily with a dilution of carbolic acid and sea water. A system of surveillance was instituted to examine cargo and passengers at ports, and inspection checkpoints and detention camps were a common feature for those using the railways. The Indian response to this massive invasion of privacy was to flee the city, conceal plague patients in hidden lofts and cupboards, chase out inspectors, and attack Europeans in the street.

This pattern of state intervention was unique in the history of colonial India, meddling with caste and religious practices, the disposal of the dead, and the free movement of people. These stringent activities came to a halt in 1902 when it became clear that it was the poorer classes who suffered most severely, and that fewer Europeans died from plague each year than from cholera. As state intervention ceased the panic subsided, although plague mortality continued to rise, reaching its peak between 1903 and 1907 [18, pp. 204-210].

Although the French biologist P. L. Simond had shown in 1898 that the plague was associated with rats, the part played by rat fleas was not firmly established until 1908 [19]. Moreover, the Indian Plague Commission held the view that a reservoir of infection was residing in microbes on the ground, subsequently spread by contact among humans [18, p. 216]. Particular emphasis was thus placed on the insanitary and filthy conditions of Indian towns and villages as a "predisposing cause" [19, p. 61].

The British response was in large part shaped by the fear of illness and death. Diseases, however, are not read for their biological characteristics alone. The new germ theory of disease, which had been readily adopted by most Europeans during the late decades of the nineteenth century, played an incisive role in race relations.

Whole populations were now labeled as "contaminants" in ways not previously considered. Armed with a newfound sense of confidence created by the contributions of Pasteur and Koch to the emerging field of bacteriology, colonial governments began to view their newly annexed populations both as inferior and as reservoirs of alien germs [20]. British hypotheses about the nature of disease in India were joined to imperial notions of the social, behavioral, and cultural characteristics of Indian populations. The unsanitary conditions of the towns and villages were increasingly portrayed as innate and natural to the subcontinent [18, p. 212].

In their attempts to conquer the disease, the British first assaulted the bodies, clothing, bedding, and houses of those (mostly poor people) seen as sources of contamination. Their second assault was directed at the growing political assertiveness of the Indian middle classes, especially those "native gentlemen" increasingly viewed as a threat to British supremacy. Attention focused on the municipalities of Bombay, Calcutta, and Pune. Here the plague crisis was said to be evidence that Indians could not manage their own affairs. In 1898, using the plague as justification, the British declared a decade of shared municipal government to be a failure, returning the ratio of nominated to elected councillors in favor of the British [19, pp. 77-78].

The plague in India was thus the setting for a complex interplay of suffering, perception, coercion, and response. It let loose British anxieties about India as a repository of disease, as well as a concern about the potential collapse of British rule [18, pp. 225-226]. The Indian response revealed widespread mistrust of Western medicine, plague administrators, and the increasing hegemony of the middle classes. As Arnold observes, the epidemic provides an extended "commentary on the developing relationship between indigenous elites, subaltern classes and the colonial state" [19, p. 56].

NEUROSYPHILIS IN EUROPE

A second shorter example of the epidemic as a cultural and socio-political construct shows that venereal disease, usually an object of odium and revulsion [21] may elicit different reactions in different contexts.[9] Stigma did indeed accompany an epidemic of gonorrhea and syphilis in late eighteenth-century France, but the outbreak of neurosyphilis in Europe around 1870 (a consequence of an epidemic of primary syphilis 10 to 15 years earlier) brought little disgrace to its victims [22]. Those who suffered in the earlier eighteenth-century epidemic were predominantly rustic migrant laborers or tradesmen who acquired the disease in

---

[9] Merrill Singer suggests that a similar story might be told about the outbreak of gonorrhea among middle-class American youth in the 1960s and 1970s. At that time, gonorrhea was not greatly feared (because it was believed to be readily treatable), and was to some degree seen as a badge of sexual prowess. As a result, the disease was a source of some humor.

the cities and returned to their villages where they infected their wives and children. The victims of the outbreak of neurosyphilis, on the other hand, were primarily middle-class young men, said to be due to the greater use of prostitutes by students than working class males. Whereas the earlier epidemic was seen as evidence of sin and degeneration, an attitude that prevented many rural women from seeking timely medical care, neurosyphilis carried no such stigma. Viewing themselves as a community of sufferers, the young men visited the same resorts and hotels, even entertaining one another at the same dining tables. Some spas actively recruited "ataxics"[10] without being branded as leper colonies. The town of Lamalou in southwestern France even had a statue of an ataxic patient in the town square. Nor were neurosyphilis patients segregated when admitted to hospitals [22, p. 55).[11]

Neurosyphilis, however, did arouse some apprehension. While certain patients manifested psychiatric complications in the form of depression, a large proportion suffered from so-called "expansive" or manic behavior. Grandiose conduct, said to be an early warning sign, was of intense importance to middle-class families, since the patients tended to go on buying sprees that threatened to deplete the family fortune. Neurosyphilis was thus not stigmatized by its association with sexual transmission, but was instead a disease that threatened the foundation of the middle class [22, pp. 55-60].[12]

As these examples illustrate, epidemics derive their significance from a conjunction of social and political circumstances in the context of (often) high mortality and individual suffering. Since this phenomenon that we call an "epidemic"—the interaction of biological and social events, social perception, and collective response—has a certain physical, social, and historical specificity, can we say that epidemics have anything in common?

WHAT EPIDEMICS HAVE IN COMMON

Recent research on the nature of epidemics suggests that the shock of pestilence elicits quite similar responses in very different historical and geographical contexts [24, 25]. As social phenomena, epidemics are said to have a familiar dramaturgical form. They "start at a moment in time, proceed on a stage limited in

[10]Ataxia—loss of coordination of the muscle, especially at the extremities. Ataxia occurs at a later non-contagious stage of neurosyphilis.

[11]The French writers Baudelaire, the Goncourt brothers, Flaubert, Maupassant, and Daudet celebrated syphilis, which they felt made them representatives of a more creative humanity. For the English, syphilitic insanity was never seen as the "fleur du mal" [see 23].

[12]The neurosyphilis epidemic halted in 1910 with injections of Salvarsan, which effectively treated primary infections. Although we are now seeing early forms of neurological syphilis associated with AIDS, an epidemic of tertiary syphilis may not follow, since primary and secondary syphilis associated with AIDS is now treated with antibiotics, and also since patients may not survive to develop tertiary syphilis.

space and duration, follow a plot line of increasing and revelatory tension, move to a crisis of individual and collective character, then drift toward closure" [24, p. 2]. As Victor Turner has also observed, severe misfortune and illness precipitate a crisis, mobilizing communities to produce a pageant of ritual responses in which common values are stressed and the actors reaffirm fundamental social conventions and conformist dictates [26].

In addition to a common dramaturgy, many historical forms of pestilence are considered to have shared additional features. They were all seen by their contemporaries as being transmitted from person to person. Even when theories about their origin combined notions of miasma and contagion, they were said to arise in the "stench" of filthy local conditions. Once recognized, the social response usually involved flight. Carriers of diseases were identified as scapegoats and stigmatized—foreigners in Renaissance Italy and modern Hawaii,[13] immigrants to the United States [28], as well as inferiors and "polluters" of different kinds—untouchables in India, ex-slaves in Africa, or Jews at the time of the Black Death.

Epidemics are also said to have elicited religious and ritual responses that promised effective action—processions in Merovingian Paris and Renaissance Europe, and ecstatic or prophetic cults in Athens and Africa. In addition, outbreaks of disease are often associated with social upheavals, war, famine, migrations, and sometimes pilgrimage [29].

Epidemics thus appear to share a common "architecture" or perhaps "choreography" as well as a number of sociological features. Since they are also mirrors held up to society, however, we need to distinguish the unique from the apparently universal in each epidemic, an exercise that the advocates of "contemporary history" propose as a contribution to health policy [1, 30, 31]. Attention to particular settings allows us to better understand the political and economic contexts that give rise to epidemics and to their interpretation. I would like to return, therefore, to consider the unique and apparently universal aspects of kuru in Papua New Guinea and AIDS in the United States. (The history and political economy of AIDS elsewhere in the world requires separate analysis.)

WHAT KURU AND AIDS DO AND DO NOT HAVE IN COMMON

Kuru and AIDS have much in common. Both appear to be following the familiar dramaturgical form of progressive acknowledgment, collective agreement on an explanatory framework, and a negotiated public response, although the kuru epidemic, which began earlier, is drifting toward closure. Appearing on the

---

[13]Measles, whooping cough, influenza, and smallpox were all introduced by visitors to Hawaiian shores in the nineteenth century. TB may have arrived as early as 1778, because it was present among the crew of Captain Cook's command. It certainly stepped ashore with the first missionaries, several of whom had TB when they arrived [see 27].

borderlands of the North Fore territory in the Eastern Highlands of Papua New Guinea around the turn of the century, kuru reached the South Fore in the 1930s, surged to a peak in the 1950s and 1960s, and settled down to its current incidence of about eight to ten cases a year. AIDS, as we know, began officially in 1981, and for some population groups the crest is yet to come.[14]

Following a period of initial ambivalence, both diseases precipitated a sense of crisis, mobilized communities, and produced a pageant of ritual and secular responses that have predominantly stressed common values and conformist dictates.

In the early days of both epidemics, physicians informed the scientific world that they had encountered a new medical phenomenon, although in the case of kuru, the Fore had earlier established this fact for themselves.

In both cases also, the naming and definition of the diseases was an exercise in cultural analysis, a meta-discussion about social acceptability, and perceived social dangers. For kuru, the Fore first noticed the patients' tremor, which they likened to the swaying of the casuarina tree, and thus called the new disorder "cassowary disease" by the further analogy that cassowary quills resemble waving casuarina fronds. Others took account of the patient's emotional lability and called the disease "negi nagi," meaning silly or foolish person. Since cassowary disease was thought to be caused by the assault of ghosts of the dead, and negi nagi by anthropomorphic spirits, neither was considered to be truly alarming. When the Fore observed that the victims were uniformly dying, however, they reasoned that mere spirits or dead ancestors were not the causative agents. Instead, living sorcerers were judged to be responsible. This theory, which assigns etiology to the malevolence of male competitors outside a limited range of kinship and residence, was a statement about the nature of perceived social dangers and unacceptable behaviors. The Fore gave the name "kuru" to this sorcery-caused illness, a word meaning shaking or fear, an apt description of the tremor exhibited by sufferers, and a name subsequently adopted by Western science. For the Fore, "kuru" was a term that had a certain political, social, and descriptive resonance.

The sufferers and their kin played no role in the initial naming of AIDS. Newspapers, however, spoke of "gay cancer," "gay pneumonia," and "gay plague" at a time when the disease still lacked a scientific name [38, p. 10]. (The Australian press had similarly distanced its audience from the sufferers of kuru by calling it "the laughing death.") As we know, the final naming of HIV disease was a product of fierce competition in the field of international science [39]. The names HIV disease and kuru thus carry an imprint of their own social and political histories.

---

[14]By 1992 AIDS had become the leading cause of death for men between the ages of twenty-five and forty-four, and the fourth leading cause for women in the same age group (mainly partners of drug users) [see 32].

Epidemiology played a key role in both contexts, defining important dimensions of each disease condition before the infectious agents were identified [40]. Epidemiologists also advised both audiences that they were experiencing an "epidemic." For the Fore, this too confirmed something they already knew. The Fore were aware that the disease predominantly killed women, not men, and had disoriented many aspects of social life. In this horticultural society women are especially valued as laborers, producing the food that sustains both people and animals. "See how few pigs we have," one Fore orator announced in 1963. "Think how many women the sorcerers must have killed." The seriousness of the situation was further underlined during the late 1950s and early 1960s when a number of international investigators, medical and anthropological, began intensive research, and government patrols were stepped up to monitor the course of the disease. The presence of outsiders, associated in Fore eyes with a powerful colonial government, gave extra stimulus to their activities of self-enquiry and revelatory disclosure, since they held themselves responsible for the plague that had fallen upon them.

This broad comparison of kuru and AIDS shows that they have many features in common, but it also begins to reveal some important differences. Each epidemic mobilized regiments of caretakers to care for the ill and to keep the issue alive in the eyes of those they believed could ultimately furnish a remedy. Close kin and fellow residents provided the care, solace, and political action for the victims of kuru.[15] AIDS has elicited a more fragmented body of actors.

In many regions of the United States voluntary agencies arose to serve particular communities affected by AIDS, especially in gay and minority communities where people were alienated from mainstream institutions [36-38].[16,17] San Francisco responded swiftly with a public-private initiative providing a complex of services in hospital wards, hospices, and care at home, with buddy-to-buddy counseling, a model of care that was widely emulated elsewhere. The "San Francisco model" provided service to predominantly white gay men. Published reports to the contrary, minority communities also mobilized in response to high rates of HIV infection in their midst, where AIDS is associated with IV drug use [40, 41].

In New York, the Gay Men's Health Crisis (founded in 1981) and the AIDS Coalition to Unleash Power (ACT UP) (organized by 1987) took on the direct action needed to keep the heat on the government and the scientific community. Political activists had their own persuasive effect, creating a climate for more temperate lobbying groups to influence policy makers in the Public Health

[15]For a period of time during the 1960s and 1970s a government and mission-sponsored hospital cared for kuru patients.

[16]As Nina Glick-Schiller notes, the burden of AIDS care in the United States often falls heavily on female kin [see 39].

[17]In the kuru epidemic, men cared for their ailing wives and motherless children.

Service. As a result, access to certain drugs was expanded before the Food and Drug Administration had completed its approval process, Burroughs Wellcome was pressed to lower the price of the drug AZT, and Congress increased the allocation of funds for AIDS research. Drug trials were opened up to women, racial minorities, and children, increasing our understanding of the different ways HIV attacks the body.

The most overt organizational feature of ACT UP was its strategic use of anger for political purposes. Rage was seen as a way to fend off despair, and to unite a diverse group of "victims" committed to direct action[18] When ACT UP's manifesto was exported to Australia, however, activists resisted this emotional style, indicating that emotions are not mere functions of an inner psychological state, but may be institutionally organized. The strategic use of anger, which accentuates the predicament of exclusion from formal decision making, had limited utility in the Australian context where the national AIDS strategy drew upon a tripartite relationship among government, medicine, and community representatives. ACT UP's expressions of rage and other forms of protest in the United States thus arose in a special matrix of power relations [42].

The Fore and a segment of the gay community each followed paths of political action to publicize their anguish, but their methods and targets were markedly different. While Fore kuru sufferers and their kin explored the therapies of indigenous and Western curers, their political leaders assembled enemy groups to examine the demographic and social emergency. In the context of these emotional assemblies, reputed sorcerers publicly confessed past activities, and the leaders appealed to those sorcerers still in hiding to come forward and to relinquish their evil practices. Every day for three and a half months, in a cascade of oratory, men and women denounced the excess of deaths that was seen as endangering the future.[19] The Fore terrain would be a wasteland, they said, unless they overcame the narrow competition and small loyalties that had driven them apart. These daily congregations provided an occasion for ritual and verbal affirmations of unity, and for restating fundamental principles to which they could all subscribe. Underlining Fore lines of authority, men spoke for women, senior males for juniors. An idealized picture emerged of harmony among kin and neighbors, as orators attempted to "re-write" the constitution of Fore society [43].

AIDS media events have been of a different order. ACT UP's calculated use of the media draws upon the gay community's skill in graphic arts, not oratory. The urban landscape has been covered with advertisements or cartoons that generate countercultural images to replace the racist, homophobic, and misogynist

[18]ACT UP's mission statement declares them to be a non-partisan group united in anger and committed to direct action to end the AIDS crisis. The motto "Silence = Death" is said to speak to the power of catharsis.

[19]In the preceding months, similar meetings had been held by the North Fore where the epidemic was showing signs of decline. The South Fore was hoping to achieve the same results.

ideologies identified with the church and federal government. When they zapped the Stock Exchange, members of ACT UP took photos of the event, then smuggled the cameras out to give to the Associated Press, thus stage-managing their own media sensation [44].

ACT UP is not alone in taking a critical sense toward the government and scientific authority. The so-called "AIDS social movement" [45] includes many people working in AIDS educational and service organizations, journalists, writers, social scientists, and people with AIDS. Diversity within the movement is reflected even among activists. San Francisco ACT UP, for example, has split into two chapters. One chapter works to eradicate homophobia, racism, and sexism, and the other is concerned with issues of treatment and the quest for drugs [46]. New York ACT UP is also divided between the science-oriented Treatment and Data Committee (concerned with the data from randomized clinical trials), and the committee advocating acupuncture and Chinese herbs [45]. Similarly, the emphasis by middle-class gay communities on cure over prevention has limited relevance for heterosexual people of color in urban centers, where "prevention" must address issues of poverty, homelessness, racism, violence, drug abuse, and access to health care [46]. That is, the diverse nature of the epidemic and of local interests becomes more apparent as the virus progresses through different communities. Disputes over the AIDS Memorial Quilt have become a locus for the clash of identity politics "where issues of race, gender, sexuality and class are in conflict" [47].

In addition to its fractured political shape, the AIDS epidemic is a peculiarly post-modern plague in the self-conscious, reflexive, and bureaucratically structured detachment with which we regard it. As the historian Charles Rosenberg notes [24, pp. 11-12], countless social scientists and journalists watch us watch ourselves, a reflexive process that has become a characteristic of America's experience with AIDS.[20]

AIDS also arrived in the midst of an information revolution, which generated a wide range of rapid-dissemination tools such as PCs, CD-ROM, and on-line databases. Well-educated grassroots groups in the white gay community used these tools for AIDS prevention, involving basic researchers, clinicians, and patients themselves. The combination of media attention and active patient involvement means that researchers, clinicians, and patients often confront new data almost simultaneously. AIDS activists have thus narrowed the gap that has developed in Western medicine between the producers and consumers of knowledge. At times, the roles are even reversed [49].

The Fore, on the other hand, had not experienced a gap between the production and consumption of knowledge. Indeed, the funerals and other public gatherings

---

[20]A post-modern, post-structuralist literature on AIDS discourse discusses language, signification, and the representation of the disease [see 48].

called to discuss the emergency were simultaneously media events and laboratories of enquiry. To confirm the Fore theory of causation, which they knew differed from that of Western medicine, sorcerers were asked to renounce old technologies of death to ensure a peaceable future. These orchestrated events were designed to interrupt the epidemic and to arrive at a common explanatory framework. Like the Indian response to British intervention during the bubonic plague, the Fore similarly confirmed an ideology that would protect the identity and integrity of Fore society within a new colonial state.

In this small-scale, relatively homogeneous New Guinea society, a common set of understandings about the cause of kuru spread rapidly throughout the region. Produced with an eye on the Australian Administration, which they feared would punish them for their excessive and continued use of sorcery, the assemblies manifested an element of self-consciousness. Still, the Fore gatherings were not post-modern happenings.

A final broad area of both overlap and departure concerns the context in which the two diseases appeared. While recent literature suggests that epidemics often occur in times of crisis such as war, famine, or mass migration, both kuru and AIDS in the United States emerged in the context of somewhat less dramatic social upheavals. Kuru appears to have begun at a time when the Fore were converting to the production of sweet potato as a dietary staple. This led to more intensive cultivation methods, the exploitation of new lands and to the keeping of the domestic pig [50]. As diets changed, men claimed prior right to pork and women added human flesh as a small supplement to the diet of themselves and their children, providing the means of transmitting the infectious kuru agent from the dead to the living [43]. The Fore may have first encountered the apparently new kuru pathogen as they cut down forests and intruded into new ecological settings, an explanation recently suggested to account for the emergence of "new" infections in other populations [51]. As with AIDS, the origin of the first case is a matter of speculation, although in each epidemic, social recognition of first cases can be geographically narrowed.

AIDS in the United States spread in the context of a different set of disturbed and changing socio-political conditions. Although diverse and localized in its expression, the United States AIDS epidemic can be described as having two broad forms, related to different social conditions and modes of transmission. AIDS is concentrated among disenfranchised inner-city residents, where poverty, poor housing, high infant mortality and low birthweight babies, death by violent means, and diseases that have nearly disappeared in all industrialized countries are present in epidemic form. AIDS, like TB, has found a place in impoverished and socially and medically underserved communities, where disrupted family networks, high rates of injection drug use, and problems with alcohol are also present [36, 52]. AIDS is thus not properly viewed in isolation. Social and biological conditions in the United States combine synergistically to affect mortality and life expectancy as well as the transmission of disease. The term *syndemic* has recently been used to call attention to the interactive nature of health and social problems among poor, inner-city, AIDS-affected communities [53]. AIDS thus spread among drug users in the turmoil of social conditions that led to increased use of injectable heroin, group living, needle "sharing," and multiple sexual partnerships. As we now know, many male injection drug users subsequently passed the disease to their sexual partners, and their female sexual partners to their children.

The homosexual transmission of the disease also arose as an extension of the social changes that began in the 1960s and early 1970s, when the lesbian and gay liberation movements led activists to destigmatize same-gender desire and to promote libertarian values. At that time, the gay community's territorial, institutional, and cultural base expanded. By the 1970s, a gay (largely white and middle-class) male culture had emerged with its pattern of sexual availability, multiple partners, and reciprocity in sexual techniques that facilitated the spread of AIDS and other STDs [36]. As a result, AIDS in the United States (as elsewhere) should not be considered a single epidemic. Unlike kuru, which is more uniformly expressed and experienced, the HIV pandemic is a more complex phenomenon, a series of superimposed epidemics in different subpopulations, requiring different approaches to treatment and prevention. The earlier decline of AIDS in white middle-class gay communities is thus due to changes in personal behavior that do not depend on structural changes in society [54].

Both the kuru and AIDS epidemics thus arose in the context of marked social change in which individuals adopted novel or "experimental," but quite different, forms of behavior (cannibalism, drug use, sex) that did not foretell their grim outcome.

WAYS IN WHICH THE TWO
EPIDEMICS DIFFER

With some departures, then, the two epidemics appear to have much in common. At times they even seem to be variations on the same theme. They differ markedly, however, in a number of areas.

First, kuru and AIDS differ significantly in their rates of transmission. The rapid spread of AIDS in the United States depended on the quarantine of distance being broken by air travel, the connections of trade and tourism, the many opportunities for viral transmission offered by the residential density of HIV-infected people in both the gay and urban drug-using populations, and on the overlap in the two risk behaviors.

Kuru spread more slowly over many decades as cannibalism disseminated from the Northern borders of Fore territory to the South. Evidence of the diffusion of cannibal practices comes from ethno-historical accounts of their gradual adoption told by people who remember and participated in these events, and in the matching, delayed appearance of the disease in Southern locations [43, 55].

Moreover, the opportunities for viral transmission occurred less frequently, requiring access to the body of a kinsperson who had died of kuru, although one dismembered corpse might be the transmission route for a number of new infections [56, 57].

From a biological standpoint, the two epidemics are again dissimilar in that the clinical course of kuru is remarkably uniform, having remained the same in over thirty years of observation. AIDS, on the other hand, is an acronym for a spectrum of diseases that are variably manifest in different patients. Further, kuru has been predominantly a disease of females, and AIDS in the United States a disease of males, a situation that is changing for each disease, more slowly in the case of kuru.[21]

The incubation periods for the two diseases also appear to differ, although in each case the range is still being defined. Kuru patients survive for an average of twelve months from the onset of symptoms, but the incubation period before symptoms appear varies greatly. (There is no marker available such as an HIV antibody test to determine the presence of an infectious agent.) Since the youngest person now succumbing to kuru is approximately forty years of age, we are looking at a disease with a latency period in some persons of over thirty-five years, consistent with transmission of the infectious agent by cannibalism before the mid-1950s when cannibalism ceased.

Recent data on long-term survival of men infected with HIV come from a study of a San Francisco City Clinic Cohort of 445 men. The cumulative proportion of men who have developed AIDS continues to increase, but a minority of men (21%) are still free of symptoms after more than ten years, suggesting that they may not develop the disease, that there is a less lethal HIV strain, or that the latency period as with kuru, is longer than we had conceived [59].

The two epidemics differ most significantly when it comes to stigma. AIDS is a stigmatized disorder, kuru is not. The stigma of AIDS is one of its most notable and unpleasant features [60]. However, as we know from the history of leprosy [20] and syphilis, stigmatized diseases are not subject to a continuous history of stain, nor are they all used for the same didactic purposes. How should we understand the heavy load of stigma associated with AIDS in the United States?

[21]Kuru is now seen only in the long incubation group, that is, among adults who consumed human flesh in childhood. Kuru among adult males has thus increased. AIDS is also changing with time and treatment. Internationally, the gender gap is closing on the number of HIV-infected women. It is estimated that by the mid-1990s, *global* adult HIV infections of women will equal that of men. In addition, the use of AZT and prophylaxis for PCP are already resulting in an increased incidence of lymphoma as patients live longer. Our epidemiological understanding changes also each time the disease is redefined [see 58].

CHRONIC DISEASE AND STIGMA

Infectious diseases are usually thought of as either acute or chronic. Acute infectious diseases have a short latency and infectious period, a short illness, and either transient or permanent immunity, as in the cases of polio and smallpox. Chronic infections, on the other hand, have long periods of infectiousness, and are either fatal or have slow recovery rates that lead to no permanent immunity. AIDS and kuru are both fatal chronic infectious disorders.

Chronic diseases often result in experiences of illness which, in Western cultural settings, are said to shape the patient's conception of self. Thus, many patients with chronic conditions are said to experience the fusion of self with sickness, or diagnosis with identity. This results in what have been called the chronic "I am illnesses," such as leprosy,[22] and such non-infectious disorders as schizophrenia, anorexia, and epilepsy, in contrast to the chronic "I have illnesses" such as TB, some cancers, and non-infectious disorders [61].

Sue Estroff suggests that the "I am illnesses" are more stigmatized, entail more disruptive or disapproved behavior, are more likely to involve cognitive function, and are more offensive to moral convention. They also include illnesses where attributions of blame for the condition rest with the individual.

Following this suggested classification, AIDS, which is heavily stigmatized, should fall into the "I am" category. AIDS, however, is an "I have illness," defined perhaps by the political activity of its first perceived target population, which quickly provided us with the referential term "People With AIDS." It is nevertheless significant that AIDS is still primarily associated with the "I am" condition of homosexuality even as the majority of new infections are among drug users and their female sexual partners. Popular perception, which *does* fuse diagnosis with identity—AIDS with homosexuality—allows stigma to re-enter by another route.

The special sexual stigma attached to AIDS arose at the outset when HIV disease was first viewed as a specific subset of sexually transmitted diseases, a potent image that has continued to frame discussion. The greater stigma of same gender sex thus erases "white" and "middle class," which in other contexts are taken to be virtues. The stigma of intravenous drug use has a different aura, since it is associated (correctly or not) with heterosexual behavior. Moreover, the prior "I am" condition here is minority status. Minority AIDS sufferers are thus presented with multiple overlapping "embattled identities" [62, p. 103]—African American, Latino/Latina, and then gay, bisexual, or drug user, a series of discriminations that becloud the single "I am" of drug use [63, 64]. Given the early media portrayal and popular perception of AIDS as primarily a disease of gays, many African-American AIDS sufferers have been fearful of being associated with its additionally stigmatizing consequences [64, p. 161].

---

[22]Leprosy patients in the United States currently resist this self-definition.

STIGMA AND KURU

Kuru, by way of contrast, was never a stigmatized disorder. Patients suffer no ostracism, disparagement, or mark of disgrace when the symptoms become apparent. Here, the structures of blame focus not on the sufferer but on sorcerers, adult men with whom the victim's husband or kin group feel the animus of competition. Sorcerers are thus depicted as infamous killers, though not social outcasts.

In normal times, the sorcerers belonging to one's own group are looked upon as worthy protectors, and sorcerers of the political opposition as dangerous miscreants. At the height of the kuru epidemic, however, when the search for individuals responsible for specific cases of illness appeared to be having no effect, blame and stigma were linked in the general image of the "rubbishman." Rubbishmen were said to be those sorcerers who remained in hiding, avoiding the public assemblies in which people were committing themselves to a healthy and sorcery-free future. During these emotional gatherings, orators denounced rubbishmen who were said to be recognizable by their lack of finery, dirty appearance, or by some physical impediment. Said to exist in all communities, these maligned absentees were in fact hard to locate. Never named, they were characterized as marginal individuals who failed to participate in the exchanges of wealth seen as essential to the reproduction of the social order.[23] Fore public discussions thus began to depict a society in which some men (whose wives were dying of kuru) would soon become rubbishmen, while others (potentially more dangerous in the eyes of the senior generation) were the reluctant wealth-sharers and participants in social exchange. Adult men who voiced these dual fears were thus attempting to shore up older structures of dominance, and simultaneously, to head off an emerging social order in which individuals who acquired wealth might keep it to themselves.

The women enduring the disease suffered no stigma. Once their symptoms began, they struggled to control their shaking limbs and to participate fully in daily life. As they gradually became immobilized, unable to work in the gardens, to care for their children, or to attend social gatherings, they spent the daytime hours at home, watched over by a small child, marooned, but not outcast.

---

[23]The marginal status of so-called "rubbishmen" and some gays is somewhat ambiguous. Fore rubbishmen are said to be undesirable riffraff, and at the same time secret users of a powerful technology. Similarly, middle-class gay white men are viewed by some as polluted, but in large cities, they may command considerable economic resources. Merrill Singer notes [personal communication] that IV drug users are also seen as rubbishmen and, in popular imagery, fit the Fore model as hidden, dirty, anti-social, and threatening, much like the image of the virus itself.

DEMOCRATIC EPIDEMICS, UNDEMOCRATIC EPIDEMICS, AND STIGMA

The stigma of AIDS is related to another important dimension by which the two epidemics differ. AIDS is an undemocratic affliction. In so-called "democratic epidemics" [65], communicable diseases cut across class, racial, and ethnic lines and threaten the community at large. Faced with such diseases (smallpox, polio in the 1950s), a sense of mutual vulnerability is said to prevent communities from stigmatizing and making outcasts of the ill. AIDS in the United States, however, although present in most communities, is socially and geographically localized. Identified with specific groups, it is increasingly concentrated in zones of poverty, in particular neighborhoods, or in the persons, where it is not perceived to threaten the community at large. It is also transmitted by socially disapproved behaviors and among social groups already the focus of disdain.

Kuru, by way of contrast, touched all hamlets and regions of the Fore domain, and few families were left unaffected. Although it afflicted mainly women, not perceived as the equals of men, the disease was not restricted to individuals viewed as expendable. Moreover, the Fore considered the true targets to be the patient's husbands and brothers, diminished by their loss of productive and reproductive labor. That is, kuru was not making outcasts of the ill, but was viewed as a weapon men used to reduce the social credit of competitors. Undiscriminating in its targets, kuru threatened to make rubbishmen of them all.

The public stress on solidarity rather than excessive conflict, on cooperation rather than selfish action underwrote a gift exchange economy which enchains people in obligatory exchange relations, and where there is no place for a Western conceptual separation of the individual and society. Kuru arose in a social context which does not lend itself to the identification of the person and the disease, or to stigma associated with the particular behaviors or social attributes of identifiable people.

AIDS in many ways appears to be epidemiologically "pre-adapted" for use as a stigmatizing tool, while kuru, which spread through the entire population, does not. Nevertheless, both theories of disease causation bring together a similar cluster of ideas concerning unproductive and marginal individuals and death by disease.

STIGMA, POLLUTION, AND SOCIAL DIFFERENTIATION

The shared theme of disease and social marginality points to an interesting relationship, historically and ideologically, between infectious disease and social differentiation. Historically, social class differences in life expectancy emerged for the first time in Europe during the eighteenth century [66]. Before that time, much of the mortality was caused by epidemics of infectious disease against which wealth was no protection. By the mid-eighteenth century, differences in mortality and life expectancy by region and social class can be attributed to a marked reduction in pandemics (plague and typhus), to population growth that made the crowd diseases (measles and smallpox) a more benign affliction of childhood, and to the better living conditions, dietary practices, nursing care, and nutritional status of the peerage. These conditions provided better protection against the most important remaining causes of illness and death—the infectious diseases of childhood and the pneumonia-diarrhea complex. Infant mortality among the aristocracy declined more rapidly than it did among the general population, and the life expectancy of aristocrats increased beyond that of the rest of the population for the first time [67, p. 355].[24]

The "undemocratic" nature of the AIDS epidemic, especially in the inner cities of the United States, is thus not the inevitable result of an encounter with infectious disease, but stems from a convergence of social, ecological, and biological factors that lead to its increased concentration in certain regions and among certain social groups.

The link between infectious disease and social differentiation has a second ideological dimension. The notion that AIDS punishes socially marginal people for deviant behavior echoes widely held nineteenth-century American views that the "vicious poor" and lower orders rightly suffered most during the cholera epidemic of 1832 [68]. The theme continues throughout the great era of immigration from the 1830s to the early twentieth century [28], and surfaces again in the discriminatory attitudes toward Haitians in the early days of the AIDS epidemic.

The moral view that established or governing groups have better health by dint of their position in society, a notion firmly held by the British in India, thus has a long history in Western thought and experience. The idea no doubt gained substance from the longer life expectancy of the European peerage, beginning in the eighteenth century, and from the nineteenth century linking of wealth and survival, as the relationships among sanitation, lifestyles, morbidity, and mortality were better defined.[25] Nevertheless, cultural codes played a key role in establishing the link between prestige and infectious disease. "Hygienic" behaviors were widely adopted in nineteenth-century Europe in the absence of any scientific rationale. In Sweden, ideals of cleanliness were not a simple product of increased knowledge about the origins of disease, but stemmed from a profound distinction between the way the bourgeoisie and the peasantry categorized the world and drew boundaries between themselves and others [69]. An expanding middle class came to define its own way of life as a national culture, even as a matter of "human

---

[24]In this case, the vicious poor were most often Irish immigrants living in tenements, rather than respectable, servant-employing, church-going Americans [see 68].

[25]Certainly the great social theorists of the nineteenth century, Engels and Virchow, understood the relationship between the political economy and poor health.

nature." New attitudes toward time, gender constructs, child socialization, notions of work and leisure, of public and private, and ideologies of home and family life, were accompanied by new conceptions of health and cleanliness, as well as by changing perceptions of sexuality and bodily functions [69, p. 6]. Important cultural codes were transmitted through "trivial everyday routines." "Table manners, for example, were not so much a lesson in eating as indirect instruction in the art of self-control" [69, p. 271]. A similar history can be told about bourgeois concepts of cleanliness, the growth of private space and of self-discipline in nineteenth-century France [70].

A crucial turn in Western attitudes toward the body began in the seventeenth century, with the imposition of new kinds of social control and the cultivation of confessional techniques for internalizing social imperatives [71, 72]. By the nineteenth century, a new science of sexuality had become an instrument for affirming bourgeois ideas of health and family structure. The heterosexual, monogamous couple was seen as the foundation of social life, and all other forms of social relationship were portrayed as abnormal.

In recent decades a great "sexual sermon" [72, p. 7] has swept through out societies, displacing the earlier Western focus on sanitary etiquette and manners in the construction of the bourgeois "self." The response to AIDS in the United States is a compelling example of the way in which sexuality has replaced hygiene as a disciplinary tactic for defining the self, and for affirming a social order based on certain middle-class cultural values.

The identification of AIDS with the pollution of "out of category" [73] sexuality has allowed conservative and religious elements in American society to organize a political backlash against the gay liberations of the 1960s and 1970s. It has also prevented us from acquiring the knowledge about sexual behavior that could help impede the spread of the disease. In France, a country less subject to moral panic about such issues, a recent government survey of sexual behaviors is now available, while U.S. efforts to launch a national survey have foundered on opposition from a recent Washington Administration influenced by conservative lawmakers allied with the radical Christian right [74].[26] The persuasive power of "pollution talk" also sustains the perception that AIDS is spread by superficial contact, even though this has been demonstrated not to be the case. American doctors, for example, are said to be more likely than their Canadian or French counterparts to believe that care of patients infected with the virus is dangerous, and are also more reluctant to care for AIDS patients than comparable groups in Canada and France where, significantly, there is no policy to exclude gay men from the military.[27] While anthropologists have given much attention to the capacity of pollution

[26]A study was subsequently carried out, funded by private foundations [see 75].
[27]Popular views associating gays and the dangers of HIV were given fresh life in June 1995 when Secret Service agents wore rubber gloves to escort a delegation of gay elected officials at the White House [see 76].

ideologies to stratify societies by caste and gender, the AIDS epidemic indicates that the "pollutions" of sexual behavior are being used by the Christian right to further fragment and stratify the American electorate and to expand their own political base. To the more familiar exclusions of wrong race, wrong class, and wrong gender, we are now increasingly pressed to add wrong sexual orientation. The moral disciplines that helped to define persons and to secure the position of the new middle classes in the nineteenth century are now applied to more intimate behaviors. In the relatively homogeneous communities of the Fore, the themes of disease, unacceptable behavior, and social marginality took on different shape. Debates about sorcery, not sexuality, depicted a category of "polluted" persons who could not be named, but whose non-reciprocal actions were characterized as a potential threat to the present social order.

FRAGMENTED THEORIES: FRAGMENTED SOCIETIES

It is perhaps a truism to observe that theories of disease causation are tied to particular social forms. Fore theories of disease origin (and therapeutic practice) stem from a relatively egalitarian social order that at the height of the epidemic still retained a fair degree of harmony between world view and personal inter-action. The idea that a person with kuru, as well as their close kin, are victims of the socially disruptive activities of a hostile opponent is an explanation that is shared by women and men, young and old, indigenous therapists and their clients, even in 1997.

AIDS, by way of contrast, produces a more fragmented set of causation beliefs from a more divided society. Physicians and laypersons no longer share similar views of the way the body functions, or the nature of therapeutic remedies. Antipathy to science has come a long way since the nineteenth-century therapeutic revolution during which views of physicians and patients concerning the mechanisms that determine health and disease began to diverge [77]. Followers of alternate medicine who focus on choice and self-help, now find support from some scientific observers who question the assumption that AIDS is caused by a virus [78-80].

While mainstream views about the origin of AIDS are themselves frag-mented, some minority populations also reject orthodox views. These minority views constitute the ideological counterface of the stigmatizing process. AIDS is here considered to be genocide in the form of germ warfare, introduced by the United States government (or resulting from lack of attention to an accident in government-sponsored research) with the purpose of eliminating unwanted persons, specifically homosexuals, drug-users, and poor inner-city African Americans and Latinos [81-83]. This interpretation reflects the experience of those who live in communities where disproportionately high levels of AIDS are compounded by inadequate health services, low incomes, and rates of infectious disease (TB, syphilis, hepatitis, gonorrhea, measles, mumps, and whooping cough) that would not be tolerated in less impoverished zones.[28] As we know from the Tuskegee Syphilis Study [21], and from the recent French hemophilia scandal, the government is sometimes implicated in killing rather than saving people [85, 86]. As one AIDS patient at Harlem Hospital recently observed: "AIDS is a designer disease. It was designed to hit gays and blacks, but it got out of control and by mistake it hit Rock Hudson and some rich white folks . . . so I think they will try to find a cure" [83].

Similar counter-histories and structures of blame occur during epidemics in other socially stratified societies. During the Indian plague, rumors of intentional ruin were carried in Indian newspaper accounts suggesting that the British were systematically poisoning hospital patients, or the village well, or the bread distributed in famine camps. Another set of rumors proposed that the plague did not exist at all, but had been invented to enable government servants to plunder the people, or for doctors to spread the fear of the disease in order to improve their business [19, pp. 70-73]. Such rumors show more than a deep suspicion about the nature of Western medicine and the complicity of dominant groups in spreading disease. They are also ethical statements and meta-commentaries about the perceived state of social relations.

At the height of the kuru epidemic, the Fore did not have a fragmented theory of disease. Certain that kuru sorcery causes death, the Fore were concerned instead with its excessive use. While the great Fore assemblies of the 1960s elicited general agreement about the way sorcery works, the meta-level discussion concerned a struggle about the place of sorcery in Fore society and the danger of fragmenting social relations. Older men conceded that knowledge of sorcery was generationally specific, conveyed at the time of initiation, but entrusted now to few young men. Younger men observed that they had never participated in sorcery assaults, did not know how to perform them, and suggested that they would all be better off if all their energies were directed toward "development" and a new social and moral order based on cashcropping, business, and education.

By the 1990s, participants in this generational debate were further apart. The younger generation, especially those who had converted to Christianity and had better access to town earnings, now argued more strongly for "development" over adherence to "traditional" payments of several kinds.[29] The willingness to question sorcery (its necessity, not its efficacy) and to opt for "development" signals a

---

[28]A recent study of the association between socioeconomic status and survival following HIV infection showed that a significant risk of death for low income men persisted despite adjustment for age at infection, CD4 count, treatment with various drugs, and year of infection. The finding is consistent with the association of lower socioeconomic status and increased morbidity and mortality observed within large populations and in other diseases [see 84].

[29]In 1991, Seventh Day Adventists said they had tabooed death payments in 1988, and were then discussing the merits of dispensing with brideprice. That is, certain segments of the population had already begun to withhold resources from the traditional forms of exchange, freeing wealth for individual investment and consumption by young men with town earnings.

shift in ideas and practices conceived as essential to an emerging social order that encourages individual effort, wage labor, local markets, and galloping consumerism. The kuru epidemic thus provided the occasion for a moral debate about the positive and negative aspects of certain kinds of political and economic behaviors.

In sum, epidemics unmask opposed interests kept subdued in less critical times, conveying partisan views about the "correct" reproduction of the social order. In the context of a changing society, the kuru epidemic allowed some individuals to question the legitimacy of the format for producing, controlling, and distributing resources, giving a new tilt to generational tensions. The response to the plague unmasked a complex of antagonisms in colonial India, and the differential response to syphilis in eighteenth- and nineteenth-century France was a lesson in the way dominant groups telegraph and protect their positions in a changing social order.

The AIDS epidemic, which raised the spectre of new ways to die, presented some segments of the American public with more information about the diversity of sexual behavior and the desperate condition of the poor than they were ready to hear, triggering its own set of moral debates about the control and distribution of resources. As the epidemic changes course, a barrage of unequal participants continue to broadcast competing versions of the apocalypse as they attempt to reconfigure society and their own place in it.

REFERENCES

1. E. Fee and D. M. Fox (eds.), *AIDS, The Burdens of History,* University of California Press, 1988.
2. *New York Times,* C3, November 29, 1994.
3. D. L. Kirp, citing J. Mann, *The Nation,* p. 93, July 18, 1994.
4. *New York Times,* C9, July 13, 1992.
5. *New York Times,* Section 2, p. 20, 1992.
6. *New York Times,* C3, June 19, 1992.
7. J. Pressman, AIDS and the Burdens of Historians, *Journal of the History of Sexuality, 1*:1, pp. 137-143, 1990.
8. D. T. Richardo, The AIDS Information Explosion, *AIDS and Society,* 5:2, 1994.
9. *New York Times,* E5, July 26, 1992.
10. *Science, 242,* p. 858, 1988.
11. S. Prusiner, J. Collinge, J. Powell, and B. Anderton (eds.), *Prion Diseases of Humans and Animals,* Ellis Horwood, Chichester, England, 1992.
12. J. Lederberg and P. Slack, Essays, *Social Research,* 55:3, 1988.
13. A. W. Crosby, *America's Forgotten Pandemic. The Influenza of 1918,* Cambridge University Press, Cambridge, 1989.
14. P. Slack, Introduction, in *Epidemics and Ideas,* T. Ranger and P. Slack (eds.), Cambridge University Press, Cambridge, 1992.
15. D. Schneider, Typhoons on Yap, *Human Organization, 16*:2, p. 15, 1957.
16. *The Lancet,* July 19, 1991.

17. D. Rosner and G. Markowitz, *Deadly Dust. Silicosis and the Politics of Occupational Disease in Twentieth-Century America,* Princeton University Press, Princeton, New Jersey, 1991.
18. R. Chandavarkar, Plague Panic and Epidemic Politics in India, 1896-1914, in *Epidemics and Ideas,* T. Ranger and P. Slack (eds.), Cambridge University Press, Cambridge, pp. 204-210, 1992.
19. D. Arnold, *Touching the Body: Perspectives on the Indian Plague, 1896-1900, Subaltern Studies V,* Ranajit Guha (ed.), Oxford University Press, Delhi, pp. 55-90, 1987.
20. Z. Gussow, *Leprosy, Racism, and Public Health, Social Policy in Chronic Disease Control,* Westview Press, Boulder, 1989.
21. A. M. Brandt, *No Magic Bullet. A Social History of Venereal Disease in the United States Since 1880,* Oxford University Press, New York, 1987.
22. E. Shorter, What Can Two Historical Examples of Sexually-Transmitted Diseases Teach Us About AIDS? in *Sexual Behaviour and Networking: Anthropological and Socio-Cultural Studies on the Transmission of HIV,* T. Dyson (ed.), Editions Derouaux-Ordina, Belgium, pp. 49-64, 1991.
23. E. Showalter, *Sexual Anarchy Gender and Culture at the Fin de Siecle,* Viking, New York, 1990.
24. C. E. Rosenberg, What Is An Epidemic? AIDS in Historical Perspective, *Daedalus, 118*:1, pp. 1-17, 1989.
25. T. Ranger and P. Slack (eds.), *Epidemics and Ideas. Essays on the Historical Perception of Pestilence,* Cambridge University Press, Cambridge, 1992.
26. V. Turner, *Schism and Continuity in an African Society. A Study of Ndembu Village Life,* Manchester University Press, Manchester, 1957.
27. A. W. Crosby, Hawaiian Depopulation as a Model for the Amerindian Experience, in *Epidemics and Ideas,* T. Ranger and P. Slack (eds.), Cambridge University Press, Cambridge, pp. 175-202, 1992.
28. A. M. Kraut, *Silent Travellers. Germs, Genes and the "Immigrant Menace,"* Basic Books, New York, 1994.
29. T. Ranger and P. Slack, *Epidemics and Ideas,* Cambridge University Press, Cambridge, 1992.
30. C. E. Rosenberg, Disease and Social Order in America: Perceptions and Expectations, *Milbank Quarterly, 64*:1, pp. 34-55, 1986.
31. V. Berridge, AIDS: History and Contemporary History, in *The Time of AIDS,* G. Herdt and S. Lindenbaum (eds.), Sage Publications, California, 1992.
32. *AIDS and Behavior, An Integrated Approach,* National Academy Press, Washington, D.C., 1994.
33. M. D. Grmek, *History of AIDS,* Princeton University Press, Princeton, New Jersey, 1990.
34. R. Schilts, *And The Band Played On,* St. Martin's Press, New York, 1987.
35. W. H. Foege, Plagues: Perceptions of Risk and Social Responses, *Social Research, 55*:3, pp. 331-343, 1988.
36. A. R. Jonsen and J. Stryker (eds.), *The Social Impact of AIDS in the United States,* National Academy Press, Washington, D.C., 1993.
37. S. C. Ouelette-Kobasa, AIDS and Volunteer Associations: Perspectives on Social and Individual Change, *Milbank Quarterly, 68*:2, pp. 280-284, 1990.
38. S. M. Chambre, Volunteers as Witnesses: The Mobilization of AIDS Volunteers in New York City, 1981-1988, *Social Service Review,* pp. 531-547, 1991.
39. N. Glick-Schiller, The Invisible Women: Caregiving and the Construction of AIDS Health Services, *Culture, Medicine and Psychiatry, 17*:4, pp. 487-512, 1993.

40. M. Singer, Z. Castillo, L. Davison, and C. Flores, Owning AIDS: Latino Organizations and the AIDS Epidemic, *Hispanic Journal of Behavioral Sciences, 12*:2, pp. 196-211, 1990.
41. M. Singer, C. Flores, L. Davison, G. Burke, and Z. Castillo, Puerto Rican Community Mobilizing in Response to the AIDS Crisis, *Human Organization, 50*:1, pp. 73-81, 1991.
42. R. Ariss, Performing Anger: The Strategic Function of Emotion in the Social Response to AIDS, *Mankind*, (in press).
43. S. Lindenbaum, *Kuru Sorcery: Disease and Danger in the New Guinea Highlands*, Mayfield Publications, Palo Alto, California, 1979.
44. D. Harris, A Blizzard of Images, *The Nation*, pp. 851-852, December 31, 1990.
45. S. Epstein, Democratic Science? AIDS Activism and the Contested Construction of Knowledge, *Socialist Review, 21*:2, pp. 35-64, 1991.
46. R. M. Wachter, Sounding Board. AIDS, Activism, and the Politics of Health, *The New England Journal of Medicine*, pp. 128-133, January 9, 1992.
47. M. Sturken, Conversations with the Dead, *Socialist Review*, pp. 165-195, 1992.
48. P. Treichler, AIDS, HIV and the Cultural Construction of Reality, in *The Time of AIDS*, G. Herdt and S. Lindenbaum (eds.), Sage Publications, California, pp. 65-98, 1992.
49. D. Indyk and D. Rier, *Grassroots AIDS Groups: Marginal Innovators?* paper presented at the American Sociological Association meetings, Cincinnati, Ohio, August 23-27, 1991.
50. E. R. Sorenson, *The Edge of the Forest*, Smithsonian Institute Press, Washington, D.C., 1976.
51. A. Gibbons, Where are 'New' Diseases Born? *Science, 261*, pp. 680-681, 1993.
52. M. Singer, Z. Castillo, L. Davison, and C. Flores, Owning AIDS: Latino Organizations and the AIDS Epidemic, *Hispanic Journal of Behavioral Sciences, 12*:2, pp. 196-211, 1990.
53. M. Singer and C. Snipes, Generations of Suffering: Experiences of a Treatment Program for Substance Abuse During Pregnancy, *Journal of Health Care for the Poor and Underserved, 3*:1, pp. 222-234, 1992.
54. S. Lindenbaum, Knowledge and Action in the Shadow of AIDS, in *The Time of AIDS*, G. Herdt and S. Lindenbaum (eds.), Sage Publications, California, pp. 319-334, 1992.
55. S. Lindenbaum, *Fore Fieldnotes 1991*, 1993.
56. J. D. Mathews, R. M. Glasse, and S. Lindenbaum, Kuru and Cannibalism, *The Lancet, 2*, p. 449, 1989.
57. R. L. Klitzman, M. P. Alpers, and D. C. Gajdusek, The Natural Incubation Periods of Kuru and the Episodes of Transmission in Three Clusters of Patients, *Neuroepidemiology, 3*:3, p. 20, 1984.
58. J. Mann, *World Overview of the Heterosexual Transmission of HIV*, speech given at the Royal Society of Medicine, London, March 30, 1993.
59. S. Buchbinder, M. Katz, N. Hessol, P. O'Malley, J. Bamjart, and S. Holmberg, Healthy Long-Term Positives: Men Infected with HIV for More than 10 Years with CD4 Counts of More than 500 Cells, *Abstracts, International Conference on AIDS*, Amsterdam, July 21, 1992.
60. M. Clatts, All the King's Horses and All the King's Men: Some Personal Reflections on Ten Years of AIDS Ethnography, *Human Organization, 53*:1, pp. 93-95, 1994.
61. S. E. Estroff, Identity, Disability and Schizophrenia: The Problem of Chronicity, in *Knowledge, Power and Practice*, S. Lindenbaum and M. Lock (eds.), University of California Press, Berkeley, pp. 247-286, 1993.
62. R. Murphy, *The Body Silent*, W. W. Norton, New York, 1990.

63. W. G. Hawkeswood, *"I'm a Black Man who Just Heppens to be Gay,"* The Sexuality of Gay Black Men, paper delivered at the American Anthropological Association meetings, New Orleans, December 2, 1990.
64. E. Quimby, Anthropological Witnessing for African Americans: Power, Responsibility and Choice in the Age of AIDS, in *The Time of AIDS,* Sage Publications, California, 1992.
65. J. Arras, The Fragile Web of Responsibility: AIDS and the Duty to Treat, *Hastings Center Report, 19*:2, pp. 10-20, 1988.
66. S. J. Kunitz, Speculations on the European Mortality Decline, *Economic History Review, 36*:3, pp. 349-364, 1983.
67. S. J. Kunitz, Making a Long Story Short: A Note on Men's Height and Mortality in England from the First through the Nineteenth Centuries, *Medical History, 31,* pp. 269-280, 1987.
68. C. R. Rosenberg, *The Cholera Years,* University of Chicago Press, Chicago, 1962.
69. J. Frykman and O. Lofgren, *Culture Builders. A Historical Anthropology of Middle-Class Life,* Rutgers University Press, New Brunswick, New Jersey, 1987.
70. G. Vigarello, *Concepts of Cleanliness: Changing Attitudes in France Since the Middle Ages,* Cambridge University Press, New York, 1988.
71. M. Foucault, *Power/Knowledge,* Pantheon Books, New York, 1980.
72. M. Foucault, *The History of Sexuality, Vol. 1, An Introduction,* Vintage Books, New York, 1980.
73. M. Douglas, *Purity and Danger. An Analysis of Concepts of Pollution and Taboo,* Praeger, New York, 1966.
74. P. Aldous, French Venture Where U.S. Fears to Tread, *Science, 257,* p. 25, 1992.
75. E. O. Laumann, J. H. Gagnon, R. T. Michael, and S. Michaels, *The Social Organization of Sexuality,* University of Chicago Press, Chicago, 1994.
76. *New York Times,* A. 7, July 19, 1992.
77. C. E. Rosenberg, The Therapeutic Revolution: Medicine, Meaning, and Social Change in Nineteenth-Century America, in *The Therapeutic Revolution,* M. J. Vogel and C. E. Rosenberg (eds.), University of Pennsylvania Press, pp. 3-26, 1979.
78. *New York Times,* September 10, 1992.
79. *New York Times,* letter by Duesberg, September 29, 1992.
80. P. Duesberg, Infectious AIDS: Stretching the Germ Theory Beyond Its Limits, *International Archives of Allergy and Immunology, 102*:2, pp. 118–127, 1994.
81. H. L. Dalton, AIDS in Blackface, *Daedalus, 118,* pp. 205-228, 1989.
82. A. Pivnick, *Victims and Saviors: The Meanings of Motherhood and Children among Poor, Drug-Using Women,* Ph.D. dissertation, Columbia University, 1991.
83. S. Lindenbaum, *Harlem Fieldnotes 1990.*
84. R. S. Hogg, S. A. Strathdee, K. J. P. Craib, M. V. O'Shaughnessy, J. S. G. Montaner, and M. T. Schechter, Lower Socioeconomic Status and Shorter Survival following HIV Infection, *Lancet, 344,* pp. 1120-1124, 1994.
85. M. Balter, French Scientists May Face Charges over CJD Outbreak, *Science, 261,* p. 543, 1993.
86. D. Butler, French Ministries Face Public Trial in HIV Blood Affair, *Nature, 370,* p. 243, 1994.

SECTION II

Gender, Ethnicity and Class in AIDS Risk in the Inner-City

CHAPTER 3

Articulating Personal Experience and Political Economy in the AIDS Epidemic: The Case of Carlos Torres

Merrill Singer

Carlos Torres (pseudonym), a twenty-eight-year-old Puerto Rican injection drug user, is struggling to overcome his drug habit, struggling to "get his life together," struggling to be supportive to his wife who is in jail on drug charges and his children who are living with her parents in Puerto Rico, and, in addition to these daunting challenges, he is struggling to come to terms with the fact that he recently tested positive for exposure to the human immunodeficiency virus. Carlos is scared and confused and, like many people with HIV disease, desperate for understanding and for reprieve. Using narrative material from life history interviewing with Carlos as part of Project COPE[1] in Hartford, Connecticut, this chapter locates his troubled life and experience within the encompassing contexts of the working class Puerto Rican community in the United States, the street drug scene, the health crisis of the urban poor, and the encompassing American socioeconomic structure. The objective of this chapter is to explore the intersection of individual biography and political economy, the critical link that unites the innermost experiences of the individual with the widest kinds of social-historical phenomena.

[1] A study of AIDS risk prevention among drug users supported by a grant (#1R18DA05750) from the National Institute on Drug Abuse.

Approaching the AIDS epidemic from this vantage is an extension of the insight of C. Wright Mills that "Neither the life of an individual nor the history of a society can be understood without understanding both" [1, p. 1]. Examining an individual case within the context of contemporary history and social structure, it is argued here, serves as one means of bridging the micro-macro dilemma that has emerged as a fundamental problem in the contemporary health social sciences [2, 3]. As DeWalt and Pelto emphasize, "articulating the linkages between microlevels and macrolevels" has become "among the most vexing issues in social science research" while at the same time being "a most promising area for current research and theory building" [4, p. 1]. The approach to micro-macro problem offered in this chapter provides a means of repersonalizing the subject matter and the content of the social science of health research by focusing on "the particular, the existential, the subjective content of . . . suffering" as both *lived* event and experience [5, p. 137], while, at the same time, not submerging the strong conditioning impact of class, gender, and ethnic relationships on human life and experience.

There is a great need for this kind of unified micro-macro focus in behavioral AIDS research, especially there is need for an approach that recognizes that not only is the personal political but that the political is personal as well. Unfortunately, too often in social science of AIDS research discourse remains frozen at the abstract and impersonal level. As HIV/AIDS spreads through a population and as the statistics begin piling up, there is a regrettable tendency to lose sight of the real people behind the mounting numbers. Unless AIDS strikes home and is diagnosed in a family member, friend, or acquaintance, it is possible to go on believing that AIDS is a distant shadow, one that does not befall "people like us." Attitudes like this have been found even among people who engage in very high risk behavior, such as injection drug users. As Mayes comments with reference to difficulties she encountered after publishing a novel about a middle-class woman with AIDS:

> The critics . . . were not interested in reading about the downfall of an attractive, successful professional, probably much like them. People who spread or had AIDS could not be viewed as *like them* [6, p. 84].

This kind of distancing allows the individual to avoid thinking about the people who die of AIDS or suffer with its painful symptoms. And it allows risk behavior to continue in the face of a lethal epidemic.

In response, one of the missions of what has come to be called the "AIDS community"—the set of people whose lives and behaviors have been significantly affected by the disease—has been to make sure they avoid burying the names, the distinctive life stories, and the poignant social memories of all of the individuals who die of AIDS. The Names Project, for example, created a giant AIDS quilt with hundreds of panels, each devoted to the unique memory of a single person who died of AIDS, for this precise purpose. Efforts like this are designed to keep a human face on the AIDS crisis, to never forget that AIDS kills people not numbers.

Farmer has suggested, "One way to avoid losing sight of the humanity of those with AIDS is to focus on the experience and insights of those who are afflicted" [7, p. 262]. Sufferer experience, an arena long neglected in the social science of health, increasingly has become a topic of research interest in recent years. But there are alternative ways of presenting and analyzing sufferer experience, including those that do not go far beyond the individual level. Scheper-Hughes, for example, has argued that in the AIDS epidemic the primary job of the social scientist is to be a "clerk of the records," carefully recording but never interpreting or analyzing the lives of people with AIDS [8]. The objective is to become "a minor historian of the ordinary lives of people often presumed to have no history" [9, p. 419]. Sufferer experience, in this approach, is recorded in order to maintain an account of the human cost of AIDS [10].

By contrast, from the perspective presented in this chapter, sufferer experience is treated as a social product, one that is constructed and reconstructed in the action arena between socially constituted categories of meaning and the political-economic forces that shape the contexts of daily life. Recognizing the powerful role of such forces, however, does not imply that individuals are passive or lack the agency to initiate change, and it certainly does not mean that they are insignificant or faceless. Instead, it means that people respond to the material conditions they encounter in terms of the set of possibilities created by the existing configuration of social relations and social conditions. Within this framework it is possible to remain sensitive to the individual level of experience and necessary to do so if we are ever to create a more humane health care system and more humane lives for all people.

Thus, in attempting to understand Carlo's reaction to and experience of AIDS, I begin with the difficult health and social conditions that have defined an important aspect of Puerto Rican life in the United States.

PUERTO RICANS, POVERTY, AND AIDS

Carlos' life as a Puerto Rican man in the United States, as a drug injector, and as a sufferer of HIV disease is fully comprehensible only in terms of the wider context of these "personal" descriptors. By 1985, there were 2.6 million Puerto Ricans living in the United States, about one-third of the total Puerto Rican population [11]. Labor migrants, Puerto Ricans constitute an important section of the post-World War II new working class created to fill a demand for low-wage unskilled labor. In Wolf's terms, the ingathering of this multinational work force on U.S. soil reflects "the general tendency of the capitalist mode to create a 'disposable mass' of laborers out of diverse populations, and to then throw that mass into the breach to meet the changing need of capital" [12, pp. 379-380].

Throughout its history, Wolf adds, the capitalist mode has exercised labor control through ethnic segmentation, allocating "different categories of workers to rungs on the scale of labor markets, relegating the stigmatized populations to the lower levels and insulating the higher echelons from competition from below" [12, p. 380]. Puerto Ricans are one group that consistently has been relegated to the bottom labor markets, and they are characterized by all of the expressions of social distress and suffering that goes along with occupying this rung in the U.S. social hierarchy. A review of the sociodemographic characteristics of U.S. Puerto Ricans reveals that they comprise one of the youngest and fastest growing ethnic subgroups in the country. Additionally, they are "more likely than non-Hispanics to drop out of school, be unemployed, and live in poverty" [13, p. 1]. As of 1987, only 53.8 percent of Puerto Ricans twenty-five years of age and older were high school graduates, compared to 63.4 percent of African Americans, and 77 percent of Whites [14]. Also in 1987, a time during which the national unemployment rate stood at 7 percent, the rate for Puerto Rican men was over 12 percent. While almost 10 percent of all non-Latino families in the United States live in poverty, among Puerto Ricans this figure stands at 38 percent [14]. Related to this is the fact that 30 percent or more of Latino twelve- to seventeen-year-olds live in single parent households, most of which are headed by women. Fifty-two percent of all Latino female-headed households live below the poverty line (compared to 27 percent of white female-headed households), while among Puerto Ricans this figure is 63 percent. Bean and Tienda conclude, "Puerto Ricans exhibit the least socioeconomic success of all of the groups, as well as many of the sorts of demographic behavior that are often associated with economic disadvantage" [15, p. 400]. In no small way, it is the personal misery and alienation produced by this disadvantage, combined with the insulting colonial status of Puerto Rico, that underlies a disproportionate level of involvement in injection drug use by Puerto Ricans. And it is this frequency of involvement with injected drugs that has fueled the AIDS epidemic among U.S Puerto Ricans, most of whom are concentrated in high infection areas of the Northeast [16].

Hartford, Connecticut, Carlos' adopted home, exemplifies the contemporary situation for most Puerto Ricans living in the United States. While Puerto Rican migrants to the United States initially headed to New York City, and helped to create the largest concentration of Puerto Ricans away from the Island, by the 1980s the majority of U.S. Puerto Ricans lived outside of New York City. Increasingly, Puerto Rican migrants, most of whom are displaced workers who "could not be integrated into the capital-intensive industrializing economy of Puerto Rico" [17, p. 200] have moved to other U.S. cities, large and small, in an effort to find jobs and a decent place to live. As Backstrand and Schensul indicate,

Reflecting this national trend, Connecticut has experienced a 481 percent increase in the number of Puerto Rican residents since 1960s, 230 percent between 1970 and 1980. . . . Paralleling the state as a whole, Hartford's Puerto

Rican population has grown rapidly: 400-500 percent since the 1960s, and doubling between 1970 and 1980 [18, p. 10].

Between 1980 and 1990, there was another 58 percent increase in the Puerto Rican population of Hartford, producing a city population that is now approximately one-third Puerto Rican. The initial attractant to Hartford was the tobacco fields that lie north of the city, a place that is well suited to growing the outer layers of certain kinds of cigars. Not uncommonly these fields have been owned and operated by the same companies that produce tobacco and employ agricultural workers in Puerto Rico. However, the tobacco industry can absorb only a limited number of workers and many Puerto Ricans who migrated to the city to be with loved ones and find better paying jobs quickly turned from agricultural to industrial employment. Unfortunately, Puerto Ricans began moving to Hartford in large numbers just as the booming industrial era was coming to a close. Throughout the region metal, machinery, textile, weapons, and other factories were shutting down or moving South, laying off workers in waves as one field of production after the other fell victim to the changing needs of capital. While the city still retained its standing as an insurance and banking center, not many jobs were available in these industries for unskilled Puerto Rican workers with limited formal education.

With the collapse of its industrial base, the outmigration of skilled workers, and the substitution of unskilled workers from the South and the Caribbean, Hartford was transformed. Today, Hartford is the fourth poorest moderate-size city in the country. It has the fourth highest per capita crime rate in the nation, with drug-related activity accounting for 80 percent of all city crimes. Over 25 percent of households in the city have incomes below the poverty level and over 30 percent are on welfare. Fifty percent of high school students live in single-parent house-holds under the poverty line [19]. These conditions are especially evident in the Puerto Rican community, as seen in several recent community studies. In 1988, the AIDS Community Research Group (ACRG), a community consortium, con-ducted a study of AIDS knowledge and risk behavior in an ethnically mixed section of Hartford. The study was designed to locate and interview an ethnically stratified random sample of individuals living in a clearly delineated neighbor-hood. Only 42 percent of the Hispanic sample, almost all of whom were Puerto Rican, had completed a high school education, and 17 percent had six or fewer years of schooling. Less than 70 percent of these respondents had full- or part-time employment. Forty-two percent reported household income from some form of public assistance. The average monthly income was $999 compared to $1,233 for African Americans and $1,812 for Whites.

The difficult social reality of Puerto Ricans in Hartford has been described in some detail in a series of articles entitled, "Two Connecticuts: Separate and Unequal" printed in the city's single remaining daily newspaper, the *Hartford Courant*. One article in the series (Sept. 25, 1988) culled federal, state, and local sources and reported that: 1) the infant mortality rate among non-whites in Hartford is 24.3 per 1,000 live births, more than triple the statewide average for white babies; 2) only 42 percent of Hispanic children (compared to 86% of white children) live with both parents; 3) almost 55 percent of Hispanic children (under age 16) are living below the federal poverty line; 4) only 42 percent of Hispanic children in the city's public schools perform above remedial standards (compared to 74% of white children); 5) among Hispanic adults, 62 percent have less than a high school education; 6) the average household income for Hispanics is half that of whites; 7) statewide 32 percent of families on welfare are Hispanic (although they compose only 4% of the state's population); 8) Hispanics account for 25 percent of clients at shelters for the homeless; 9) 24 percent of inmates in state prisons in the state are Hispanic; and 10) Hispanic families in Hartford are poorer than Hispanics nationally, with 25 percent earning less than $5,000 a year in 1980. Other reports have shown that many Hispanic families in Hartford live in over-crowded and deteriorating apartments that are exorbitantly priced, leaving few resources for food, health care, and other family needs [3]. High levels of stress due to poverty, cramped space, language barriers, unfamiliarity with the surrounding environment, and limited culture-appropriate social programming have left many Puerto Rican families feeling powerless, depressed, and alienated from the wider society. As another of the *Hartford Courant* articles concluded, "All too often, researchers say, the lesson learned by Black and Hispanic children is a lesson in self-hate" (Nov. 20, 1988).

As Wallace has demonstrated, deteriorating social conditions and disrupted community networks in the Northeast contribute significantly to increased AIDS transmission for several reasons [20]. First, under these conditions, the appeal of drug use skyrockets. On the one hand, there are few meaningful and socially valued life options available. Opportunities to gain a prestigious job, material comfort, or social recognition in mainstream society through conventional routes are meager. The social support needed to overcome adversity is limited, while the daily insult of ethnic discrimination and disparagement, in the schools, in stores, and in the workplace, is so common as to *almost* escape notice. Mood-altering drugs, on the other hand, are ubiquitous, available for illicit sale on street corners throughout inner-city neighborhoods. Today, street drug sales in Hartford are controlled primarily by youth gangs who directly manage the trade in some key locations (i.e., high volume sites) and "lease" space and sell drugs to other dealers in less lucrative locations. For example, on June 15, 1995, Hartford police arrested a twenty-three-year-old high-ranking member of Los Solidos (The Solids), a primarily Puerto Rican local gang, for possession of 3,000 single-dose $10 bags of heroin with intent to sell [21]. This arrest was preceded by a series of drug-related police actions against Los Solidos and their rivals in other gangs.

Second, in the Northeast, drug injection is the means of drug consumption that has been passed on as each aging generation of drug users has taught up-and-coming siblings, friends, and potential customers how to get on the road to chemical escape. The response of the dominant society has been to pass laws to control the working-class drug user. To augment laws against drug use and possession, a number of states, including Connecticut, implemented statutes to restrict access to the equipment needed to inject drugs. Syringe prescription and possession laws allowed law enforcement officials to arrest drug users for carrying syringes even if they were not in the possession of drugs. On the street, police have used these laws to regularly stop known drug users, threaten them with arrest, extract information from them, and smash any syringes in their possession even if they do not arrest them. As a result, drug injectors have attempted to limit the frequency with which they carry syringes with them. Instead, many have turned to "shooting galleries" as sources of needles. In these sites, which are often set up in apartments by drug users who gain access to drugs by providing a safe place to "shoot up" to their fellow addicts, renting out used syringes as well as drug cookers and syringe rinse water came to be the norm. A similar type of location in Hartford is the base-house, where cocaine addicts gather to smoke either powder cocaine or crack-cocaine, the latter of which is commonly called "rock" in Hartford.

A review of cumulative AIDS data for the United States indicates that individuals born in Puerto Rico have both the highest incidence of AIDS among Hispanics in the United States as well as the highest incidence associated with injection drug use [22]. Additionally, existing AIDS data reveal the special dynamics of the epidemic in the Northeast, where Puerto Ricans constitute the largest Latino subgroup. Brown and Primm note that this region "has both the highest cumulative incidence of AIDS among minority populations and the greatest prevalence of AIDS associated with the abuse of injectable substances" [23, p. 7]. The relative risk for AIDS for Latinos is seven times higher in the Northeast than other parts of the country [22]. For example, although Latinos, primarily Puerto Ricans, represent 6 percent of Connecticut's overall population,[2] they comprise 18 percent of adult and 24 percent of pediatric AIDS cases. Approximately 60 percent of Latino cases are among injection drug users. Among Project COPE participants, 42 percent of the Latino injectors in our sample tested HIV-positive compared to 19 percent of White injection drug users.

CARLOS IN CONTEXT

One of these participants is Carlos. During interviews, Carlos talked of his difficult life in matter-of-fact terms, revealing, but not recognizing through the telling of his tale, the close connection between unique biography and general historic process. Child of a broken home, he was raised in a low-income substance-involved female-headed home in the inner city. He recalls:

---

[2] Up from 4 percent in 1988, as noted on p. 66.

I grew up in Puerto Rico with my mother. My father used to be an alcoholic. We used to get big whippings, you know and my mother got divorced and she moved to New York. And she started meeting different people. Different men coming into the house and I was still young, seven. I started seeing all sorts of things, my mother getting beat up by my father, then she left him and ended up with another guy; same problems again. They would party a lot; there would be bottles of booze. I started off with booze first. I was going to school drinking everyday. And from there I started meeting people that weren't drinking, they were messing around with drugs. I was thirteen the first time I used drugs.

The illicit drug Carlos was first exposed to was cocaine and it left an indelible imprint on his life thereafter. Like his mother and father, he turned increasingly to substance use as a means of getting by and coping with life's miseries. He reports:

When I first snorted cocaine I didn't know what it was. I seen my friend, he was shooting it so one day I decided to try it. I stole 50 bucks from my mother. I was mad at her about something and I stole 50 bucks from my mother and bought two bags. He helped me shoot the first time, but from then on I learned how to do it myself. I got involved with this girl and she got pregnant when I was fourteen. I went to live with her and her mother at their house. But the drugs got worse because I began doing it three and four times a day. I'd go outside and steal and do all kinds of things. I was losing a lot of weight just because of the drugs, my clothing didn't fit me. I'd think about problems. I'd go to sleep and I'd think about my mother getting into an argument with my father. I'd think about when I used to get beat up by my stepfather, seeing my sister getting beat up by my stepfather, my brother getting drunk. I'd start thinking about all of that, that's why I'd get high. Sometimes I don't sleep. I don't sleep nights. I still got that problem. I start thinking about things I'm not supposed to be thinking about, you know? And it hurts. Sometimes I get the feeling like I want to do some drugs.

While living with his girlfriend's family, Carlos supported himself with a paper route. He used this job as a ploy to track when his customers were not at home so that he could burglarize their apartments. Eventually, he was caught and sent to juvenile prison for two years. Although he continued to use contraband drugs while in prison, he was able to stop using by the time he was released and returned home to resume his relationship. He says:

I was off drugs for maybe about three months and then I got handed too much pressure. I had a job, I was doing good. But I ended up on drugs again so she left me. First one left me, a second one left me. I didn't even care anymore. I went back to visit my mother. She pretty much knew I was on drugs, so she wanted to keep me closer to her. But she couldn't afford living with me and giving me money for the drugs and if she didn't give them to me, I would steal it from her. I met another lady. I was working seven days a week to support my habit. You know, I was living by myself when I met her, a beautiful lady. Instead of taking care of her I hooked her into drugs. I made $700 a week working seven days a week. So I give her $300 and I take $400 dollars for me. I'd take a ride to New York and I'd buy four bundles of drugs to last me a whole week. And I used to do that every week. She was asking me one day what I was doing with my money. And we got into an argument. I was drinking, and I was on cocaine. She got mad so I gave her a taste of coke. She got to like it after a while. We just started shooting drugs together. Then they raided the house and they found heroin and cocaine at the house. They couldn't catch me, I dove from a second story window. She didn't want to jump, she got scared, so she got busted. So she took all the blame for everything. She went to jail.

The police found a large supply of cocaine in Carlos' apartment because he had converted it into a base house. Carlos allowed fellow cocaine addicts to "get off" in his apartment in exchange for "a taste" of each user's cocaine supply. In addition, he rented the bedrooms of the apartment to use for sex, a common practice in this type of "house" [24].

Once his partner was arrested, Carlos began to reassess his life. He began trying to make sense of his problems, to come to terms with his sense of responsibility and guilt, and to understand the type of man he is. He comments:

The questions just came into my head again and again: am I good, am I bad? Back and forth. I used the drugs. I have problems. I ain't a kid who cares. And now she's in jail. She knows that I have the AIDS virus but just because of that she ain't gonna leave me. I talked to my counselor from Project COPE. He tells me things that I can't understand. He says "You do this and this and cooperate with life, don't hide it using drugs. You're clean, you're doing good, now you gotta get a job. You'll have all the material things again." But I got too many pressures in my mind worrying about my wife in jail.

Carlos also is trying to understand his HIV disease, while seeing his infection as one more expression of the cruel hand of fate that has so deeply shaped his life. Nervously, he says:

When I found out about coming out positive, the counselor started asking me if I knew about AIDS. I said I don't know about it. I just knew that I was sick. Well, he sat right down there and explained it, you know, how to keep myself safe, how not to infect anybody. This guy gave me condoms. I use them, when I have relations with somebody. The guy told me, "Make sure that you don't harm nobody else, protect that person, protect yourself." I said, "That's what I'm gonna do, I'm gonna take it easy." So far I'm doing good, my family's helping me out a lot. They don't get mad at me like before when I used to do drugs. They'd say, "I don't want you here, you're all drugged up, get out of here." They still don't trust me, but I tell them, "Hey trust me, if you knock me down, I'm gonna feel bad. I might go back on cocaine if it's too much pressure. I'm not gonna be able to hack it, especially now that I'm sick." And I gotta understand AIDS but I don't understand it too good. I want to save my kids. I want to find out what I can do to protect them and to protect me. Some people who use drugs don't have AIDS, those are the lucky ones. They're lucky, you know? I hung around with the wrong people.

Through all of this Carlos struggles to retain hope, clinging to the idea that he will be all right if he is careful now, holding fast the wish that his wife's release from prison will usher in a return to a safer, less frightening time. Also he is preoccupied with understanding how he got infected and who might have "given" him the virus. And he worries that he may have infected his wife. He ruminates constantly on these issues but can reach no resolve. He notes:

> I know AIDS is cyclical and you can help yourself or make it worse. Sometimes you still need some counseling, you gotta hear it from somebody else's mouth telling you you've got it. I don't understand it, but I don't want to get sicker than I'm supposed to. I don't know how I got it. My brother-in-law, my wife's husband, has AIDS. He's had AIDS for awhile. He doesn't know how long he's gonna live, but he's doing the best he can. He's not using drugs and now he's trying to stretch out his life a little bit more. Maybe from him I got it, I don't know. He came to the house, we shared needles. I just don't know how I got AIDS. I don't know about my wife either. She has to be positive too, I came out positive and she used the same needles that I used. Sometimes when I left my needles without cleaning them she wouldn't clean the needles and she would just pump it right up herself. And we'd have crazy sex sometimes in bed, you know, without condoms.

Try as he may, Carlos cannot really come to terms with his situation. He feels alone and dependent, worried that he has brought calamity down upon his own life and the lives of his wife and children. In his torment, he thinks of drugs, the one solace in a life of false starts and difficult turns, a life of limited options in which personal agency has been activated only within a narrow track produced by forces and relations beyond Carlos' immediate awareness. Enrolled by his drug counselor in an inpatient drug treatment program, he fights the regimentation that it imposes. After a life of free wheeling, drug-induced excitement, he finds it hard to set limits. Drugs have become an integral part of his life, an immediate escape from social constraint and from an emotionally threatening social reality. Consequently, he quickly drops out of treatment and returns to the streets, to his drug-using friends, to a way of life that will certainly bring him death from a frightening disease that he feels he cannot escape, cannot stop, and cannot really understand. Until then, he can at least find brief respite from his fears through a drug-induced euphoria and that is what he chooses. A year later, he has still not recontacted his counselor. Perhaps he has found another program, perhaps he is in the hospital, perhaps, like many drug users, he died of violence even before he died of AIDS.

CONCLUSION

As with all people, the content and character of Carlos' life and experience are unique, a complex configuration that reflects both innate disposition and the particular set of experienced personalities and events, times, and places that conjoin and intermingle giving each life the singular and distinctive quality we term personality. As a consequence, describing Carlos' life and his confrontation with AIDS as mechanically determined from above would degrade not only his self-hood and personal significance, but the special ability of the social sciences and life history research to bring to light the intricate details and hidden interconnections of lived experiences as well. Carlos' boyish innocence and self-centered irresponsibility, his painful guilt and nagging memories, his confusion and fear, his manipulation and loneliness, his deep longing for a woman like his mother who will not desert him despite his shortcomings all combine and shape his distinctive AIDS narrative. Yet the broad outlines of Carlos' story are hardly his alone. On this plane, there is a redundancy across the lives of many urban Puerto Rican men who as teenagers learned from their peers how to deflect the dissonance and degradation of daily life by turning to the use of ever-present mood altering substances. Graduating quickly from alcohol and marijuana use to mainline heroin injection (and in recent years, cocaine injection or smoking), they learned how to get the strongest "high" for the lowest cost.

In short, they learn that there is a way to "beat the system" or so it seems. They may live in rat infested apartments, be denied access to socially valued types of employment, be subject constantly to the distrustful and condemning eyes of store-owners and cruising police, and endure a hundred other reminders both large and small of their social worthlessness, but they have a way to "get high" nonetheless. While drug use may have painful consequences, so do many other aspects of life as a social pariah. And with drugs, at least, it is possible to escape the pain, at least temporarily. And so the cycle continues.

Ironically, with AIDS, the prevailing structure of inequality has, as it always does, the last say. Because of a shortage of new syringes in the drug underground, injection commonly involves either direct needle sharing or indirect sharing (through renting, borrowing, finding, or stealing) of a previously used needle. While direct sharing with a close friend or lover may express intimacy, indirect sharing or sharing with someone who is not emotionally close tends to be frustrating (because you have to wait for others to take their turn before you can get high or because you are forced to use a dull needle that is painful to insert). Either way the behavior can be understood as an adaptive response to the criminalization of syringe buying without a prescription. Sharing, not only of syringes but of bags of "dope," containers to cook or melt the drugs in, cotton to filter the drugs with, and water to rinse clogged needles, have become common practices. All of these behaviors emerged in response to the illegal and clandestine nature of drug use and they all have the capacity to assist the transmission of HIV from one person to another.

As a result of this intertwined set of factors, many Puerto Rican men (and women) now suffer from HIV infection or full-blown AIDS. In all of this, individual biographies merge like streams that feed a common river cascading down a steep and boulder-strewn riverbed. Consequently, treating Carlos' biography and experience independent of wider social-historical phenomena would be a distortion. Carefully fitting the two together, by contrast, including contextualizing unique instance within the fold of a broader pattern, identifying the range of freedom likely within politically and economically determined channels of possibility, and documenting both individual and collective effort and systemic response, offers a road to knowing both the special qualities of the individuals whose lives have been touched so deeply by AIDS and the social structures and social conditions that have brought these particular individuals together as the otherwise faceless cases that comprise this menacing epidemic. This approach propels us to break through the defensive wall of denial and Otherness that have allowed the human immunodeficiency virus to spread continually to new population segments and it forces us to seek social responses to the AIDS crisis that move beyond individual behavior change.

REFERENCES

1. C. Mills, *The Sociological Imagination*, Oxford University Press, Oxford, 1959.
2. M. Singer, Cure, Care and Control: An Ectopic Encounter with Biomedical Obstetrics, in *Encounter with Biomedicine: Case Studies in Medical Anthropology*, H. Baer (ed.), Gordon and Breach Science Publishers, New York, 1987.
3. M. Singer, F. Valentín, H. Baer, and Z. Jia, Why Does Juan Garcia Have a Drinking Problem?: The Perspective of Critical Medical Anthropology, *Medical Anthropology*, *14*:1, pp. 77-108, 1992.
4. B. Dewalt and P. Pertti, *Micro and Macro Levels of Analysis in Anthropology*, Westview Press, Boulder, 1985.
5. N. Scheper-Hughes and M. Lock, Speaking "Truth" to Illness: Metaphors, Reification, and a Pedagogy for Patients, *Medical Anthropology Quarterly*, *17*, pp. 137-140, 1986.
6. S. Mayes, *It Can Happen: An Essay on the Denial of AIDS. In Confronting AIDS Through Literature*, J. Pastore (ed.), University of Chicago Press, Chicago, pp. 84-90, 1993.
7. P. Farmer, *AIDS and Accusation: Haiti and the Geography of Blame*, University of California Press, Berkeley, 1992.
8. N. Scheper-Hughes, *Discussant Comments*, presented at the Ethnicity, Gender and the Experience of AIDS, 90th Annual Meeting of the American Anthropological Association, Chicago, 1991.
9. N. Scheper-Hughes, The Primacy of the Ethical, *Current Anthropology*, *16*:3, pp. 409-420, 1995.
10. G. Whitmore, Bearing Witness, in *The AIDS Reader*, N. McKenzzie (ed.), Meridian, New York, pp. 586-594, 1991.
11. C. Rodriguez, *Puerto Ricans: Born in the U.S.A.*, Unwin Hyman, Boston, 1989.

12. E. Wolf, *Europe and the People Without History,* University of California Press, Berkeley, 1982.
13. E. McKay, *Changing Hispanic Demographics,* National Council of La Raza, Washington, D.C., 1988.
14. Bureau of the Census, *Persons of Spanish Origin in the United States: March 1986 and 1987, Advance Report,* Department of Commerce, Current Population Reports, Series P-20, No. 416, Washington, D.C., 1988.
15. F. Bean and M. Tienda, *The Hispanic Population of the United States,* Russell Safe Foundation, New York, 1989.
16. M. Singer and Z. Jia, AIDS and Puerto Rican Injection Drug Users in the United States, in *Handbook on Risk of AIDS,* B. Brown and G. Beschner (eds.), Greenwood Press, Westport, Connecticut, pp. 227-255, 1993.
17. C. Rodríguez, Economic Factors Affecting Puerto Ricans in New York, in *Labor Migration Under Capitalism: The Puerto Rican Experience,* History Task Force (eds.), Monthly Review Press, New York, pp. 239-264, 1979.
18. J. Backstrand and S. Schensul, Co-Evolution in Outlying Ethnic Communities: The Puerto Ricans of Hartford, CT, *Urban Anthropology, 11,* pp. 9-38, 1982.
19. M. Singer, Providing Substance Abuse Treatment to Puerto Rican Clients Living in the Continental U.S., in *Substance Abuse Treatment in the Era of AIDS: Volume II,* O. Amuleru-Marshall (ed.), Center for Substance Abuse Treatment, Washington, D.C., 1995.
20. R. Wallace, Urban Desertification, Public Health and Public Order: 'Planned Shrinkage,' Violent Death, Substance Abuse and AIDS in the Bronx, *Social Science and Medicine, 31:7,* pp. 801-813, 1990.
21. M. Swift, City Drug Bust Nets $30,000 in Heroin, *Hartford Courant,* B-1, B-2, June 18, 1995.
22. R. Selik, K. Castro, and M. Pappaioanou, Racial/Ethnic Differences in the Risk of AIDS in the United States, *American Journal of Public Health, 79,* pp. 1539-1545, 1988.
23. L. Brown and B. Primm, Intravenous Drug Abuse and AIDS in Minorities, *AIDS and Public Policy Journal, 3,* pp. 5-15, 1988.
24. J. Inciardi, D. Lockwood, and A. Pottieger, *Women and Crack-Cocaine,* Macmillan Publishing Co., New York, 1993.

CHAPTER 4

Love, Jealousy, and Unsafe Sex among Inner-City Women

E. J. Sobo

INTRODUCTION

The majority of women who develop AIDS are poor inner-city Blacks.[1] While Blacks comprise about one-eighth of the American population, they account for about half of all women with AIDS [1]. Black women are about fourteen times more likely than White women to be diagnosed with AIDS [2]. This is not because Black women practice risky sex more frequently than other Americans—they generally do not [3-8]. However, for poor Black women, poverty and racism increase the chances of HIV transmission during unsafe sex. Substandard health care, the frequency of intravenous drug use and untreated venereal infection [9], the negative effects of racial and economic oppression on men's approach to heterosexual intercourse [10-13], and the high prevalence of HIV in inner-city environments increase the chances that unprotected sex among poor urban Blacks will involve HIV transmission.

As Kline and colleagues [3] suggest, much of the literature dealing with hetero-sexually transmitted HIV/AIDS among women describes a model in which impoverished minority women engage in unprotected sex for material gain or because of financial coercion and their lack of a developed sense of power or agency [e.g., 9, 14-16; see also 17]. Poverty does play a key role in enabling HIV

---

[1] I use the term "Black," as did most participants in the research to be described.

transmission, and economic conditions (and the political circumstances that engender them) do circumscribe the range of sexual options that are open to poor urban women, but the women who participated in this study explained their preference for condomless sex with reference to love, not money [18]. That is, at least for these women, the link between macro-level conditions and micro-level sexual decisions is mediated by cultural ideals for heterosexual relations and gender roles. These ideals, themselves linked with political-economic conditions [19-22; cf. 23, 24], are the main immediate drivers of unsafe sex; they leave most women emotionally and socially dependent on relationships with men and affect their perceptions of risk such that unsafe sex seems a safe bet [25; see also 3].[2]

This chapter describes the links between low levels of condom use and inner-city women's experiences and understandings of heterosexual relationships. Specifically, I examine the causes, contexts, and mechanisms of HIV/AIDS-risk denial, which enables and necessitates unsafe (condomless) sex.[3] I focus on the relationship between women's conjugal and extraconjugal relationships and the unsafe sex that HIV/AIDS-risk denial entails (for efficiency's sake, I use conjugal to refer to both legal and common-law or paraconjugal unions). The findings come from a study conducted in 1991-1993 that attempted to identify and explore barriers to safer sex among clients of the Maternal and Infant Health Care Program (M&I) in Cleveland, Ohio, with the aim of improving the efficacy of M&I HIV/AIDS education [25, 32, 33].

BACKGROUND: PREVIOUS RESEARCH

Accepted Models of the Sexual Economy of Blacks

Much of the existing literature on sexuality among poor inner-city Blacks focuses on the overt and immediate economic reasons for the apparent cultural emphasis on the instrumental dimension of sex [cf. 3]. For example, it is thought that women must compete for men because they need men's money; and a willingness to have sex as men want it (i.e., without condoms) narrows the competition [16]. The high level of non-monogamous heterosexual intercourse recommended for and often achieved by men is traced to their lack of economic opportunity and their related dependence on favorable peer evaluations and

---

[2] Many Blacks favor marrying later than whites do and many condone single parenthood [13], but both groups hold the same basic ideals for conjugal relations [e.g., 10-12, 21, 26]. The correspondences between Black women's marriage and gender-related aspirations and those of mainstream U.S. women, findings from risk-perception research [e.g., 3, 27-31], and my own exploratory comparative work [32] suggest that the condom-use and other HIV/AIDS-related patterns and processes that I describe in this chapter can also be found among White and perhaps other U.S. women as well as among poor urban Blacks.

[3] All condomless sex is unsafe sex, even when one's partner swears that s/he is monogamous, because as participants said, "You never know."

tendency toward hyper-masculine compensatory behavior involving sexual conquests and overt misogyny [10-13; see also 15; for statistics on non-monogamy see 34[4]; also see 38, pp. 51-57; 35]. Women who depend on men for money can be forced by circumstance to ignore the infidelities of their male partners while engaging in "survival sex" [36, p. 153].

Like men, some women have multiple partners, but most Blacks think this disrespectable [4]. Multiple partnering among women has generally been analyzed primarily as a strategy by which resource bases are expanded [15, 21; see also 16, 39]. Even having children, which is desirable whether in or out of wedlock, can be understood this way. Conceiving—which involves unprotected sex—can be a strategic choice, given the lack of alternatives or career opportunities. Having a baby can be a way of trying to establish economically indispensable structural links with or through men. Moreover, having responsibilities to a child is often a prerequisite for membership in resource-sharing female support networks [40; see also 21, p. 121].

Less instrumental views of procreative sex do occur in the literature. For instance, Anderson [10; see also 11] notes that Black men are often eager to sire offspring because babies provide proof of their manly heterosexual activity. In regard to women, Mays and Cochran explain that having a baby can be a way of bringing joy and unconditional love into one's life; further, each child born holds the promise of achieving great things [41]. Such cultural forms, shaped by political and economic forces, may actually be more important for women's sexual behavior than the direct financial ramifications that political and economic forces have.[5] While ultimate causality lies with the political economy, proximate reasons for unsafe sex—and those perceived as being most important by decision-making social actors—may be tied to the cultural constructions of heterosexual conjugality that political and economic conditions help to generate. Certain economic data indicate that the notion that women are dependent on men for financial survival may be in error [18].

As is widely noted, a disproportionate number of Black males are unemployed, underemployed, imprisoned,[6] or victims of homicide [e.g., 12]. This limits the

---

[4] African Americans were underrepresented (by about half) in Blumstein and Schwartz [34], education levels were higher than is average for our participants and, because of sampling methods, the study is not generalizable. But it is the only study to my knowledge that explores extra-conjugal affairs among unmarried, cohabiting couples as well as married ones. As the figures do not include non-cohabiting couples, of which there are many in poor, urban communities, I also cited Bower [35], whose figures apply to both white and African-American men. A "substantial" number of heterosexually-coupled men cheat bisexually [36, p. 91; 37, p. 152].

[5] Sex workers and drug users are in many ways an exception; this hypothesis would not generally apply to women while they are members of these groups.

[6] Women's risk for HIV infection rises with male incarceration rates, because homosexual relations are common in prison. Furthermore, heterosexually-coupled men often cheat bisexually [36, p. 91; 37, p. 152]. Covert bisexuality is probably more common among Black men than whites because of the ways that African-American identity is constructed [34, 42].

material benefits that women can get from heterosexual partners. Indeed, W. Wilson explains that some Black women, knowing that the supply of marriageable or employed men is small, choose to build families and network connections without the perceived burden of a husband or boyfriend [43]. Pittman and colleagues comment on the stereotypic "image of Black females as independent baby-makers" [13, p. 340] that has emerged partly in relation to this (and which in certain ways contradicts the stereotype of financial dependence that materialist theories reflect); Pittman and colleagues also point out that Black women are socialized to be economically independent, as does P. Wilson [44]. As Kline and colleagues report, "Rather than occupying financially dependent roles in relationships with men, [poor urban] women [are] often forced to assume economic control" [3, p. 450]. Growing up, Black girls often learn early to assume adult responsibilities and they experience a more egalitarian family structure and have less traditional sex-role expectations than whites [45]. As Weinberg and Williams note, women often provide male lovers with money rather than the other way around [46; see also 21, p. 110].

These exceptions notwithstanding, the literature on Black heterosexuality generally ignores economic self-sufficiency among women when discussing behavior deemed puzzling, deviant, or immoral (such as unsafe, premarital, or non-monogamous sex), preferring to ascribe such conduct to simple financial necessity [for an exception, see 3]. Through a focus on immediate neediness, scholars can provide women with "rational" motivations and they can adopt an ostensibly non-judgmental stance: profit-seeking makes sense according to capitalist logic (which itself helps create needy underclasses), and hunger can be used to excuse or explain moral breeches. I do not deny the force of financial need in certain cases; however, I argue that emotional and social needs are sufficient motivations for having unsafe sex, and they are the motivations that the sample of women involved in this research recognize. Further, as I shall show, these kinds of needs have as much to do with political and economic conditions as more tangible financial needs do.

Unsafe Sex and AIDS Risk Denial

Among most inner-city women as among most U.S. women, cultural ideals make committed sexual unions with men essential for achieving status and attaining happiness [25, cf. 6, 12, 47].[7] According to these ideals, a healthy relationship involves a healthy, disease-free partner—a partner who need not bother with condoms for this partner carries no germs. Without such loyal male partners, women can be subject to shortages of emotional and social resources. Manlessness

---

[7] Some people, including some lesbians and gays, do not accept this. The research does not deal with populations that reject mainstream conjugal ideals.

can leave women feeling unloved or lonely, and it can lower their self-esteem and status. Women actively use unsafe sex as part of a psycho-social strategy for building and preserving an image of themselves as having achieved the conjugal ideal. It often is noted that, in addition to indicating social distance [27; cf. 48, p. 100], using condoms announces that partners are not sexually exclusive and signals a lack of mutual trust. Accordingly, condom use denotes failure in a relationship.[8] Conversely, because of the trust and closeness that it connotes, unsafe sex signals the perfect union [25].

Women can build status and self-esteem by presenting themselves to others as having attracted loyal, upstanding partners and as having attained perfect intact unions. Women commonly pattern stories about their relationships with men on either or both of two narrative forms: the "Monogamy Narrative" and the "Wisdom Narrative." The latter involves claims of having used wisdom in making partner choices; the former involves claims of having an excellent and monogamous relationship [25].

The Political and Economic Context of Women's AIDS Risk Denial

In stratified or class societies, the cultural emphasis on women's role in relation to men as privatized (legal or common-law) wives rather than as blood relatives such as sisters is related to women's subordination to men [20, 22; see also 21, pp. 113-114, 124-125]. Structural subordination of women is culturally reinforced in many ways. For example, as Ortner explains, "In marriage a woman's distinctively feminine (as against generically human) attributes—mainly centering on biological reproduction—are highlighted, whereas in kinship roles they are not. Thus in marriage a woman is more open to being seen as a radically different type of human being" [50, p. 400; parenthetical material in original]. Women are generally seen as lesser human beings when the role of wife is emphasized: they are seen as beings whose completion lies in their articulation with men. This idea holds for many urban Black women as well as for mainstream Whites (see note 2); as I shall show, it is one of the main motivators of unsafe sex.

The fact that most impoverished urban women draw self-esteem from their relationships with men (as do most mainstream U.S. women) is linked to patriarchal social organization. It is further linked to industrial capitalism and the family romance that this political and economic system has fostered. The cultural

---

[8] Condom use also signals instrumental rather than expressive motivations for sexual congress: a woman who uses condoms is likened to (or is) a prostitute, as her sexuality appears unrelated to a desire to establish or maintain a long-term relationship. In reality, prostitutes do tend to use condoms with clients; however, they tend to practice unsafe sex with boyfriends because condoms imply a distance and a profit motive that is inappropriate in the context of a personal relationship [49, pp. 260-261; see also 27].

idealization of monogamy and of the type of loving loyal family relations that monogamy narratives entail exist in "symbolic opposition to work and business, in other words, to the market relations of capitalism"; they exist in opposition to "the market, where we sell our labor and negotiate contract relations of business, that we associate with competitive, temporary, contingent relations" [51, p. 34].

Women who participate in households do a disproportionate share of the labor by which the work force is maintained and reproduced. Rapp explains that they are paid off in a "coin called love" [19, p. 184], both by men who may participate in these households, and by other household members, as all attempt to actualize the ideas associated with family (regarding the function of the unemployed work force in relation the employed work force, see [21, pp. 127-129]). Moreover, as participants in the capitalist economy, we think of the family in terms of expressive relations and love rather than instrumental relations and money, which we associate with "the market" [19].[9] We seek to organize our households according to our notions of family, and these notions "absorb the conflicts, contradictions, and tensions actually generated by those material, class-structured relations that households hold to resources in advanced capitalism" [19, p. 171; see also 51]. In doing so they also provide "an implicit critique of capitalism" [22, p. 3].

Family Ideology, Household Reality

The ideology of family serves to guide us as we seek to form and organize households. Many poor inner-city Blacks, like many Whites, seek to cohabit with a spouse in a nuclear household (see note 2). The concept of family that these women hold can function as a shock-absorber [19], but households that women form in relation to the concept cannot always withstand the pressures of the political-economic environment in which they are built. As Rapp notes, "The tension generated by relations to resource base can often tear households apart" [19, p. 174].[10]

In a now classic study, Stack shows that among urban impoverished Blacks, economic oppression and related resource shortages discourage stable household formation to begin with [21, e.g., p. 91]. Moreover, kin networks often discourage single members from forming conjugal unions, because this would mean the few resources that those individuals would otherwise contribute to the group will be siphoned off to spouses [21, pp. 113-115, 124-125]. The welfare system can discourage conjugal cohabitation through its policies as, for example,

---

[9] As Thorne notes, the two realms of home or family and market interpenetrate and expressive and instrumental relations are not in actuality mutually exclusive [22].

[10] For instance, when money is in short supply and rent goes unpaid, eviction and the dispersal of household members can follow. Substance use, itself tied to the tensions generated by political-economic conditions, also can lead to a household's disintegration, sometimes in tandem with state intervention [regarding the link between unemployment and alcoholism, see 52].

by providing more aid to single women than to married women or cohabiters [21, p. 113].[11]

Household stability is further undermined by male responses to unemployment and underemployment. As noted earlier, most scholars explain women's sexual decisions with reference to simple and immediate financial need, failing to consider macro-level and ideological factors. In comparison, men's actions are more often explained not as financially-motivated but as emotionally-driven responses to macro-level forces. It is widely argued that poor urban men denied access to jobs or decent wages also are denied access to self-fulfillment through the classic male act of supporting a spouse and children.

Beside alcohol use or domestic violence [19; 24, p. 44], partial or complete desertion is a common response to the inability to contribute to one's partner's and children's welfare. Inner-city men often figure desertion not as a sign of failure but as one of the ultimate signs of manliness. For example, a poor Black man can explain "the failure of his [conjugal relationship] by the theory of manly flaws." Conceding that to be head of a family and to support it is a principle measure of a man, he claims he was too much of a man to be a man" [11, p. 214]; that is, his manly appetite for sex with other women and other extra-conjugal excitement kept him from tying himself to one woman. Multiple partnering and prolific sexual virility come to serve as substitute measures of manhood.

As an alternate to desertion, men can express ascendancy in the context of conjugal relations by acting with the power vested in them as family head or patriarch to control their female partners. Among White working-class households, this control often takes the form of denying women the right to work outside of the home [24]. Male dominance is generally a reaction to cultural, social, or material stresses that put "men in the position of fighting literally and figuratively to maintain an old or to forge a new sociocultural identity" [53, p. 181]. The stresses on Black men, as mentioned above, include economic and racist oppressions that make fulfilling the male provider role extremely problematic.[12]

---

[11]As Stack further notes, "Welfare law conspires against the ability of the poor to build up an equity" [21, p. 127]. This, plus welfare law's more direct impacts on household structure, leads to a situation in which most households are unstable. While on the one hand stable households buoyed by the idea of family can reproduce an army of reliable workers, a certain amount of system-supported household instability and poverty also can be beneficial to industrial capitalism. As Stack notes, "Inequities are not unfortunate accidents. They are necessary for the existence of the existing economic order" [21, p. 127]. The system helps create a large pool of easily expendable unemployed in part because the ready supply of unskilled workers puts pressure on those who are employed. Lower-class employees will be more likely to work hard and less likely to complain about being underpaid when they know that they can be easily replaced [21, p. 128].

[12]They also include a problematic identification with powerful female caretakers. As Sanday notes, summing up an argument presented elsewhere by the Whitings, "male dominance displays are a reaction to perceptions of female power" and they are "motivated by the need to break a primary identity with powerful women" [53, p. 182; see also 54]. Further, male irresponsibility or desertion may be motivated by the expectation of male irresponsibility [regarding the "theory of manly flaws," see 11; regarding male socialization for irresponsibility in African-Jamaican culture, see 55].

The impact of macro-level political and economic forces differs in relation to race and class as well as in relation to gender, and so the forces that encourage generic women's dependence on men for esteem and status also encourage in poor urban Black women a resourceful attitude of financial independence [13, 44]. Black women have always worked outside of the home [56], and their incomes are often steadier than their men's [18; 21, p. 113]. So male control in these households would more often involve control over the main conjugal partners' movements and the extent of their partners' extraconjugal relationships.

As is widely argued, women often interpret and talk about men's controlling attitudes and actions as expressions of caring protection. This interpretation helps to maintain existing gender-linked power structures (which exist both in micro-level household relations and in macro-level political and economic relations) even while easing the tensions and rationalizing the problems that such power disparities involve. It exists in relation to women's emotionally-driven desire for ideal conjugal relations and to the macro-level forces which support the construction of this desire.

Social Factors and Health-Related Action

It is well known that the level of support offered by an individual's social circle influences health behaviors. As Orth-Gomer and Unden note in their review of the literature on measures of social support, "The frequency of social contacts, the number of available persons and the amount of social activities seem to have a substantial effect on health and survival" [37, pp. 291-293; 57, p. 83; also see 58, 59].

Participants in the preliminary phase of the study reported keeping to themselves and maintaining few friends outside of their relationships. That is, many women reported having small or weak extraconjugal support systems. At the same time, they talked about their desires for conjugal closeness and described how these were accommodated or even met through unsafe sex [see 25]. This led me to hypothesize that women with lower levels of extraconjugal support might depend more on their conjugal partners to meet their emotional and social needs, and I tested the hypothesis in a second phase of research, which this chapter concentrates on.

Bott's work on conjugal relations and social networks in urban London documents correspondences between extraconjugal support and conjugal style [23]. It examines the impact of social network strength on variables such as conjugal recreation and decision-making patterns, which can be joint or segregated. In Bott's study, couples without extensive or tightly-knit extraconjugal networks were more socially and emotionally interdependent and had a joint style of relating to each other. Conjugal partners embedded in strong networks had a segregated style and relied more on extraconjugal network members for social and emotional support than they did on each other.

Women with smaller external support systems may necessarily be more dependent on their partners for social and emotional resources. Accordingly, they might experience a more intense need to idealize and justify their partnerships and to deny the possibility of conjugal problems.[13] In a study of couvade in Colombia, Browner found that the number and severity of pregnancy-related symptoms that women reported for their male partners were inversely correlated with the strength of the women's social networks [60]. Women who felt more socially isolated tended to focus on the strength and excellence of their conjugal bonds and on the way that couvade symptoms in their partners expressed this.

A correlation may exist between unsafe sex and weak extraconjugal social support just as correlations existed between partner-centered conjugal relations and weak external networks in Bott [23], and between couvade symptom reports and social isolation in Browner [60]. To facilitate testing this hypothesis, Dressler's definition of "social support" as "the perceived availability of help or assistance from other persons during times of felt need" and his definition of a "social support system" as "a subset of an individual's ego-centered social network" [61, p. 19] were followed.

METHODS

Ethnographic focus-group and interview data collected in an earlier phase of the larger study [regarding methods, see 25] were used to devise a questionnaire for collecting quantitative data on the effects of economic factors and of social network strength on sexual risk taking. The questionnaire, which includes a brief demographic background section and several questions about sexual practices, focuses mainly on economic and social network data (questions regarding HIV testing also were posed [see 32]). Because many clinic clients have low literacy skills, the instrument uses simple language and mainly yes or no, forced choice, and Likert-type scaled questions.

To identify the extent of male financial contributions to female households, respondents were asked if they relied on anyone at all for money regularly, if their partners were employed, and if they ever received financial help from them. Respondents also were asked to indicate on Likert-type scales how often their partners gave them certain kinds of non-monetary gifts (like food, clothing, small appliances, or help around the house), if at all [regarding economic data, see 18].

The extensivity of respondents' extraconjugal support systems was ascertained by asking for the sex, age, and general relational status (friend, relative, or neighbor) of the individuals that each deemed important. Respondents then were asked if they needed or wanted help with child care or housework, money, or advice, and if such help was forthcoming. Other questions measured how often the

---

[13] I thank Jill Korbin for this suggestion.

respondent relied on her social support network (if at all) and identified the persons who provided the most help. Finally, respondents were asked how often they felt "all alone in the world," with "no one to turn to for help." The questions measured how good each woman felt about different aspects of her social support network and how effective this network was for her as a whole.

In addition to questionnaires, the second phase of the research involved interviews: qualitative data were collected to supplement and inform an understanding of the frequencies generated from the questionnaire data. The interview protocol was designed and administered with the help of M&I staff members, and also with insights gained from several clinic clients who met in a focus group to discuss the preliminary data after we finished with the questionnaire. Interviews were conducted using open-ended verbal probes to elicit personal opinions and information regarding participants' financial strategies, the quality and extensivity of their conjugal and extraconjugal relations, and their condom-use patterns. Women's personalities and their particular concerns regarding relationships were taken into account in conducting each interview: the agenda remained flexible [see 62] so that unanticipated information could be collected when it arose [cf. 63]. Each interview lasted about one and a quarter hours. The interview material included below was transcribed verbatim from audio tapes; repetitions and some non- grammatical phrases are excluded for ease in reading where doing so does not alter meanings. Pseudonyms rather than real names are given.

The Subjects

According to M&I record-keeper Anne Gulbranse, in 1991 90 percent of M&I clients were impoverished, and 25 percent had some history of substance use problems (substance use, as defined by M&I, includes alcohol as well as crack cocaine and heroin use). About one-in-four clinic clients were first-time mothers, and almost all clients had something—nutritional status, income (or lack thereof), drug habit—placing them in the generic M&I "at risk" category. One-in-three (34.2%) women served by the M&I clinic that served as a research site reported ever having had an STD, and University Hospitals, the facility that would serve M&I women involved in this study, reported an HIV prevalence of 0.5 percent (P. Toltzis, personal communication).

Thirty M&I clinic clients receiving prenatal care (and so receiving HIV/AIDS education) were recruited to complete the questionnaire by Donna Dayse, an HIV/AIDS educator.[14] Consent was verbal and each woman was paid $5. Of the thirty women, there were twenty-five Blacks (83.3%), four Whites (13.3%), and

---

[14]Later, sixty more questionnaires were collected, for a total of ninety [33]. This chapter was completed before the whole set could be analyzed.

one Latina (3.3%).[15] As Table 1 shows, the average participant was about twenty-eight years old and a mother of two (adolescents were excluded for legal and logistic reasons). Most women had completed the eleventh grade. While all respondents lived impoverished inner-city lives, twenty-six (86.7%) of the thirty women had a regular income: fourteen (46.7%) had jobs; eleven (36.7%) received public assistance, one (3.3%) both had a job and got assistance. Twenty-one (70%) had husbands or boyfriends.

After the questionnaire phase, M&I staff members recruited twenty-five clinic clients to be interviewed by the author. Again, consent was verbal. Each woman was paid five dollars. All interviewees had at least some African heritage; twenty-two (88%, *n* = 25) self-identified as Black or African American; three (12%) self-identified as being mixtures of African and other nationalities.[16] All participants lived impoverished inner-city lives. As Table 1 shows, the average interviewee was about twenty-eight years old and a mother of two (again, adolescents were excluded). She had completed the twelfth grade. Twenty-one (84%) of the twenty-five had a regular income: five (20%) had jobs; twelve (48%) received public assistance; four (16%) both had jobs and got assistance. Because of the need to learn more about heterosexual relationships within this community, all interviewees had male sexual partners.

Findings from the interviewees and questionnaire respondents are described in the section that follows. With the exception of the condom use data provided below, the frequencies reported were generally derived from the questionnaire (as I do not wish to misrepresent the significance of the frequencies presented, which

---

[15]I draw heavily on literature concerning African-American sexuality and home-life in framing my presentation of data. One of the scholars who reviewed this article noticed that all participants were not Black and also that gender relations and other political-economic issues were key factors in my arguments. The reviewer asked, appropriately, "Does ethnicity matter?" Put simply, I do not think that it much does. Racism and related ethnic responses can involve community-level AIDS risk denial [see 25], and they do impact on the expression of gender relations. But data suggests that the gender power structure, and the ideal of heterosexual monogamy that it entails, is itself the main force behind individual decisions to forego condoms. The majority of women who participated in the research were African American and, while I might have used the generic phrase "women" throughout this chapter and I might have refrained from discussing African-American sexual and household traditions, I did not consider it appropriate to whitewash that methodological fact. I have very little data from women who belong to other ethnic groups and I did not wish to suggest to readers that my conclusions apply on any scientific basis to members of these other groups. I also do not wish to suggest that my conclusions can be generalized beyond the population studied. However, it is my belief that the hypotheses will not be falsified if tested among other groups of women. This belief is strengthened by pilot data that I collected from middle-class Whites [see 26].

[16]These three women (12%, *n* = 25) were of African heritage plus "Indian," "American Indian," and "Italian and Irish," respectively. Interestingly, patterns related to the self-identifications made by the other twenty-two women suggest that self-identifying as African American rather than as Black correlates with condom use. Of the twenty-five interviewees, twelve (48%, *n* = 25) self-identified as African American and ten (40%) self-identified as Black. But of the seven condom-users, five (71.4%) self-identified as African American. I am developing an analysis of the apparent relationship between pro-active identity politics, self-esteem, and condom use elsewhere [33].

Table 1. Participant Characteristics

	Questionnaire Respondents (N = 30)	Clinic Interviewees (N = 25)
Number of Black women	25 (83.3%)	25 (100%)
Average age (years)	28	28
Average number of children	2	2
Average education (grade)	11	12
Number with a regular income	26 (86.7%)	21 (84%)
Number conjugally partnered	21 (70%)	25 (100%)

describe findings from small convenience samples, I provide the raw numbers that underlie them and I do not include chi-square test results). Discourse taken from interview transcripts is used to help provide a context for interpreting the meanings of the frequencies. The similar ways in which the two sets of women were recruited and the fact that they were all M&I clients support such cross-referencing.[17]

RESULTS AND EXPLANATORY HYPOTHESES

Condom Use and Conjugal Status

All of the women were sexually active. Twenty-nine of the thirty questionnaire respondents provided condom-use information. Twelve (41%) reported using condoms that last time that they had sex; seventeen (59%) said that they did not. A larger proportion of the twenty-five interviewees (72%, $n = 18$) said that they had not used condoms during their last sexual encounters. However, all interviewees were involved in relationships while eight (27.6%, $n = 29$) of the questionnaire respondents who provided condom-use data were not. While fifteen (88.2%) of the seventeen non-using questionnaire respondents were involved with steady sexual partners (i.e., husbands or steady boyfriends), only six or half (50%) of the twelve women who used condoms had steady partners. In sum, thirty-five (64.8%, $n = 54$) women did not use condoms, and these non-users were more likely to be involved in steady conjugal relationships than the condom users were.

---

[17]While some of the women who completed the questionnaire were not in relationships, all interviewees were; interview data is used accordingly to avoid generating moot hypotheses.

Even in the preliminary phase of data collection, it was clear that most women did not use condoms because they did not consider them appropriate or necessary within the context of a committed, loving relationship. Participants' own words and stories express this best. Josephine explained that she saw no need for condoms because "I know my man ain't, you know, doing 'this and that' (i.e., cheating)." Gloria proclaimed, "If my husband comes to me and hands me some condoms, I think I'm going to shoot him because I know then that he's out there doing something that he ain't got no business doing." Janet, who explained that women often have sex to "feel loved, needed, wanted," pointed out that with unsafe sex there is "nothing in between you both physically and emotionally. You are the closest to him that you can be." Quality of relationships and condom use are presented as inversely correlated.

Among the questionnaire respondents, involved non-users of condoms (hereon, "non-users") had been involved with partners for much longer than most involved condom users. Only two of the six steadily involved condom users had been involved for five to nine years; none had been involved for over ten years. In contrast, seven of all fifteen steadily involved non-users had been involved for more than five years; five of these seven—one-third of all fifteen—had been involved for over ten years.

According to clinicians, clients report that condom use is harder to initiate after a relationship has been established than in the early stages of courtship. Gloria and Josephine's above-noted testimonials about how out-of-place condoms are in established and supposedly intact relationships make clear why this might be so: except when justified in terms of birth-control (which makes little sense to men whose partners have been sterilized or use birth-control pills), condoms connote distrust, disrespect, and disease. Women in long-term relationships may be more dependent on men for self-esteem and status than women who are not as involved and so may be less willing to confront such connotations. This is explored later, when extraconjugal social support patterns are examined.

Men as Providers? Quantitative Findings

The questionnaire included questions regarding income. Interestingly, a greater proportion of condom users (50%, $n = 12$) than non-users (41.7%, $n = 17$) received aid (in cash or kind) from men. Most of the women reported being on their own financially. Nineteen of the thirty respondents (63.3%) were household heads. In response to a general and open-ended question about regular financial assistance from individuals, eleven (37%) reported receiving regular financial assistance from a partner, friend, or relation. Eight of the eleven women (72.7%) receiving money regularly got it from sexual partners. In other words, just over one-fourth (26.7%) of all thirty women reported receiving financial assistance from a man.

Paychecks and public assistance paid directly to the women prove to be more reliable income sources than men. Fifteen questionnaire respondents (50%) brought in paychecks; twelve (40%) got federal or state aid (had we asked directly about food stamps and other non-liquid assistance, the frequency of aid reported might have been higher). Even after accounting for one woman who got both a paycheck and aid, twenty-six women (86.7%) drew resources regularly in their own names. While this certainly does not mean that impoverished women do not need the financial help that men sometimes provide, it does indicate that women contribute far more to their household budgets than theories focusing on the instrumental dimension of heterosexual relations imply.[18]

Condom-Use Decisions

Men do not play prime breadwinner roles, and they do not overtly rule in the sexual arena. Seventeen questionnaire respondents, or about two-thirds (68%) of the twenty-five women who provided information about both last condom use and condom-use decision making, said that the decision to use or not to use condoms is a joint one. One woman (4%), a non-user, said that the man decides unilaterally (i.e., on his own, for the couple). The remaining seven (28%) make the decision for themselves.

Decision-making styles may be related to condom use decisions. Women who made condom-use decisions for themselves were more likely to use condoms. While ten of the seventeen women who made condom-use decisions jointly (58.8%) did not use condoms, only two of the seven self-motivated women decided to forego them. Further, neither of the two self-motivated non-users had jobs, while three of the five self-motivated users did.[19] Perhaps employment's seeming significance stems less from the money that it brings—which for many menial jobs is actually less than federal and state assistance programs would provide—than from the sense of accomplishment and independence that it engenders.

Self-motivated or unilateral decision making on the part of women involves and demonstrates independence and agency. Joint decision making also shows that women are active participants in the sexual arena. Further, joint decision making

[18]Because only a certain amount of information could be collected without overwhelming participants, the actual amount of money brought in by poor inner-city women was not ascertainable in the round of data collection described in this article. More detailed information regarding finances was collected in a later phase of the project [see 33].

[19]Employment status for joint deciders was about the same whether or not the decision was to use or not to use. Three (42.9%) of the seven jointly deciding users were employed, as were five (50%) of the ten jointly deciding non-users.

is popularly associated with good conjugal communication.[20] Agreeing to unsafe sex reflects a real and active desire to signal commitment.

Male Providers? Qualitative Findings

Clinic women did not feel as if they were coerced into unsafe sex by financial dependence on men. They did mention money when describing their relationships, but they focused more on talk about emotional ties, the personal characteristics of their mates, and the social status and self-esteem that being in a relationship brings. Love, not money, binds these women to men. For instance, June, who works seasonally selling flowers at intersections, noted in her assessment of her partner that he was a "good listener" and a "caring" man who showed his love: "If it's like your birthday or something coming 'round, he doesn't necessarily go out and buy me a dozen roses, but the phone rings and he be singing 'Happy Birthday'."

Twenty-three-year-old Shelly, who until six months prior to the interview had been in prison for drug and robbery charges, said of her partner, "He's worrying about me—physically, mentally, romantically; he's worrying if I'm OK." Sarah, who at age twenty-one dreams of being a nurse, said that her partner was "always supporting me with whatever choice I choose; I do the same for him, I'm always there for him. [If we] need advice, [we] sit down and talk about things." She described her feelings of love, as well as her status-related concerns: "It's just like being in heaven, you know. It's nice, it's wonderful! It's just a nice feeling, waking up knowing that, 'Wow, I got a guy who really cares for me.' I can do something with a guy instead of walking around being with girls."

Very few interviewees pointed to the attractiveness of men's money when talking about their partners' best qualities. "Take a man as whatever they are, not for what they got," advised Bernice. When women did mention money, it was usually in the context of an explanation of the good things that the willingness and ability to work say about a man (or in the context of talk about gifts or dinner dates, which I shall return to later). Working men are not lazy, and they have goals. Still, the women felt that jobs are not always easy to come by, and so they did not interpret unemployment itself as a bad sign regarding a man's character.

[20]It is possible that, because of this association, people interested in casting their relationships in good light for social reasons and those with the inner emotional need to see their conjugal situations as ideal can strategically or defensively claim to make decisions jointly even when coercion or elected acquiescence occurs. Nonetheless, the perception of joint participation in the decision is real. To complicate matters, I must note that women who participated in the first phase of the research told us that male resistance to condoms and to female requests that they use them is omnipresent: men very frequently unilaterally say "no." Women may claim this to rationalize their own need for unsafe sexual contact and to conceal the extent of their responsibility for it. But if men do generally refuse condoms, as data so far indicates, many of the myriad reports of jointly decided upon condomlessness may represent strategic efforts to recast that which must be (i.e., unsafe sex) as that which is chosen.

All of the interviewees had plans for their futures that included financial independence and, in some cases, home ownership. Twenty (80%) of the twenty-five women saw themselves as already financially independent. Clarissa gets food stamps and welfare. She says:

> I'm the whole family, yeah. [My husband] keeps calling me the man of the house. I feel like I'm doing a good job. I was telling my kids the other day, I said, "Whenever you need something"—they don't have the most expensive clothes, but when I really need something—paper, books, shoes, I get it.

Marvelle echoed this sentiment: "The welfare is [minimal]," she said, "but I do know how to budget money. I don't actually depend on [my partner]."

The M&I clinic I worked in is located in a neighborhood in which exactly 850 in 1000 live births in 1990 were to unwed mothers [64]. Of all households with children in this neighborhood, 64 percent were female headed; 30 percent were headed by married couples [64]. Most of the women I talked with did say that at times making ends meet could be difficult; likewise, most had methods for meeting financial challenges. Clarissa, who at the age of twenty-eight was expecting her fourth child, explained one of her strategies for stretching money: "I keep food stamps. When I get them, I go to the grocery store, get something. But the prices go down after a certain time of the month so I give my sister $200 or $100 to hold for me, and then by the time end-of-the-month comes, like I say, I got food."

Most of the women did not view conjugal relations as financially lucrative. Most of the interviewees who got money from their partners said that they did not need the money and that they did not manipulate their men to get it. But, as Vicki said, "I just take it anyway. I don't turn nothing down. If he's gonna give me something then I have it." Twenty-one-year-old Sarah, who made about $200 a month doing hair for her girlfriends, received about $75 every two weeks from her boyfriend but, she explained, "I don't expect it. It really don't matter, you know. If he gives it to me, he gives it to me, and if he don't, he don't."

Women enjoyed the feeling of being able to provide for themselves and their children. "It's such a good thing you can't even describe how good it feels," said Nicole; "Being independent—it's just like an inside victory, you know." Roberta explained:

> I feel like I am my own woman. When you're independent, you stand on your own two feet. When I [find] a man that takes that away from me—you know, do so much for you till you feel dependent on him—I don't know if I would let anybody do that because I like being independent. I feel strong. I don't feel like I'm better than no one else but I just feel strong within myself.

One of the main reasons for wanting to be one's "own woman" was uncertainty: men employed or devoted today may be neither employed nor devoted tomorrow. As Shelly said, "There's gonna be a time when he ain't gonna be able to do that, you know." Michelle observed, "There may not be a significant other so therefore you might have to be the one to take care of yourself." The acknowledged uncertainty of inner-city life and of love (and so of men's efforts) made the ability to provide for one's own household crucial, and the sense of achievement (the "inner victory") that self-sufficiency brought was important. So was the avoidance of self-loathing. Bernice, a serious, soft-spoken, self-sufficient twenty-four-year-old mother of one, describes the loss of self-esteem that dependence can bring and that she, like all of the other women, would rather avoid. She also comments on the fickleness of men.

> I would be disgusted with myself. I just wouldn't feel good 'cause I made myself bound and my child bound. [I'd] feel like I'd be going backwards instead of forwards. I want to be a strong person and not so much dependent on other people to help me out. I feel good when somebody got their hand out asking me for something, that feels good, you know, that somebody can count on me. It's not wrong or anything [to count on somebody], but sometime in your life you just got to stop and do something for your own self. I have never counted on my baby's father, you know, never count on him. He did try to do his part and I appreciate that, but I never counted on him. [If I would have waited] on him to bring Pampers or milk, my baby would fall asleep soaking [and hungry]. You can't wait like that—you got things to do, people to take care of.

Women say that they do not actually depend on men's money, and they explain this in terms of their own self-esteem as well as the high risks that relying on male aid would involve. But focusing on dollar amounts when trying to gauge women's reliance on men excludes many kinds of valued contributions. Even confirmed bread-winning women talk of male gifts (generally, clothing) and dinners out [see 18]. Nice as they may be, items or favors bestowed are not liquid like cash. While women can allocate cash as they see fit, gifts in kind or of labor leave women like wards, with little liberty to manage their own affairs or to make decisions regarding spending priorities. And, as with most donations, the recipients—the women—often have little say about important details such as the style of dress received, or the kind of food that partners bring them to cook, or when (finally?) the year-old hole in the door will get fixed. This plus the lack of liquidity may lessen the practical value of male offerings to women, and the offerings may be experienced as indexing controlling or oppressive conjugal relations.

Bernice, who spoke above, described the power plays that accompany accepting gifts of cash or kind from men: "They think they have the upper hand or something." They will "get all worked up and stuff, 'Well I did this for you,' and stuff like that, trying to make theyself look big." Women especially disliked having to ask for things because this seemed to magnify men's power. Rachel, a mother of two who had just entered a drug addiction recovery program, explained her feelings with examples:

> [You feel] "Oh I need these shoes," and then you have to explain why you gotta have this other pair of shoes and they know you got other shoes in the closet. . . . I didn't like to have to go and explain to him why I wanted to go get this or that. To go through with him [demanding], "What's wrong with this dress here?" When you got your own money you're in control.

Male gifts can also hold an abundance of positive emotional value for women: they can be taken as welcome signals of love and good intentions. A man who gives his wife or girlfriend gifts, services or money lives up to—or at least begins to live up to and implies that he intends to live up to—the cultural ideal of benefaction and caring for one's partner and, if children are involved, one's family. Presents are taken to symbolize love. This is one reason for women's ostentatious display of male gifts to them, like rings.[21] Presents also help women maintain their denial of HIV/AIDS risk, which characteristically needs constant reinforcement ("You see, he *does* love me") and which entails unsafe sex. Moreover, when men give presents wives and girlfriends may, in turn, demonstrate that they trust in their partners' interest in their welfare by reciprocating for that love with condomless sex.

There is more to romance than finance: with few exceptions, for the participants in this research, condomless sex is not directly purchased. Women may capitulate more readily to partners' demands for unsafe sex when partners give them money or gifts because the giving is seen to entail love and the fulfillment of duty; it is seen to imply caring and respect—qualities unexpected from adulterous men. Women reckon that partners who look like they intend to provide support do love them and do not intend to have sex with outside partners. The receipt of male offerings and favors reinforce the denial of HIV/AIDS risk that women actively use unsafe sex to bolster, confirm, and maintain (space in this chapter is limited; for further information on finance's relation to romance, see [18]).

Affiliative Needs and Social Support: Quantitative Findings

The questionnaire asked women to complete social network lists. Respondents were then asked to indicate how happy they were with their interactions with the individuals so listed, and whether or not they felt secure and supported. Depending on their scores, respondents were ranked as "extremely supported," "supported" or, if their scores were below the median,

---

[21]Ostentatious display of male offerings sends other messages too, such as those concerning a woman's skill in catching successful men who support her well. However, the material benefits of conjugal relations do not detract from their affective worth which, in part due to culture and unless prostitution is concerned, is paramount in the context of sex (as informants' discourse showed).

Table 2. Perceived Extra-Conjugal Support and
Condom Use (N = 24)

	Condom Users	Condom Non-Users
Extremely supported	3	1
Supported	3	2
Under-supported	5	10
TOTAL	11	13

"under-supported."[22] As Table 2 shows, a pattern suggesting that a low level of social support is associated with a lack of condom use emerged.

Three times as many users as non-users felt "extremely supported"; twice as many were at least "supported." Three (27.3%) of the eleven condom users who provided answers felt "extremely supported"; three more (27.3%) felt "supported." This means that over half of the users (54.5%) had scores above the median. But only one (7.7%) of the thirteen non-users who answered the questions felt "extremely supported"; only two more (15.4%) felt "supported"; in other words, less than one-fourth (23.1%) of the non-users had scores above the median. Ten-in-thirteen (76.9%) non-users as opposed to five-in-eleven (45.5%) users felt "under-supported."

All told, exactly two-thirds (66.7%) of the nine women who felt "supported" or "extremely supported" used condoms. But only five (33.3%) of the fifteen "under-supported" women used condoms the last time they had sex; ten (66.7%) went condomless. The proportions are in exact opposition, suggesting the existence of a correlation between women's perceptions of social support and their condom-use choices.

Employment seems to have an important impact on feelings regarding social support, as Table 3 shows. Six (66.7%) of the nine women who felt good about their extraconjugal support networks ("supported" or "extremely supported") had jobs, while only half (50%) of all thirty questionnaire respondents and six (40%) of the fifteen "under-supported" respondents were employed. Moreover, while only ten (40%) of all women and only four (26.7%) of those who felt "under-supported" worked full-time, five (55.6%) of the "supported" and "extremely supported" women were full-time employees.

[22]The rank of each individual's scores within the respective ranges for the three social support questions were calculated and overall extra-conjugal social support satisfaction levels were derived. To count as "extremely supported" all three of a woman's scores had to fall in the top thirds of the ranges. "Supported" women had scores that fell in the top halves of the ranges. Insufficient data was provided by six of the thirty women and so their answers were excluded from the calculations. Interestingly, most (80%) of the women who failed to provide information were not condom users, and the questions that they did provide answers for showed that they were generally very under-supported.

Table 3 also shows that while all questionnaire respondents were sexually active, women who felt secure extraconjugally tended to lack steady partners. Five of the nine (55.6%) "supported" and "extremely supported" women were partnerless. Of the fifteen "under-supported" women, only two (13.3%) were partnerless. This difference is large and suggests an inverse correlation between having a partner and having a supportive extraconjugal network. There may even be a further correlation between being partnered, "under-supported," and non-users of condoms: less than one-third (30.8%) of the thirteen "under-supported" women with partners were condom users. In contrast, two of the four (50%) socially supported and partnered women used condoms, and four of the five supported and unpartnered women (80%) did so.

Affiliative Needs and Social Support: Qualitative Findings

Interviewee testimony informs the hypothesis that a link exists between conjugal styles, extraconjugal support systems, and HIV/AIDS risk denial. The small size of the sample notwithstanding, the testimony revealed apparently significant differences in the ways that users and non-users related to their conjugal partners, and in the quality—or at least the quantity—of their extraconjugal social relations.

Among the interviewees, none of the seven condom-users considered their partners among their two closest social companions, while nine (50%) of the eighteen non-users did so. Further, while only one (14.3%) user talked about having a jealous partner, twelve (66.6%) non-users had jealous partners (see Table 4). The interview data suggest that women with jealous partners are more dependent on their men for emotional and social resources and that their social circles are kept small by and for the men. This may lead them to be more likely to list their partners as close social companions.

Clarissa, who does not use condoms, keeps very few friends and she refrains from talking with these few on the phone when her husband is home. She describes her situation: "All my friends were male and so I had to leave them all alone, and then the one [female] friend that I had, he can't stand her 'cause she's

Table 3. Employment Status, Conjugal Status, and
Perceived Extra-Conjugal Support

	Extremely Supported or Supported (N = 9)	Under-Supported (N = 15)
Employed	6	6
Unemployed	3	9
Partnered	4	13
Single	5	2

Table 4. Conjugal Patterns, Partner Jealousy, and Condom Use

	Condom Users (N = 7)	Non-Users (N = 18)
Partner: Close companion	7	9
Partner: Not close companion	0	♦ 9
Jealous partner	1	12
No jealousy	6	6

not married." Jealous partners don't trust their women around men, and they don't like them to socialize with single girlfriends. As Marvelle explains of her boyfriend, "He figures they have an influence on me." Sarah had the same problem. "When the relationship first started off, I had a lot of man friends. [My partner] thought it was more of a sexual thing [with them]. I told him it wasn't like that: they was just friends." But she had to leave them behind in order to keep her partner happy.[23]

Marvelle says of her partner, "You would think he was older than what he is the way he thinks (i.e., like an old man): 'You don't go out. Only whores go out." Rachel's partner is jealous "constantly. He's so jealous that I think he should go—like if I'm riding in the car, if I look this way in the car (i.e., out the window), he goes 'Oh, you're looking there, why don't you just go on and get in the other car with the nigger-man?' He's extremely jealous."

Male control over female social circles is not only driven by the fear that the women will commit adultery or leave them. As Nicole explained, reputation also plays a role.

> [To socialize with] my mother, then that's OK. But like if I was to stay here [and socialize with] my boy [i.e., friend] Tom, [my partner] would be like "No." No, men are out; that's just totally no way. It's not because—I don't think [my partner gets] scared. It's just that he's the kind of guy that worries about what people think of him, so if somebody was to see me and Tom, you know, and come and tell [my partner], "Well I've seen [Nicole] with Tom," you know, it's "Oh God!"

Male jealousy limits women's social circles, forcing women to be more emotionally and socially dependent on their primary partners. Further, as Rachel's

---

[23]Jealousy also is expressed in male opinions about their partners' dress. Sarah told me, "He doesn't like me wearing tight clothes, he really don't like it. . . . He says, 'Don't you ever wear that around there ever again,' showing off my knees, my butt, and everything. I don't like that." But she also told me, "I'm gonna wear it anyway," asserting her independence. Indeed, she wore shorts to the interview. Other women with jealous, watchful men were not as self-determined as Sarah; they upheld the standards that their men set for them.

interview and a few of the other interviews revealed, male jealousy can sometimes find expression in more extreme forms of controlling behavior, like verbal and physical abuse. Women with few outside sources of support—without a sense of "home" extraconjugally—can find themselves trapped, as Rachel explained.

> [My partner] was real jealous and he got to be controlling and abusive, physically abusive towards me, but I still tried to hang in there because he had all the qualities that I wanted at that time—that I thought that I wanted in a man. When he got abusive I would say [to myself], "What do you think?" and I sat and thought about it, I said, "Well, it was my fault. I should have just shut my mouth up." I was more or less yearning for those type of men and I loved those men and I was a dope. And I was basically trying to find a home. . . . Those kind of men they protect you and then it's like they know just when to romance you in the right way and just when to try to discipline, or put their control, like when they see you kinda getting on your own and getting away from them.

"Getting on your own and getting away from them" might involve employment, which Winsome's boyfriend, like Rachel's, described in the above quote, would not allow. It always involves extraconjugal contacts, and it seems to promote independence and possible adulterous liaisons, so it threatens jealous men. Betty, who was not formally interviewed but who participated in a focus group used to help design the interview protocol, explained that some men purposefully promote women's dependence.

> If [a woman] has a lot of friends and a lot of family to talk to and stuff, she's not so dependent on that man. [She gets dependent on a man if] he don't want her to have outside friends; he don't want the family in. . . . If the family members tell her the sky blue, he say its green. The sky blue, but . . . he don't want [her] to listen to [her] family and friends.

Contradicting the monogamy ideal is extremely threatening in this kind of situation, so these women—women with jealous or controlling men—are the most likely to be non-users of condoms. Indeed, as noted, only one (14.3%, $n = 7$) condom-using interviewee portrayed her partner as jealous, while twelve (66.6%, $n = 18$) non-using interviewees did so.

DISCUSSION

With the exception of a 1992 paper by Kline et al. [3], scholars of unsafe sex have represented Black women as dependent. Like the women in the Kline et al. study, the interviewees in this research present themselves as able and willing to take care of themselves. Indeed, they need to be: unemployment, incarceration, and homicide rates make good male partners hard to come by in the inner city. This demographic or epidemiological fact plus the women's testimony and self-reports undermine materialist models of risky sex and support the argument that emotional and social dependence play a much greater role in encouraging HIV/AIDS risk denial.

The findings reported in this chapter indicate that individual HIV/AIDS-risk denial among many inner-city women is motivated by the need to maintain the belief that their relationships are "good." Standards for "good" relationships are tied to the goals of industrial capitalism and of the patriarchal and racist social structure in which the capitalist enterprise is played out. Partly in response to this structure and partly to bolster it, the family and household are mythologized by mainstream U.S. culture as sanctuaries providing relief from the market-related world of work.

The division of labor in many households serves to maintain and reproduce the work force at the largely un- or under-remunerated expense of women. In the mainstream U.S. cultural system, the conjugal relations from which such households stem are justified in terms of love, not money. Research findings bear this out: love rather than money compelled study participants into conjugal relationships.

In accordance with ideologically-driven emphasis on love as the motivation for conjugal coupling, and also in accordance with the actual political and economic conditions that foster self-sufficiency among inner-city women and limit the economic role of male partners, most study participants had a firm sense of agency and considered themselves financially independent from men. The inner-city women who participated in this research acknowledged overtly that without money households cannot run. But they did not depend on men for this money. Rather, the women provided for their households by themselves, with wages from paid labor, state or federal aid paid to them in their own names, or with the help of relatives.

While a man's love for his partner is indexed by, among other things, the offerings he makes to her and the favors that he grants her (regarding the expressive value of reciprocity and gift-giving, see [65-67]), participants said that financial coercion does not play a major role in driving unsafe sex. The women generally saw themselves as active sexual decision makers. Within the context of conjugality, the sexual arena is understood as an arena for the freely elected expression of love, rather than as a stage for market-style instrumental transactions. Freely elected condomless sex is a prime expression of the trust that love is culturally constructed as entailing.

When participants in this study reflected on their heterosexual relationships, they concentrated on their social and affective needs for status and self-esteem, which male validation and participation in monogamous heterosexual unions can bring. Much of their relationship-related talk describes a dream of fidelity, puts forth a claim of having achieved it (as in a "Monogamy Narrative" [25]), or supports a belief in its reality. Because condoms are associated with infidelity and deceptive behavior, using them implies that partners do not truly care for one another. Admitting to this is emotionally painful and shaming. Condom use undermines the monogamy-related narratives that women are encouraged to—and need to—tell; therefore, it is avoided.

Women's denial of the possibility of male adultery and their associated unsafe sex practices seem to be positively related to low levels of extraconjugal social support. Women with little extraconjugal support seemed to depend more on their conjugal partners to meet their emotional and social needs. These women might experience a more intense need to idealize and justify their relationships and to deny the possibility of conjugal problems.

The findings suggest that unsafe sex occurs most frequently among socially isolated women who, in part due to their small social networks, have few other sources of self-esteem and status aside from having conjugal partnerships with men. There seems to be a positive correlation between unsafe sex and women's feelings of insecurity about their conjugal relationships and their extraconjugal support systems. The less convinced women are that friends and relatives will take care of them, the more likely they may be to have unsafe sex—the more likely they may be to engage in wishful thinking and denial during the emotionally charged period of lovemaking. This seemed especially true for study participants without jobs, who were more likely than the employed women to forego condoms. Jobless women seem to be forced to rely on relationships with men for self-esteem as they are not able to draw it from their own accomplishments.

Employed women who felt firmly anchored in extraconjugal support systems were much more likely to insist on condom use and much less likely to be dependent on relationships with men for validation. Beyond the money their paychecks bring, jobs provide women with alternative sources for self-esteem. Further, empowerment through employment may positively affect "self-efficacy," as was seen in the correlation between self-motivated condom use and employment. A lack of "self-efficacy" among the unemployed can only be exacerbated by these women's more prominent dependence on men for status, self-validation, and financial help.

My findings suggest that the implied tie between unsafe sex and money is only loosely bound in many contexts; it is frequently mediated by cultural and psycho-social factors. While the potential for financial gain through heterosexual relations does exist and may be fantasized about just as women can dream about true love and high prestige, in reality—as reflected in the numbers of women working or bringing in government aid—and despite the obstacles of sexism, poverty, and racism, many inner-city women can and do actively seek support by themselves, in their own names. The women who participated in this research did not think of their relations with conjugal partners in instrumental terms; indeed, they provided most of their own resources [18]. Generally, however, women cannot gain status and emotional fulfillment on their own. That requires a heterosexual relationship with a man.

As mentioned, the small and nonrandom sample used in this research limits the degree to which findings can be generalized. There are other limitations that must be noted. For one thing, because of its exploratory nature, this research collected women's self-reports of male bestowals rather than directly measuring the actual monthly dollar-value of male contributions of cash and kind. For another, women's claims of independence were only indirectly confirmed. Gathering accurate income or resource allocation data poses quite a challenge, partly because of the often illegal means by which people bring resources into their homes (e.g., working "under-the-table," earning more than the welfare department would allow without cutting one's benefits, or even selling drugs). Additionally, the social desirability of male contributions may lead women to make exaggerated claims—claims that hide the low value and infrequency of men's indirect (non-cash) economic contributions to women's households and that seem to support a materialist model of romantic involvement [cf., 24].

Since women's perceptions do affect their behavioral choices whether or not these perceptions accurately reflect economic reality, reliance on self-reports is not in itself a problem. In fact, self-reports reveal patterns that objective measurements cannot expose. However, direct measurements of women's material realities should be gathered in the future so that a more precise model of the interplay between cultural ideals and women's real financial conditions may be developed. Sexual decision-making patterns also deserve more attention. While questionnaire responses indicated that the decision-making process is paramount, they also indicated that the answer categories provided in this research (joint and unilateral) were too broad. Data on perceived motivations, the imposition of unilaterally conceived plans, intentions, contexts in which decisions are made, and conversations regarding condoms are sorely needed, as are data on actual sexual decision-making practices and histories.

CONCLUSION

People who don't use condoms are often said to be "in denial" about their risk for HIV infection. The term "denial" is treated all too often as a unidimensional, self-explanatory blanket concept [27, 68]. As such, the label "denial" hides more than it reveals [cf. 52]: it constructs AIDS-related risk-taking as a self-evident, individual-level, "micro-social problem" [52, p. 79]—a problem without macro-level correlates or causes. My exploration of denial's mechanisms reveals that women's denial of their risks for AIDs and their related practice of condomless sex has "levels of meaning and cause beyond the narrow confines of immediate experience" [52, p. 100].

The data suggest that ideological constructs regarding heterosexual relations mediate the impact of political and economic forces on women's sexual decisions. They demonstrate that political economy's impact on such decisions can be indirect and complicated. Causal linkages can be quite complex; the M&I clinic data cannot be accounted for with simple models in which women's dependence on men is figured as purely financial.

Women who are less dependent on men for self-esteem and support—women who have strong extraconjugal networks that they feel good about—are most likely to use condoms. In contrast, women with small social networks or weak extraconjugal ties tend to focus on their conjugal relationships, and so tend to engage in condomless sex as an expression of the HIV/AIDS-risk denial that wishful thinking about monogamy entails. Supporting one's denial by having unsafe sex is an adaptive, psycho-socially beneficial practice in the short run, as it promotes a sense of well-being in relation to conjugal arrangements, but this strategy can have deadly long-term health costs (especially when invoked in the context of poverty, racism, and sexism).

Until far-reaching socioeconomic and cultural changes are achieved so that gender, class, and race relations are restructured, we shall have to depend upon education programs to promote safer sex. Programs aimed toward women in particular must help them to develop the desire to seek validation from their own accomplishments rather than from relations with men, as well as the practical skills necessary for abandoning the need for unsafe sex. They must frame the pro-condom message with notions of trust and love rather than of deceit and lust. They must cease to be driven by simple materialist stereotypes that ignore the roles that social and emotional factors generated by larger political-economic forces play in women's (sex) lives.

REFERENCES

1. Centers for Disease Control and Prevention, *HIV/AIDS Surveillance Report*, 5:1, 1993.
2. C. Campbell, Women and AIDS, *Social Science and Medicine*, 30:4, pp. 407-415, 1990.
3. A. Kline, E. Kline, and E. Oken, Minority Women and Sexual Choice in the Age of AIDS, *Social Science and Medicine*, 34:4, pp. 447-457, 1992.
4. M. T. Fullilove, R. E. Fullilove III, K. Haynes, and S. Gross, Black Women and AIDS Prevention: A View Towards Understanding the Gender Rules, *The Journal of Sex Research*, 27:1, pp. 47-64, 1990.
5. S. Seidman, W. Mosher, and S. Aral, Women with Multiple Sexual Partners: United States, 1988, *American Journal of Public Health*, 82:10, pp. 1388-1394, 1992.
6. D. Worth, Minority Women and AIDS: Culture, Race, and Gender, in *Births and Power: Social Change and the Politics of Reproduction*, W. P. Handwerker (ed.), Westview Press, San Francisco, pp. 111-136, 1990.
7. G. Wyatt and K. Dunn, Examining Predictors of Sex Guilt in Multiethnic Samples of Women, *Archives of Sexual Behavior*, 20:5, pp. 471-485, 1991.
8. G. Wyatt et al. 1988, as cited in *AIDS: Sexual Behavior and Intravenous Drug Use*, C. F. Turner, H. G. Miller, and L. E. Moses (eds.), National Academy Press, Washington, D.C., p. 113, 1989.
9. M. Ward, A Different Disease: HIV/AIDS and Health Care for Women in Poverty, *Culture, Medicine, and Psychiatry*, 17:4, 1993.
10. E. Anderson, *Street Wise: Race, Class, and Change in an Urban Neighborhood*, University of Chicago Press, Chicago, 1990.
11. E. Liebow, *Tally's Corner: A Study of Negro Streetcorner Men*, Little, Brown and Company, Boston, 1967.

12. W. Oliver, Sexual Conquest and Patterns of Black-on-Black Violence: A Structural-Cultural Perspective, *Violence and Victims, 4*:4, pp. 257-273, 1989.

13. K. J. Pittman, P. M. Wilson, S. Adams-Taylor, and S. Randolph, Making Sexuality Education and Prevention Programs Relevant for African-American Youth, *Journal of School Health, 62*:7, pp. 339-344, 1992.

14. K. Carovano, More than Mothers and Whores: Redefining the AIDS Prevention Needs of Women, *International Journal of Health Services, 21*:1, pp. 131-142, 1991.

15. P. Handwerker, Gender Power Differences may be STD Risk Factors for the Next Generation, *Journal of Women's Health, 2*:3, pp. 301-316, 1993.

16. D. Worth, Sexual Decision-Making and AIDS: Why Condom Promotion among Vulnerable Women is Likely to Fail, *Studies in Family Planning, 20*:6, pp. 297-307, 1989.

17. R. Jones, *The Political and Economic Dynamics of STDs*, paper presented at the 90th Annual Meeting of the American Anthropological Association, Chicago, Illinois, 1991.

18. E. J. Sobo, Finance, Romance, Social Support, and Condom Use among Impoverished Inner-City Women, *Human Organization, 54*:2, pp. 115-128, 1995.

19. R. Rapp, Family and Class in Contemporary America, in *Rethinking the Family*, B. Thorne and M. Yalom (eds.), Northeastern University Press, Boston, pp. 168-187, 1987.

20. K. Sacks, Engels Revisited: Women, the Organization of Production, and Private Property, in *Woman, Culture, and Society*, M. Rosaldo and L. Lamphere (eds.), Stanford University Press, Stanford, California, pp. 207-222, 1974.

21. C. Stack, *All Our Kin: Strategies for Survival in a Black Community*, Harper, New York, 1974.

22. B. Thorne, Feminist Rethinking of the Family: An Overview, in *Rethinking the Family*, B. Thorne and M. Yalom (eds.), Northeastern University Press, Boston, pp. 1-24, 1987.

23. E. Bott, *Family and Social Network: Roles, Norms, and External Relationships in Ordinary Urban Families* (2nd Edition), The Free Press, New York, 1971 [1957].

24. L. Rubin, *Worlds of Pain: Life in the Working-Class Family*, Basic Books, New York, 1976.

25. E. J. Sobo, Inner-City Women and AIDS: The Psycho-Social Benefits of Unsafe Sex, *Culture, Medicine, and Psychiatry, 17*:4, pp. 455-485, 1993.

26. S. D. Cochran, Women and HIV Infection: Issues in Prevention and Behavior Change, in *Primary Prevention of AIDS: Psychological Approaches*, Sage Publications, Newbury Park, California, pp. 309-327, 1989.

27. B. Sibthorpe, The Social Construction of Sexual Relationships as a Determinant of HIV Risk Perception and Condom Use among Injection Drug Users, *Medical Anthropology Quarterly, 6*:3, pp. 255-270, 1992.

28. D. F. Harrison, K. G. Wambach, J. B. Byers et al., AIDS Knowledge and Risk Behaviors among Culturally Diverse Women, *AIDS Education and Prevention, 3*:2, pp. 79-89, 1991.

29. T. Prohaska, G. Albrecht, J. Levy et al., Determinants of Self-Perceived Risk for AIDS, *Journal of Health and Social Behavior, 31*, pp. 384-394, 1990.

30. N. D. Weinstein, Perceptions of Personal Susceptibility to Harm, in *Primary Prevention of AIDS: Psychological Approaches*, V. M. Mays, G. W. Albee, and S. F. Schneider (eds.), Sage Publications, Newbury Park, California, pp. 142-167, 1989.

31. N. D. Weinstein, Unrealistic Optimism about Susceptibility to Health Problems: Conclusions from a Community-Wide Sample, *Journal of Behavioral Medicine, 10*:5, pp. 481-500, 1987.

32. E. J. Sobo, Attitudes toward HIV Testing among Impoverished, Urban African-American Women, *Medical Anthropology*, *16*:2, pp. 1-22, 1994.
33. E. J. Sobo, *Choosing Unsafe Sex: AIDS-Risk Denial and Disadvantaged Women*, University of Pennsylvania Press, Philadelphia, 1995.
34. Blumstein and Schwartz 1983, cited in *AIDS: Sexual Behavior and Intravenous Drug Use*, C. F. Turner, H. G. Miller, and L. E. Moses (eds.), National Academy Press, Washington, D.C., pp. 110-111, 1989.
35. B. Bower, Risky Sex and AIDS, *Science News*, *140*, August 31, 1991.
36. M. Muir, *The Environmental Context of AIDS*, Praeger, New York, 1991.
37. C. F. Turner, H. G. Miller, and L. E. Moses (eds.), *AIDS: Sexual Behavior and Intravenous Drug Use*, National Academy Press, Washington, D.C., 1989.
38. E. Johnson, *Risky Sexual Behaviors among African-Americans*, Praeger, Westport, Connecticut, 1993.
39. M. Freilich, Sex, Secrets, and Systems, in *The Family in the Caribbean*, S. Gerber (ed.), Institute of Caribbean Studies, Puerto Rico, pp. 47-62, 1968.
40. M. Ward, The Politics of Adolescent Pregnancy: Turf and Teens in Louisiana, in *Births and Power: Social Change and the Politics of Reproduction*, W. P. Handwerker (ed.), Westview Press, San Francisco, pp. 147-164, 1990.
41. V. M. Mays and S. D. Cochran, Methodological Issues in Assessment and Prediction of AIDS Risk-Related Sexual Behaviors among Black Americans, in *AIDS and Sex*, B. Voeller et al. (eds.), Oxford University Press, New York, pp. 97-120, 1990.
42. H. Dalton, AIDS in Blackface, *Daedalus*, *118*:3, pp. 205-227, 1989.
43. W. J. Wilson, *The Truly Disadvantaged*, University of Chicago Press, Chicago, 1987.
44. P. Wilson, Black Culture and Sexuality, *Journal of Social Work and Human Sexuality*, *4*:3, pp. 29-46, 1986.
45. G. Wingood and R. DiClemente, Cultural, Gender, and Psychosocial Influences on HIV-Related Behavior of African-American Female Adolescents: Implications for the Development of Tailored Prevention Programs, *Ethnicity and Disease*, *2*:4, pp. 381-388, 1992.
46. M. S. Weinberg and C. J. Williams, Black Sexuality: A Test of Two Theories, *Journal of Sex Research*, *25*:2, pp. 197-218, 1988.
47. V. M. Mays and S. D. Cochran, Issues in the Perception of AIDS Risk and Risk Reduction Activities by Black and Hispanic/Latina Women, *American Psychologist*, *43*:11, pp. 949-957, 1988.
48. C. Patton, *Inventing AIDS*, Routledge, New York, 1990.
49. H. G. Miller, C. F. Turner, and L. E. Moses (eds.), *AIDS: The Second Decade*, National Academy Press, Washington, D.C., 1990.
50. S. Ortner, Gender and Sexuality in Hierarchical Societies: The Case of Polynesia and Some Comparative Implications, in *Sexual Meanings: The Cultural Construction of Gender and Sexuality*, S. Ortner and H. Whitehead (eds.), Cambridge University Press, New York, pp. 359-409, 1981.
51. J. Collier, M. Rosaldo, and S. Yanagisako, Is There a Family? New Anthropological Views, in *Rethinking the Family*, B. Thorne and M. Yalom (eds.), Northeastern University Press, Boston, pp. 25-39, 1987.
52. M. Singer, F. Valentin, H. Gaer, and Z. Jia, Why Does Juan Garcia Have a Drinking Problem: The Perspective of Critical Medical Anthropology, *Medical Anthropology*, *14*:1, pp. 77-108, 1992.
53. P. Sanday, *Female Power and Male Dominance: On the Origins of Sexual Inequality*, Cambridge University Press, New York, 1981.
54. N. Chodorow, *The Reproduction of Mothering: Psychoanalysis and the Sociology of Gender*, University of California Press, Los Angeles, 1978.

55. E. Clarke, *My Mother Who Fathered Me: A Study of the Family in Three Selected Communities in Jamaica*, George Allen and Unwin, Boston, 1957.
56. B. Hooks, Re-Thinking the Nature of Work, in *Feminist Theory: From Margin to Center*, B. Hooks (ed.), South End Press, Boston, pp. 95-105, 1984.
57. K. Orth-Gomer and A. Unden, The Measurement of Social Support in Population Surveys, *Social Science and Medicine, 24*:1, pp. 83-94, 1987.
58. J. H. Medalie, G. C. Kitson, and S. J. Zyzanski, A Family Epidemiological Model: A Practice and Research Concept for Family Medicine, *The Journal of Family Practice, 12*:1, pp. 79-87, 1981.
59. D. Schmidt, The Family as the Unit of Medical Care, *The Journal of Family Practice, 7*:2, pp. 303-313, 1978.
60. C. H. Browner, Male Pregnancy Symptoms in Urban Colombia, *American Ethnologist, 10*:3, pp. 494-511, 1983.
61. W. W. Dressler, *Stress and Adaptation in the Context of Culture*, State University of New York Press, Albany, 1991.
62. J. Spradley, *Participant Observation*, Holt, Rinehart and Winston, New York, 1980.
63. L. Dorfman, P. Derish, and J. Cohen, Hey Girlfriend: An Evaluation of AIDS Prevention among Women in the Sex Industry, *Health Education Quarterly, 19*:1, pp. 25-40, 1992.
64. CUPSC (Center for Urban Poverty and Social Change), *Neighborhood Profiles: A Profile of Social and Economic Conditions in the City of Cleveland*, Vol. II, Center for Urban Poverty and Social Change, Mandel School of Applied Social Sciences, Case Western Reserve University, Cleveland, Ohio, April 1992.
65. F. G. Bailey, Gifts and Poison, in *Gifts and Poison*, F. G. Bailey (ed.), Schocken Books, New York, pp. 1-27, 1971.
66. M. Mauss, *The Gift*, Norton, New York, 1967.
67. E. J. Sobo, *One Blood: The Jamaican Body*, State University of New York Press, New York, 1993.
68. E. J. Sobo, Meaning and Its Usefulness for Inner-City HIV/AIDS Interventions, *Practicing Anthropology, 15*:4, pp. 56-58, 1993.

CHAPTER 5

Multiple Racial/Ethnic Subordination and HIV among Drug Injectors

Samuel R. Friedman, Benny Jose, Bruce Stepherson, Alan Neaigus,
Marjorie Goldstein, Pat Mota, Richard Curtis, and Gilbert Ildefonso

INTRODUCTION

Racial/ethnic subordination is a major sociohistorical fact in the United States and many other countries. Its definition and terminology are controversial, and cannot be fully resolved here.[1] For the purposes of this chapter, however,

---

[1] A note on terminology is needed. We will use the term "race/ethnicity" rather than using either "race" or "ethnicity" alone. This is because there are objectionable connotations in using either term alone (for further critical discussion of such terminological difficulties, see [1-4]).

In the anthropological tradition, "race" has been associated with physical anthropological approaches which have sometimes ascribed the negative social and personal consequences of racial/ethnic subordination to evolutionary, biological, or genetic causation. In recent sociological and political discussions in the United States, on the other hand, the term "ethnicity" has been used in two ways that seem objectionable to us: First, it is often used in ways that equate the injustices and/or inequalities faced in the U.S. by some persons descended from particular European nationalities with the much more deeply-institutionalized injustices and inequalities—both past and present—faced by African Americans, Latinos, and Native Americans (stemming initially from past enslavement in the United States or from military conquest and ensuring domination by the United States) [1, 5]. Second, "ethnicity" is often used as part of arguments that implicitly or explicitly hold that these injustices or inequalities are a product of the *cultures* of the subordinated group, rather than parts of a system of political, economic, and cultural stratification that victimizes the subordinated groups in ways that benefit the dominant economic and political classes [3].

In short, we are using "race/ethnicity" for lack of a better term. Clearly, since we see race/ethnicity as the product of sociohistorical processes of subordination, we also see racial/ethnic categories as sociohistorical constructs rather than as biological entities. Terminological difficulties become even more complex if one attempts to encompass the full global range of national, language, caste, and religious subordinations.

racial/ethnic subordination will be used to refer to a complex social pattern which includes the following major aspects:

1. *Institutionalized power imbalance*—i.e., racial/ethnic subordination is a *relationship* which is embodied in: 1) patterns of the ownership and control of corporate and other capital; 2) which people hold top political positions; and 3) differential treatment by key institutions such as criminal justice systems, employment markets (both for initial hiring and for promotion), housing markets, and school systems.
2. *Ideological stigmatization* via media representations, art, and expressions of one or another form of racist belief. Thus, racial/ethnic subordination has a cultural form as well as inhering in social structural relationships.
3. *Dignity denial:* Ideological stigmatization and power imbalance are complemented by the denial of full human dignity to the subordinated groups; this leads to deep personal hurt and psychological pain.
4. *Distributional inequality:* Members of subordinate racial/ethnic categories have less access to desirable "personal attributes" of the kind measured in censuses such as income, wealth, and education, and a concomitant increased share of unemployment, poor jobs, reliance on welfare, and membership in the reserve labor force [6-8].
5. *Dominance, acceptance, and resistance:* Racial/ethnic subordination, like all power relationships, includes elements of domination, of acceptance, and of resistance. Thus, to study or to change it, one needs to understand how the domination is organized, including its relationships to the core institutions of society; how a degree of acceptance is translated both into "legitimate authority" [9] and into deep personal damage; and how it is related to "discontent" [10] and thus to social movements to resist and/or to change one or all aspects of subordination and/or the overarching structures of society [1, 5, 10, 11-15].

For reasons which are not fully understood, HIV seroprevalence is greater in some racially/ethnically subordinated groups in the United States than among whites. AIDS case surveillance data through December 1993 (CDC, preliminary data) find that, whereas 12 percent of the United States population is African American and 9 percent is Latino, the corresponding percentages for African-American and Latino men with AIDS are 28 percent and 16 percent and for African-American and Latina women, 54 percent and 20 percent. By transmission category, African-American men comprise 19 percent of the men who have sex with men, 29 percent of the men who both inject drugs and have sex with men, 49 percent of the drug-injecting heterosexual men, 57 percent of the women drug injectors, 59 percent of the men whose risk is having sex with a woman drug injector, 50 percent of the women whose risk is having sex with a drug-injecting man, 35 percent of the women whose risk is sex with a bisexual man, 51 percent of the men whose risk is having sex with an HIV-seropositive woman whose risk is not known, 55 percent of the women whose risk is having sex with an HIV-seropositive man whose risk is not known, 51 percent of the men with no identified risk and 67 percent of the women with no identified risk. By transmission category, Latino men comprise 12 percent of the men who have sex with men, 15 percent of the men who both inject drugs and have sex with men, 30 percent of the drug-injecting heterosexual men, 20 percent of the women drug injectors, 17 percent of the men whose risk is having sex with a woman drug injector, 28 percent of the women whose risk is having sex with a drug-injecting man, 13 percent of the women whose risk is sex with a bisexual man, 25 percent of the men whose risk is having sex with an HIV-seropositive woman whose risk is not known, 22 percent of the women whose risk is having sex with an HIV-seropositive man whose risk is not known, 18 percent of the men with no identified risk, and 13 percent of the women with no identified risk. Thus, in all of these categories, African Americans and Latinos are disproportionately likely to have been diagnosed with AIDS.

HIV-seroprevalence data among injecting drug users (IDUs) in many—but not all [16]—areas of the United States also indicate that African Americans and those Latinos of Puerto Rican origin or descent are more likely to be seropositive than are whites [17-26].

These data suggest a hypothesis: That people such as Latinos and African Americans who are racially/ethnically subordinated may be at greater risk for HIV than people who are not.[2] Such a hypothesis clearly calls for further research, since it leaves open all questions of mechanism—that is, *how* it comes about (if it does) that racial/ethnic subordination is associated with higher HIV infection rates and, relatedly, why it is that in some geographical areas whites may be equally likely to be infected. To the extent that this hypothesis is true, or course, it resembles the pattern which has been observed regarding many other diseases and conditions—such as syphilis, tuberculosis, infant mortality, stroke, diabetes, and cancer mortality—which are also disproportionately prevalent among racially/ethnically subordinated people [28-30].

If racial/ethnic subordination leads to higher HIV seroprevalence, what happens to people who are subjected to racial/ethnic subordination in more than one way?[3] While research has found that white IDUs are less likely to be HIV-seropositive than African-American or Latino IDUs, few studies have measured whether

---

[2] Black Latinos who are not drug injectors also seem to face double minority status. In a study of residential segregation, Denton and Massey [27] found that Black Hispanics are segregated from other Hispanics, from Anglos, and from non-Hispanic blacks.

[3] Which is to be distinguished from the "multiple oppression" of women from racially/ethnically subordinated groups. Unfortunately, in this study, the number of Black Latinos/as both sexes is relatively small (58), of whom only thirteen are women, so we are unable to analyze gender stratification and related issues in this chapter, although we do briefly discuss other forms of multiple subordination below.

persons who are both African American and Latino are more likely to be HIV-infected than persons who engage in the same categories of behavioral risk but who are only members of one racially/ethnically subordinated group.

Two studies of IDUs from our research group have done so. A previous study [25] showed that among Manhattan methadone and detoxification clients in 1984-1985, Black-Latinos were more likely to be infected than Black non-Latinos, Latino non-Blacks, or White non-Latinos in 1984.[4] In this chapter, we show, using data from a study of street-recruited IDUs in Brooklyn from 1991-1993, that Black Latino IDUs (primarily with Puerto Rican ancestry rather than other Latino ethnicity) remain most likely to be infected. We also show that Black-Latino IDUs, relative to other Black and Latino IDUs, are indeed subordinated by presenting data which show that they are less likely to receive the benefits of society (and thus are "distributionally unequal"), and some ethnographic evidence that suggests that they may be subject to interpersonal domination and exclusion even within the drug street scene.

It is important to look at multiple racial/ethnic subordination because programs for HIV prevention and care among minority communities need to take it into account. Racial/ethnic stratification within these communities can affect the response that outreach workers and/or specific messages receive. The lines of stratification between the singly- and multiply-subordinated may also be boundaries between networks, which might tend to restrict both viral transmission and the communication of prevention messages across these boundaries.

METHODS

Six hundred and sixty street-recruited New York IDUs who provided information about their race/ethnicity were HIV tested (repeat ELISA with Western blot confirmation) and interviewed from July 1991 to January 1993. The sample was 71 percent male; 32 percent white non-Latino/a, 26 percent black non-Latino/a, 34 percent non-black Latino/a, 8 percent black Latino/a.

The interview asked about respondent characteristics: HIV risk behaviors during the last two years and the last thirty days, medical history, and roles in the drug scene. It also included questions about the characteristics and behaviors of subjects' egocentric networks—i.e., about people with whom subjects had injected drugs, had sex, or otherwise interacted in the previous thirty days; and

---

[4] Another aspect of terminology needs to be discussed here. During the collection of data for this project, many African-American leaders expressed the desire that the term "African American" be used rather than "black" or other words. The data, however, were collected asking the participants in the study whether they identify themselves as "black." Thus, in discussing the results *per se*, we will use the term "black" to be accurate in terms of what they told us; but when discussing more generally, we will use the term "African American."

about the nature and history of the relationships between subjects and their network members.

Analyses of social network-related risk use two kinds of data. Egocentric data describe characteristics of subjects' personal contacts. Sociometric network measures describe the place of subjects within the various networks that constitute the Bushwick drug scene [31]. The specific sociometric network variable used is a categorization of network location, by which seven hundred and sixty-seven subjects were assigned to four categories of increasing linkage to other participants in the study:

1. Two hundred and seventy-six IDUs who were *not* linked to other participants, whether through naming them as part of their network or through being named by another participant;
2. Two hundred and fourteen other IDUs who were members of small connected components (such that linkage was made between 2 to 7 participants), and who thus seem to have direct and indirect ties with relatively few other drug injectors;
3. One hundred and forty-six IDUs in the periphery of a large connected component with 277 members;
4. One hundred and thirty-one IDUs in the two-core of this large connected component (which means that all of the members of the 2-core are linked to at least 2 other members of the core). The drug injectors in the core of the large component thus interact with more other IDUs who themselves have links with other IDUs than do IDUs in the other categories.

Ethnographic data were also collected as part of this study. The ethnographic team: conducted direct observations in street drug settings and in shooting galleries; helped to recruit subjects for the quantitative interviews; and conducted 210 in-depth ethnographic interviews with forty-six drug injectors and twenty-two other local drug users in the Bushwick neighborhood of Brooklyn.

Statistical analyses concentrate on the differences between drug injectors who are subject to multiple racial/ethnic subordination—those who are both Latino and Black—and those who are subject to only one category of racial/ethnic subordination—those who are either Black non-Latinos or those who are Latino but not Black. (This is particularly justifiable because, as Figure 1 shows, Black non-Latinos and Latino non-Blacks have similar HIV seroprevalence rates.) These analyses present data that suggest that Black Latinos are subject to multiple racial/ethnic subordination, that their behaviors and social networks place them at greater risk of HIV than other Black and Latino IDUs, and that they are more likely to be infected with HIV than white IDUs or other Black and Latino IDUs.

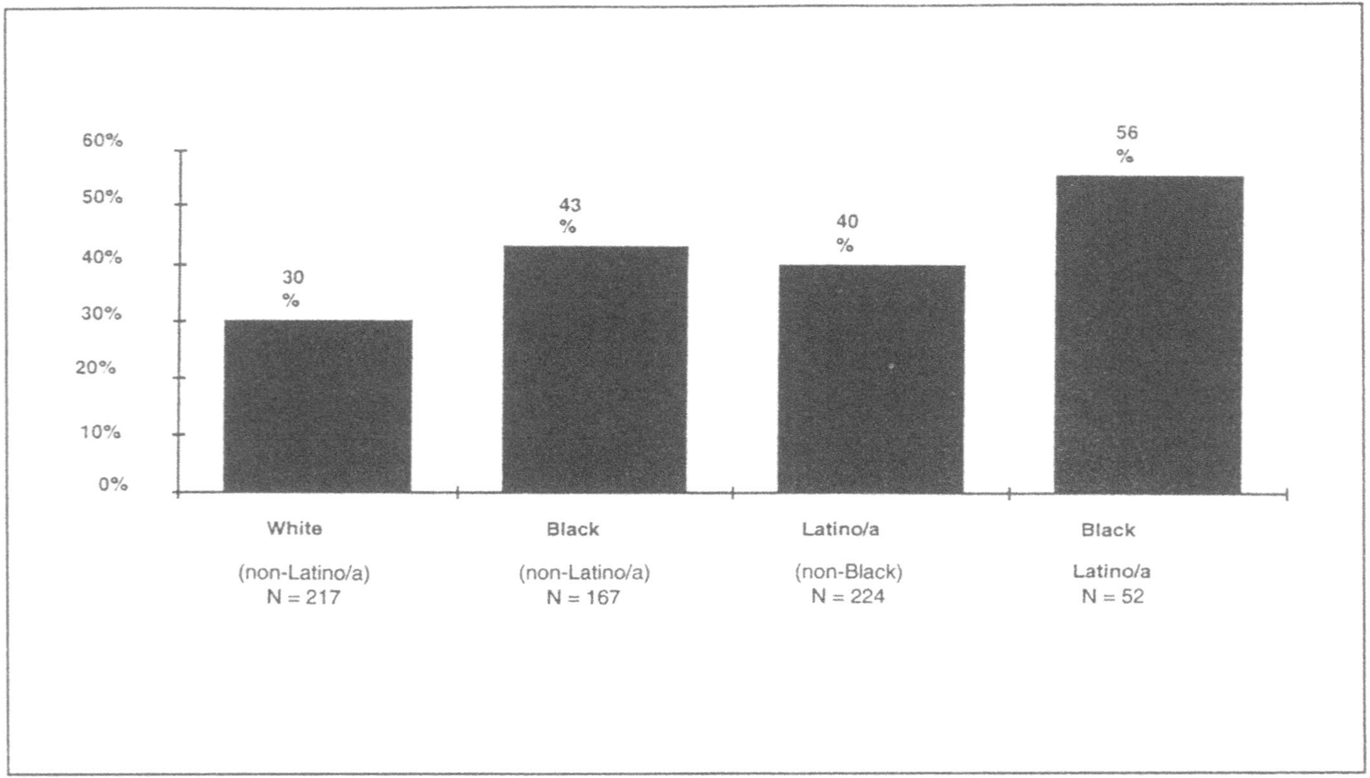

Figure 1. Percent HIV seropositive by race/ethnicity.

RESULTS

Seroprevalence was highest among Black Latinos (see Figure 1). Seroprevalence among Black Latinos (Table 1) is 15 percent higher than among those drug injectors who are Black non-Latinos or Latino non-Blacks (odds ratio = 1.82; 95% C.I. 1.02, 3.24; $p(\chi^2)$ = .042).

Black Latinos/as seem to have less access to (or make less use of) certain "mainstream" resources and institutions, and thus are "distributionally subordinated" (see Table 2). Thus, they are less likely to have homes, less likely to be in drug abuse treatment, and less likely to visit doctors. The drastic impact of homelessness on drug injectors' lives has been discussed elsewhere [32, 33], and we have previously reported that, in a multi-city dataset, homeless drug injectors are more likely to undergo HIV seroconversion than those with homes [34]. Drug abuse treatment is useful to drug injectors both as a way to keep their habits under control [7, 35] and as a way to stop using drugs, when and if they decide to do so. Treatment also helps prevent seroconversion [36, 37]. Less contact with doctors—particularly for a group who have had high HIV seroprevalence since 1984 [25]—suggests that many Black Latinos/as may be going without care for diseases and conditions that may be susceptible to treatment.

Perhaps as a direct or indirect consequence of their greater social subordination, Black Latinos are more likely than other Black and Latino IDUs to engage in a number of HIV risk behaviors such as injecting speedball, injecting in prison, injecting in shooting galleries, and injecting in outdoor settings. They also seem to play distinctive social roles in the drug scene, in that they were more likely than other minority IDUs to see drugs or syringes. Their egocentric and sociometric networks may also put Black Latino IDUs at higher risk of HIV. Black Latino IDUs know more HIV-seropositive persons, and have known more persons who have died from AIDS, than other Black or Latino drug injectors. The egocentric network data indicate that Black Latinos are more likely to have a drug-injecting network member whom they have known for a year or less. This is a measure of network turnover and thus of potential exposure to HIV-infected IDUs, and has

Table 1. HIV Seroprevalence among Minority IDUs

	Other Black or Latino/a	Black Latino/a
HIV−	231	23
HIV+	160	29
Percent HIV+	41%	56%
$p(\chi^2)$	.042	
Odds Ratio	1.82	
(95% C.I.)	(1.02, 3.24)	

Table 2. Comparisons of Black Latino/a IDUs and Other Black
or Latino/a IDUs among Subjects with HIV Results

	Other Black or Latino/a	Black Latino/a	$p\ (\chi^2)$
Demographic Variables			
Sex: % Female	30	21	.18
% Legally married	12	8	.36
Measures of Distributional Inequality			
% High school graduate	61	60	.85
% Homeless	17	30	.029
% Income < $10,000	84	77	.26
% With legal income (can include transfer payments)	76	71	.48
% Ever in drug abuse treatment	63	62	.82
% Currently in drug abuse treatment	21	8	.021
% Who have seen a doctor in last 6 months	63	46	.015
Risk Behaviors			
% Monthly injection frequency > once daily, last 2 years, for:			
All drugs	62	74	.093
Heroin	37	42	.58
Cocaine	10	17	.16
Speedball	23	42	.005
% Ever injected drugs in prison	3	11	.004
% Injected at shooting gallery in last 2 years	32	56	.001
% Injected at multi-person outside setting in last 2 years	45	69	.001
% Engaged in sex for money or drugs, last 2 years	13	13	.99
% Ever engaged in anal sex	50	52	.76
Egocentric Network Characteristics			
% Who have a Latino/a injector in network	52	77	.001
% Who have a Black injector in network	44	29	.038
% Who have an IDU network member who is at least 5 years older	33	33	.94
% Who have known at least one member of injector network for 1 year or less	32	48	.021

Table 2. (Cont'd.)

	Other Black or Latino/a	Black Latino/a	$p\,(\chi^2)$
Sociometric Network Charactertistics			
Network Location:			.001
% is Core of large connected component	12	33	
% is Periphery of large connected component	17	9	
% is Small component	29	9	
% Unlinked	41	48	
Roles in Drug Scene			
% Who sell drugs	22	38	.011
% Who sell syringes	19	43	.001

	Other Black or Latino/a (mean)	Black Latino/a (mean)	$p\,(t)$
Continuous Variables			
Age	34.5	34.6	.89
Years since first injected drugs	12.9	14.6	.18
Number of HIV+ persons subject knows	7.0	13.8	.039
Number of persons subject knew who died from AIDS	7.0	11.8	.032

been found to be related to the probability of HIV infection among newer injectors who engage in risk behavior [38] or who are women [39]. Black Latinos are more likely to have Latino/Latina injectors in their networks, and less likely to have Black injectors in their networks, which suggests that they maintain closer social ties to drug-injecting Latinos/Latinas than to Blacks.

In terms of sociometric location, Black Latinos are particularly likely to be members of the cores of large connected social network components (i.e., to have multiple links with drug injectors who also have links to yet other drug injectors)—and we have elsewhere shown that members of the cores of social networks are more likely to be infected with both HIV and HBV than are less tightly linked drug injectors [31, 40].

ETHNOGRAPHIC OBSERVATIONS OF RACIAL/ETHNIC SUBORDINATION WITHIN THE DRUG SCENE

In collecting qualitative data on the everyday lives of IDUs in the study neighborhood, the ethnographic team was guided primarily by the overarching concerns of the project—collecting data on networks of IDUs, injection behaviors, and social relationships to the larger society (including those of racial subordination). The issue of racism *among* IDUs and how that may impact upon behavior (and ultimately serostatus), however, was something that was not so readily apparent. As in society in general, racism among drug injectors is often found below the surface of face to face interaction, out of the spotlight of public scrutiny. Among the myriad of problems faced by IDUs, racism by some IDUs against others seemed, at first glance, not to be of first-order salience. In retrospect, and in light of the quantitative data presented in this chapter, the importance of racism within the drug scene itself began to take on new significance and called for a reexamination of the ethnographic data and, in some instances, re-interviewing of key informants in the field.

Ethnographic observation indicates that Black-Latino IDUs are subject to exclusion and invidious discrimination by a wide range of street-level drug market participants, including other Black and Latino IDUs. While Black-Latino IDUs were not overtly denied access to local shooting galleries and/or crack houses, they were often made to feel unwanted in these places. For example, when one Black-Latina (Dominican) IDU was asked whether she had been denied access to local shooting galleries, she replied that she could go into any place she wanted. When asked why the ethnographer had never seen her inside a local gallery run by an elderly (non-Black) Puerto Rican man, she replied that she could go in there, but "he doesn't like Black people" and she felt uncomfortable using drugs in his place. While Black Latino/as were not overtly barred from some injection locations, then, the subtle and not so subtle pressures on them to avoid particular locations had the effect of limiting the number of places to which they had access to use drugs.

It was probably no coincidence that, throughout the duration of the study period the three main *outdoor* shooting galleries in the research neighborhood were operated by HIV-positive Black Latinos/as. Although Black-Latino IDUs disproportionately used these outdoor galleries, many other drug injectors were also part of their clientele. These locations were notorious for the absence of clean injection equipment, the social marginality of their clientele, and the rapidity with which clients injected in them so as to avoid the police and/or other IDUs who might ask for a taste of their drugs. The use of harm-reduction techniques and clean injection materials was rarely observed in these locations.

The first gallery, run by the Latina mentioned above, operated in an empty lot adjacent to the major crack-selling and crack-using spots in the neighborhood. Because of its proximity to local crack markets, many IDUs who did not smoke crack tried to avoid this location, so they would not have to undergo the hassles of interacting with long-term frequent crack users. Syringe dealers also avoided working near this gallery because many of these crack users would beg syringe dealers for small change and/or an opportunity to help them sell syringes so they could have money for their next hit. As a result, there appeared to be fewer new syringes on the block, and fewer of the IDUs seemed to use clean injection equipment than at other locations in the neighborhood. On several occasions, the ethnographer witnessed IDUs at this location pick up used syringes off the ground, rinse them with water and inject with them. This behavior was not generally observed at other injection locations.

The second gallery, run by a Black-Panamanian IDU, also operated in an empty lot. This gallery was located near a local subway station and catered to many homeless IDUs who panhandled on the subway as well as those IDUs who sold scrap metal. The area immediately surrounding the gallery looked like a junkyard, strewn with garbage (like TVs, radios, etc.) that had been discarded by IDUs who had decided that the items were worthless. IDUs who frequented this gallery were almost sure to run into other IDUs and were expected to share drugs with the gallery operator and/or whoever might be "dope sick" at the time. Many clients at this gallery looked visibly "sick"—open sores on their arms and legs, large abscesses, thrush, and so on.

The third outdoor shooting gallery, run by a Black-Puerto Rican IDU, operated on a sidewalk about a block from the main heroin and cocaine selling areas. The operator of this gallery was known for being adept at injecting other IDUs in the neck and he had more than a dozen daily clients for whom he performed this service. Given that his gallery was quite visible, he also had to be quick to avoid both the police and IDUs who were desperate to get a free taste of someone else's drugs. The police knocked down his hastily constructed windshield and counter-top at least once a day, and as a result, clean injection materials were a scarce commodity at this location.

These three outdoor shooting galleries were distinct from other neighborhood injection locations. IDUs who frequented *indoor* shooting galleries in the neighborhood both engaged in more efforts to reduce their behavioral risk and also tried to hide the high-risk behaviors they continued to engage in from each other, from the ethnographic staff of this research project, and from AIDS outreach workers. IDUs who frequented these outdoor shooting galleries, on the other hand, engaged in frequent high-risk behavior without attempting to conceal it. Thus, on many occasions, they were observed sharing injection equipment (though syringes were not passed from hand to hand), backloading, scraping out used cookers for drug residue, and collecting used syringes for future use.

DISCUSSION

The data presented here indicate that the relative social positions of Black Latino/a drug injectors and other Black and Latino/a drug injectors are quite complex. The data on homelessness, drug abuse treatment use, and contact with doctors, as well as ethnographic data, however, provide considerable evidence that Black Latinos/as are in a subordinate status.

One important implication of these data which should not be overlooked is the necessity to gather data that measure multiple racial/ethnic subordination. In particular, questionnaires and ethnography should not simply assess whether people are Black or Latino; instead, they should ascertain whether they are both. *Within* the drug scene, Black Latinos seem to be enmeshed in a complicated and perhaps contradictory set of social relationships. On the one hand, the ethnography indicates that they face a degree of exclusion within the drug scene, and that this exclusion may lead them to engage more in high-risk injecting. On the other, the data presented here indicate that they are more likely than other Black and Latino/a drug injectors to sell drugs and to sell syringes. Although these drug and syringe sellers occupy low ranks in the drug dealing hierarchy, these roles nonetheless represent a modicum of power in that they function as gatekeepers between distributors and non-core consumers [40]. Syringe sellers, in particular, seem to be able to use their centrality in communication networks among street-level drug market participants to get free samples from distributors and also to get shares of the drugs bought by those drug users with few links to the market. The behavioral results of filling these roles are also complicated: Although syringe sellers sometimes engage in syringe sharing or syringe-mediated drug injecting while sharing drugs [40]—both of which practices can transmit HIV [41]; and although both Black Latino and other Black and Latino syringe sellers in this sample are more likely than other drug injectors to report backloading in the prior two years (both $p < 0.01$), Black Latinos in this sample are nevertheless *not* more likely to report engaging in either backloading or receptive syringe sharing than other Blacks and Latinos/as. Further research should be conducted so we can unravel these complicated social and behavioral patterns that occur within the drug scene.

Furthermore, Black Latinos are more likely than other drug injectors in this study to be part of the sociometric core, and to have more rapid turnover in the egocentric networks of drug injectors with whom they spend time. Membership in the sociometric core is a risk factor for HIV even after behavioral risk factors have been adjusted for [31], and network turnover may be associated with HIV infection among new injectors [38].

Black-Latino/a drug injectors engage in particularly high levels of a number of risk behaviors. First, they are less likely to be in drug treatment, more likely to be homeless, more likely to engage in social roles in the drug scene that often involve opportunities for shared access to drugs (such as selling syringes or running outdoor shooting galleries), and are members of a sociometric core group that itself has been linked to high levels of risk behaviors [31]. Second, their position at or near the bottom of the racial/ethnic subordination hierarchy in the larger society, and their subordination even within the drug scene itself, may lead to fewer options in terms of potential partners and places in which to use drugs, and thus over time *might* possibly be conducive to greater willingness to take risks. (Before concluding that this is so, more research is clearly needed. In making this kind of an argument, unless one exercises extreme care, it is possible to fall into the trap of blaming the victim [42]).

What is the relationship between these findings and HIV? The issue raised by these results is not simply one of identifying which variables are the proximate epidemiologic risk factors for HIV. It is instead a question of disentangling a complex pattern of causation and intercausality. Black Latinos and Black Latinas in New York are subjected to political, economic, and other forms of subordination from the day they are born. Those who become drug injectors remain subject to this subordination, which may well include both greater distributional inequality than is faced by other Black and Latino IDUs and, as well, a degree of discrimination within the drug scene itself, and find themselves with additional problems to the extent to which they become dependent on drugs. The specific behaviors in which they engage, and their network characteristics, are not antecedent to their racial/ethnic subordination, but are instead subsequent. Thus, it seems far more reasonable to emphasize the extent to which Black Latinos'/as' racial/ethnic subordination can lead to high-risk behaviors, high-risk networks, and lack of contact with medical systems, than the reverse. If this is so, then we can view these behaviors and networks as the proximate causes of HIV infection, and indeed we would expect that multivariate equations could be constructed in which these behavioral and network variables would be significant predictors of infection, while being Black Latino/a would lose significance. All this would mean, however, is that some or all of the effects of being subordinated both as a Black and as a Latino/a would operate by way of shaping risk behaviors and networks.

Further research is clearly needed so we can look beyond the purview of isolated drug scenes. Such research should include studies comparing cities and/or countries in terms of basic patterns of political economy such as racial/ethnic stratification, class structure, the industrial and occupational distributions of available jobs, gender relations, and how changes in these affect racial/ethnic stratification among workers; how these changes and patterns of stratification interact with social and political organizational factors and thence with drug policy and its associated stigmas and police action; and how these sometimes produce situations in which HIV (and other blood-borne agents) spread more rapidly among those who are subjected to more forms of subordination. In addition, research should be conducted to compare the extent to which Black Latinos, as persons subject to multiple racial/ethnic subordination, are more or less likely to be afflicted with other diseases and medical conditions such as hypertension, heart disease, some cancers, and—perhaps as a consequence of HIV and of crowded housing—tuberculosis.

OTHER SITUATIONS OF MULTIPLE SUBORDINATION

Racial/ethnic subordination is not the only form of social subordination faced by persons in modern society. Gender, class, and sexual orientation are also forms of social subordination. Multiple subordination of different kinds may also be related to greater probabilities of HIV and/or AIDS.

AIDS surveillance data indicate that men who have sex with men, and who are also Black or Latino, are more likely than other homosexual/bisexual men to have AIDS [43, 44, CDC Surveillance data (previously)]. Thus, among men, the combination of subordination by race/ethnicity with that by sexual orientation seems to lead to greater risk of AIDS.

Several studies have found evidence that, among drug injectors, those who both are women and also have sex with women are more likely to be HIV-seropositive [41, 45] and more likely to seroconvert [46]. In the data that form the basis for this chapter, women IDUs who have sex with women tended to be more likely to be infected, with 53 percent being seropositive as compared to 39 percent for other women IDUs ($p < 0.12$). There is some suggestion that there may be additional consequences of a third layer of subordination: ten of thirteen (77%) of Latina women IDUs who have sex with women were seropositive. This can be compared with 35 percent of seventeen non-Latina women who have sex with women ($p < 0.024$) and 39 percent of seventy-nine Latina women who do not engage in sex with women ($p < 0.011$). The reasons why women drug injectors who have sex with women are more likely to be infected have not been specified, but both Reardon et al. [45] and Friedman et al. [46] have suggested that it is likely to be due to sexual or drug-injection-related transmission from men who have sex with women. Here, it can be argued that the predisposition of men who have sex with men and of women who have sex with women preferentially to engage in risk behaviors together, rather than with heterosexuals, may be a direct or indirect consequence of social subordination of persons who have sex with the same sex.

PRACTICAL IMPLICATIONS

Immediate Issues

Data of the kind presented in this chapter pose a dilemma. On the one hand, they indicate the urgent need for immediate practical steps to reduce HIV transmission and other negative consequences of multiple racial/ethnic subordination. On the other hand, they indicate that racial/ethnic subordination itself creates problems for subordinated people, and thus should be eliminated. This latter goal, the elimination of racism, requires far greater effort and far greater social change than is needed for focused and targeted programs of AIDS prevention or even for the amelioration of certain aspects of distributional inequality. As a practical issue, then, we are faced with the dilemma of how to act so as to address both the immediate goals and the longer-term goal of ending racial/ethnic subordination.

Our research group has written a number of articles on HIV prevention [47-50]. We will thus not spend much attention here on the specifics of what is needed.

One clear need is to assure easy legal access to sterile syringes. This should be done through syringe exchange programs; through making over-the-counter sales of syringes both legal and widespread—since data from a national study of drug injectors indicate that living in a state where over-the-counter sales are illegal is a risk factor for HIV seroconversion [51]; and through the abolition of laws that criminalize the possession of syringes for the purpose of injecting drugs [47]. Programs that aim to help drug users to change their "culture of risk" into a "culture of harm reduction" are also needed; examples of such programs start with community outreach, but also include projects to encourage peers to work together to reduce their risks [52], projects that recruit leaders of local networks to encourage risk reduction [50, 53], and efforts by drug injectors themselves to set up drug users' unions to fight AIDS [49].

Expansion of drug abuse treatment is also needed to reduce HIV transmission. In this regard, however, the data presented in this chapter point out a problem. Black Latinos are less likely to be in treatment than other Blacks or Latinos. There is a clear need for research on the reasons why this is so. There is also a clear need for action to eliminate this pattern of exclusion. The responsibility to make this happen is shared by funders of treatment programs, the providers and staff of treatment programs, and by clients and neighbors of programs who might make it uncomfortable for Black Latinos to attend.

Similarly, the data in this chapter indicate that Black-Latino drug injectors are subordinated in other ways besides those of HIV or drug use per se. They are more likely to be homeless, less likely to see doctors and, within the drug scene, may face exclusion. Special efforts should clearly be made to ensure that Black-Latino drug injectors get equal access to housing and medical attention—and, we would add, that access to these necessities be made universal in society.

Within the drug scene, drug users' organizations and others should try to reduce and, indeed, eliminate racial/ethnic exclusion and discrimination. This is clearly not an easy task, since such racism within the drug scene is probably deeply rooted in racial/ethnic subordination throughout the society. Furthermore, the drug scene is an illegal and ostracized portion of society, and does not have political, judicial, or mediatory institutions to help its members resolve conflicts over issues of racism or exclusion. Research might help, but action by drug users and their friends (including experimentation to discover the most effective strategies) is probably more important.

Acting on these issues might reduce problems of multiple racial/ethnic subordination among drug injectors, and thus might help to reduce the probability that they become infected with HIV. In addition, however, the issue of racial/ethnic subordination itself needs to be addressed. It cannot be ignored simply because it is difficult to deal with. The evidence presented here—that multiple racial/ethnic subordination contributes to HIV spread among drug injectors and that it also contributes to other problems for drug injectors—is clearly only a minute part of the problems caused by racial/ethnic subordination. Racial/ethnic subordination is a gigantic problem in and of itself; the existence of racial/ethnic subordination, furthermore, often makes it much more difficult to gather the social and political forces needed to deal with other issues because racial/ethnic inequalities create friction and conflicts among those who might otherwise be able to work together. One example of this was the delay in the establishment of syringe exchanges in the United States because of differences between some African-American elites (and their constituencies) and those supporting syringe exchange.

Underlying Issues for Immediate Action

Thus, one clear need is that *racial/ethnic subordination must be eliminated.* Such a recommendation is not new, and enjoys at least lip-service support from many, perhaps most, people in the United States (and, indeed, the world). Clearly, however, the political and social structure of the United States has not functioned in ways that have eliminated racial/ethnic subordination. In a book on the *political economy* of AIDs, it is worth considering why not.

In one of his first publications, the first author of this chapter raised the issue: "How is racism maintained?" [54]. This article pointed out that racial/ethnic subordination, like any other enduring institution, existed because changing it is resisted with political and economic resources from other parts of society. The precise sources of this support for racial/ethnic subordination are, of course, controversial, and raise issues about how society as a whole can most usefully and accurately be analyzed. These analyses, in turn, point to different strategies and philosophical perspectives needed to change the society enough to eliminate (or even to seriously reduce) racial/ethnic subordination.

In a chapter of this length, it is not possible even to give a full description of our views on the political economy of racial/ethnic subordination and how it is interrelated with the rest of society, much less to defend it or to answer the critiques that others may raise. Nonetheless, it seems worthwhile to *sketch* our analysis, while recognizing that *there are many levels of historical and social complexity that we cannot even begin to address here* (such as class, gender, and sociocultural differentiation and subordination within such groups as African Americans, Latinos/as, and whites).

We favor an approach that sees racial/ethnic subordination in the United States as having grown out of the political, economic, and ecological expansion of European capitalism through the conquest or domination of Africa, the Americas, and much of Asia by Europeans and their American descendants, and through the consequent creation of labor systems that supported capitalist development in Europe and North America [1, 5, 55]. Institutionalization of these labor systems took diverse forms in different countries and, indeed, these institutions change over time in each country; for example, in the United States, enslaved African Americans were first incorporated into plantation crop production; this was succeeded in many parts of the South by tenant farming. Later yet, much of the

African-American population was incorporated into the industrial and service sectors of the working class [1, 5, 56]. Similarly, the conquest of Puerto Rico and part of Mexico by the United States led in time to a change from peasant farming to agricultural wage labor and then, for many Latinos, to industrial and service work. The institutionalization of these labor systems involved the creation or adaptation of political, educational, and religious institutions and beliefs that buttressed racial/ethnic subordination; and changes in these labor systems were accompanied by changes in these other institutions and beliefs. Racial/ethnic subordination, in turn, has buttressed the overall stability of the economic system and, indeed, of the other institutions, by creating disunity among those who might challenge the established order (although there have indeed been periods such as the 1960s when it appeared that the effect of the racial/ethnic subordination was to create instability, the system has proved to be quite able to weather such periods, in large part because of the disunity produced among workers—of blue, white, and pink collars—by the institutions of racial/ethnic subordination.)

The *political* role of racial/ethnic subordination is both important and complex. It is tied into the difficulty of maintaining social stability—a difficulty that varies in intensity over time. There are periods when stability seems assured, and others when it seems extremely precarious. A period such as the last decade has been—and such as the future seems to promise—poses special threats. Income and wealth have become more unequally distributed. The economy has seen a large-scale shift from full-time manufacturing jobs to part-time employment in other industries; and heightened competition has meant that job security and job quality have become extremely problematic. Governments have reduced many social services. In sum, it has been a period of difficulty for the majority, penury for many, and affluence for a minority. In Dickens' phrase, "It was the best of times, it was the worst of times." It was also a time of change rather than of stability.

In times like these, then, there is considerable risk of serious social unrest. The last decade saw such unrest topple regimes in a number of economically relatively developed countries such as those in Eastern Europe and South Africa. In the absence of structures or measures to prevent it, serious unrest could develop in the United States as it did in the 1930s and the 1960s.

From the viewpoint of the affluent and powerful, the threat of social movements that demand change is dangerous. Social structures that make it hard to mount a powerful challenge clearly have many benefits for the status quo. Historically, racial/ethnic divisions, both among workers and in impoverished communities, have been one of the major forces weakening social movements in America, as was evidenced in the failure of Populism in the 1890s, the racial cleavages in the labor movements during and just after both World Wars, and the melange of social movements of the 1960s. Movements of subordinated racial/ethnic groups have been weakened by class divisions, and in particular by the tendency of middle class and business owners in these groups to try to moderate their efforts [1, 5, 11].

Other fissures, such as those of gender and sexual orientation, also can sap the strength of movements. Wars on drugs can function as a way to divide potential insurgent groups into "respectable" and stigmatized groupings within a given community—as, for example, between non-users and drug users in today's African-American communities. Drug wars can also reduce the prospects of unity between the groups that contain large numbers of drug users and those that either do not do so (or can pretend not to do so)—and thus, for example, weaken the prospects for united action by African-American and white working-class and poor communities today, or by Italian American "wet" versus "Anglo-Saxon" American "dry" workers in the period before and after World War I.

Such divisions have both passive and active functions for the powerful. In the passive mode, they prevent unity without any particular effort by societal elites. That is, the differences that are built into ongoing social structures, and the awareness and valuations of these differences that are part of the culture, can create friction and hold off widespread unrest without politicians or cultural leaders having to take conscious action. On other occasions, efforts at active scapegoating may seem useful to some or all political and cultural leaders. There may be disagreements among elites about the advisability of scapegoating at any given time, and/or about the particular lines along which scapegoating should occur. Thus, different forms of scapegoating can serve as "functional equivalents." At one time, race-baiting might seem most effective; at another, such as the period immediately after World War II, a combination of red-baiting and "playing the gender card" (to expel women from many of the best jobs) might be most effective. At other times, as in the 1980s, a combination of racial division and drug-baiting may seem to some political elites like an efficacious way to forestall or weaken social challenge.

If this analysis is correct, racial/ethnic subordination will be very hard to root out. This is borne out by the failure of large-scale efforts to do more than dent the structures of racism in the United States. Although the demonstrations, mass actions, and perhaps even government programs of the 1960s changed the specifics of racial/ethnic subordination, the general pattern continues to hold true: Blacks and Latinos/as remain subject to institutionalized power imbalance, ideological stigmatization, dignity denial, and distributional inequality; and have, as a consequence, been particularly vulnerable to the decline of many manufacturing industries, to the associated decline of the economies of urban neighborhoods (and even whole cities) in which they live, and to the pressures of heightened intercorporate competition on a global basis. And, as has been extensively documented, they pay the consequences of this in poorer health care and greater exposure to many diseases, including HIV. Indeed, as we have shown in this chapter, Black-Latino/a drug injectors in New York are particularly likely to be HIV-seropositive.

Waterston has argued that drug injectors are not part of a subculture cut off from the rest of society [7]. Instead, as she sees it, they are a constituent part of the labor market and of the political economy. She presents data showing that many of them hold jobs, albeit primarily in jobs that Friedman [6] has viewed as constituting them as a potential reserve labor force for better jobs. Street Voice, a drug users' organization in Baltimore, has worked with many drug users with such jobs, and has helped them to push for improved employment conditions and for improved treatment by public and non-profit service agencies. Such struggles, however, are not easily won. As the *Street Voice* newsletter and Waterston both argue, the existence of a mainly racially/ethnically subordinated reserve labor force has many economic and political advantages for capital, and is deeply institutional-ized—and these advantages are only increased by the possibility of scapegoating and demonizing a part of this subordinated labor reserve as drug injectors. If these social arrangements have as one of their consequences an increased spread of HIV and AIDS, this social tragedy will be lamented widely, and will lead to a number of narrowly targeted projects to retard HIV spread. It will not, however, lead those who benefit from the current distribution of economic and political power to publicize the linkages between the economic and political structure and HIV spread, much less lead them to push for major changes in the system of racial/ ethnic stratification or in the political economy.

The existence of this system of racial/ethnic stratification, then, and its interac-tion with class society, is a social fact that seems to encourage the spread of HIV. It is an obstacle to efforts to reduce the spread of AIDS and, indeed, to ameliorate its effects upon those who themselves become infected or whose family members or friends become infected. It can be argued that as HIV and AIDS become more concentrated among racially/ethnically subordinated groups, the concern and funds of government and corporations will become harder to mobilize. This can, however, be reversed—to the extent that the racially/ethnically subordinated mount social movements that are powerful and disruptive enough to demand attention, and particularly if this mobilization coincides with larger-scale social movements of workers and others that might parallel those of United States labor in the 1930s of Solidarnosc in Poland during 1980-1981.

The question that remains, for research, for social experimentation, and ulti-mately for mass action, is how to organize the needed social movements. One facet of this question is to find ways in which two apparently disparate kinds of movements can reinforce each others' efforts: First, the relatively narrow-focus efforts around issues of HIV prevention, HIV care, and protecting the rights and needs of drug injectors—specifically including those aspects of these struggles that involve fights against racial/ethnic subordination; and second, wider social movements such as those that aim for 1) universal access to quality housing, 2) health care, 3) the abolition of racial/ethnic subordination, and/or 4) other sub-ordinations such as those by gender and sexual orientation, 5) changes in the social conditions under which socially-necessary labor is performed, and 6) the associated economic system. Much remains to be learned about how such move-ments can be formed; how they can be strengthened; what they should do with their power; and how they can most usefully think about issues of philosophy and social change.

REFERENCES

1. J. A. Geschwender, *Racial Stratification in America*, William C. Brown, Dubuque, Iowa, 1978.
2. D. McBride, *From TB to AIDS: Epidemics among Urban Blacks since 1900*, SUNY Press, Albany, New York, 1991.
3. S. Steinberg, *The Ethnic Myth: Race, Ethnicity, and Class in America. Updated Edition*, Beacon Press, Boston, 1989.
4. D. Y. Wilkinson and G. King, Conceptual and Methodological Issues in the Use of Race as a Variable: Policy Implications, in *Health Policies and Black Americans*, D. Willis (ed.), Transaction Publishers, New Brunswick, New Jersey, 1989.
5. J. M. Bloom, *Class, Race, & the Civil Rights Movement*, Indiana University Press, Bloomington, 1987.
6. S. R. Friedman, Structure, Process, and the Labor Market, in *Labor Economics*, W. Darity, Jr. (ed.), Kluwer-Nijhoff, Boston, pp. 175-218, 1984.
7. A. Waterston, *Street Addicts in the Political Economy*, Temple University Press, Philadelphia, 1993.
8. W. J. Wilson, *The Truly Disadvantaged*, University of Chicago Press, Chicago, 1987.
9. M. Weber, *The Theory of Social and Economic Organization*, The Free Press, Glencoe, Illinois, 1947.
10. W. A. Gamson, *Power and Discontent*, Dorsey, Homewood, Illinois, 1968.
11. R. L. Allen, *Black Awakening in Capitalist America*, Doubleday Anchor, Garden City, New York, 1970.
12. F. Fanon, *The Wretched of the Earth*, Grove Press, New York, 1963.
13. A. Memmi, *The Colonizer and the Colonized* [trans.], Beacon Press, Boston, 1967.
14. R. Sennett and J. Cobb, *The Hidden Injuries of Class*, Vintage, New York, 1972.
15. J. C. Scott, *Domination and the Arts of Resistance*, Yale University Press, New Haven, 1990.
16. M. L. Williams and J. Johnson, Social Network Structures: An Ethnographic Analysis of Intravenous Drug Use in Houston, Texas, in *AIDS and Community-Based Drug Intervention Programs: Evaluation and Outreach*, D. G. Fisher and R. H. Needle (eds.), Harrington Park Press, Binghamton, New York, pp. 65-90, 1993.
17. D. D. Chitwood, J. R. Rivers, M. Comerford, and D. C. McBride, A Comparison of HIV-Related Risk Behaviors of Street-Recruited and Treatment Program-Recruited Injection Drug Users, in *AIDS and Community-Based Drug Intervention Programs: Evaluation and Outreach*, D. G. Fisher and R. H. Needle (eds.), Harrington Park Press, Binghamton, New York, pp. 53-63, 1993.
18. S. R. Friedman, J. L. Sotheran, A. Abdul-Quader, B. J. Primm, D. C. Des Jarlais, P. Kleinman, C. Mauge, D. S. Goldsmith, W. El-Sadr, and R. Maslansky, The AIDS Epidemic among Blacks and Hispanics, *The Milbank Quarterly, 65*(suppl. 2), pp. 455-499, 1987.
19. S. R. Friedman, M. Sufian, and D. C. Des Jarlais, The AIDS Epidemic Among Latino Intravenous Drug Users, in *Drug Abuse in Hispanic Communities*, R. Glick and J. Moore (eds.), Rutgers University Press, New Brunswick, New Jersey, pp. 45-54, 1990.
20. S. R. Friedman, P. A. Young, F. R. Snyder, V. Shorty, A. Jones, A. L. Estrada, and NADR Consortium, Racial Differences in Sexual Behaviors Related to AIDS in a

Nineteen-City Sample of Street-Recruited Drug Injectors, *AIDS Education and Prevention, 5,* pp. 196-211, 1993.
21. S. R. Friedman, D. C. Des Jarlais, J. A. Wenston, and J. L. Sotheran, *Stable Racial/ Ethnic Differences in HIV Seroprevalence among IDUs,* paper presented at 1st National Conference on Human Retroviruses and Related Infections, Washington, D.C. [abstract 285], 1993.
22. R. A. Hahn, I. M. Onorato, T. S. Jones, and J. Dougherty, Prevalence of HIV Infection among Intravenous Drug Users in the United States, *Journal of the American Medical Association, 261,* pp. 2677-2684, 1989.
23. B. A. Koblin, J. McCusker, B. F. Lewis, and J. L. Sullivan, Racial/Ethnic Differences in HIV-1 Seroprevalence and Risky Behaviors among Intravenous Drug Users in a Multisite Study, *American Journal of Epidemiology, 132,* pp. 837-846, 1990.
24. R. A. LaBrie, W. E. McAuliffe, R. Nemeth-Coslett, and L. Wilberschied, The Prevalence of HIV Infection in a National Sample of Injection Drug Users, in *Handbook on Risk of AIDS,* B. S. Brown and G. M. Beschner (eds.), Greenwood Press, Westport, Connecticut, pp. 16-37, 1993.
25. M. Marmor, D. C. Des Jarlais, H. Cohen et al., Risk Factors and Infection with Human Immunodeficiency Virus among Intravenous Drug Abusers in New York City, *AIDS, 1,* pp. 39-44, 1987.
26. O. C. Nwanyanwu, S. Y. Chu, T. A. Green, J. W. Buehler, and R. L. Berkelman, Acquired Immunodeficiency Syndrome in the United States Associated with Injecting Drug Use, 1981-1991, *American Journal of Drug and Alcohol Abuse, 19,* pp. 399-408, 1993.
27. N. A. Denton and D. S. Massey, Racial Identity among Caribbean Hispanics: The Effect of Double Minority Status on Residential Segregation, *American Sociological Review, 54,* pp. 790-798, October 1989.
28. J. E. Becerra, C. J. R. Hogue, H. K. Atrash, and N. Perez, Infant Mortality among Hispanics, *Journal of the American Medical Association, 265*:2, pp. 217-221, 1991.
29. Council on Scientific Affairs, Hispanic Health in the United States, *Journal of the American Medical Association, 265*:2, pp. 248-252, 1991.
30. K. G. Manton, C. H. Patrick, and K. W. Johnson, Health Differentials between Blacks and Whites, *The Milbank Quarterly, 65*(suppl. 2), pp. 129-199, 1987.
31. S. R. Friedman, A. Neaigus, B. Jose, R. Curtis, M. Goldstein, J. L. Sotheran, J. Wenston, C. A. Latkin, and D. C. Des Jarlais, Network and Sociohistorical Approaches to the HIV Epidemic among Drug Injectors, in *The Impacts of AIDS: Psychological and Social Aspects of HIV Infection,* J. Catalán, B. Hedge, and L. Sherr (eds.), Harwood Academic Publishers, Chur, Switzerland, in press.
32. M. Beardsley, M. C. Clatts, S. Deren, W. R. Davis, and S. Tortu, Homelessness and HIV Risk Behaviors in a Sample of New York City Drug Injectors, *AIDS & Public Policy, 7*:3, pp. 162-169, 1992.
33. R. Rockwell, S. R. Friedman, J. L. Sotheran, J. A. Wenston, and D. C. Des Jarlais, Homelessness, Race, HIV Testing and Drug Treatment among Injection Drug Users in New York City, in *The Political Economy of AIDS,* M. Singer (ed.), Baywood Publishing, Amityville, New York [this volume], pp. 131-147, 1998.
34. S. R. Friedman, B. Jose, S. Deren, D. C. Des Jarlais, and A. Neiagus, Risk Factors for Human Immunodefeciency Virus Seroconversion among Out-Of-Treatment Drug Injectors in High and Low Seroprevalence Cities, *American Journal of Epidemiology, 142*:8, p. 864, 1995.
35. R. C. Stephens, *The Street Addict Role: A Theory of Heroin Addiction,* SUNY Press, Albany, New York, 1991.

36. D. S. Metzger, G. E. Woody, A. T. McLellan et al., Human Immunodeficiency Virus Seroconversion Among Intravenous Drug Users In and Out-of Treatment: An 18-Month Prospective Follow-Up, *Journal of the Acquired Immune Deficiency Syndrome, 6*, pp. 1049-1056, 1993.

37. J. C. Soto, F. Lamonthe, J. Bruneau et al., *High Risk of HIV Seroconversion among Street Intravenous Drug Users in Montreal,* paper presented at the Eighth International Conference on AIDS, Amsterdam, The Netherlands [abstract ThC 1550], 1992.

38. A. Neaigus, S. R. Friedman, B. Jose, M. Goldstein, R. Curtis, and D. C. Des Jarlais, *Latino Race/Ethnicity and Injecting at Outside Settings are HIV Risk Factors among New Injectors,* paper presented at the 121st Annual Meeting of the American Public Health Association, San Francisco, 1993.

39. S. R. Friedman, B. Jose, A. Neaigus, M. Goldstein, R. Curtis, and D. C. Des Jarlais, *Female Injecting Drug Users Get Infected with HIV Sooner than Males,* paper presented at the 121st Annual Meeting of the American Public Health Association, San Francisco [session 3137], 1993.

40. R. Curtis, S. R. Friedman, A. Neaigus, B. Jose, M. Goldstein, and G. Ildefonso, Street-Level Drug Market Structure and HIV Risk, *Social Networks, 17*, pp. 229-249, 1995.

41. B. Jose, S. R. Friedman, R. Curtis, M. Goldstein, J.-P. C. Grund, T. P. Ward, and D. C. Des Jarlais, Syringe-Mediated Drug-Sharing (Backloading), *AIDS, 7*, pp. 1653-1660, 1993.

42. W. Ryan, *Blaming the Victim,* Vintage Books, New York, 1971.

43. R. M. Selik, K. G. Castro, and M. Pappaioanou, Racial/Ethnic Differences in the Risk of AIDS in the United States, *American Journal of Public Health, 78*, pp. 1539-1545, 1988.

44. R. M. Selik, K. G. Castro, M. Pappaioanou, and J. W. Buehler, Birthplace and the Risk of AIDS among Hispanics in the United States, *American Journal of Public Health, 79*, pp. 836-839, 1989.

45. J. Reardon, M. J. Wilson, G. F. Lemp, J. A. Gaudino, D. Snyder, M. Elcock, and S. Nguyen, *HIV-1 Infection among Female Injection Drug Users (IDU) in the San Francisco Bay Area, California 1989-1991,* paper presented at the 8th International Conference on AIDS, Amsterdam, The Netherlands [abstract #ThC 1553], 1992.

46. S. R. Friedman, D. C. Des Jarlais, S. Deren, B. Jose, and A. Neaigus, *HIV Seroconversions among Street-Recruited Drug Injectors in 14 United States Cities,* paper presented at the Eighth International Conference on AIDS, Amsterdam, The Netherlands [abstract PoC 4251], 1992.

47. D. C. Des Jarlais and S. R. Friedman, AIDS and Legal Access to Sterile Drug Injection Equipment, *Annals of the American Academy of Political and Social Science, 521*, pp. 42-65, 1992.

48. D. C. Des Jarlais and S. R. Friedman, AIDS Prevention Programs for Injecting Drug Users, in *AIDS and Other Manifestations of HIV Infection. Second Edition,* G. P. Wormser (ed.), Raven Press, New York, pp. 645-658, 1992.

49. S. R. Friedman, W. de Jong, and A. Wodak, Community Development as a Response to HIV among Drug Injectors, *AIDS 92/93, 7*(suppl. 1), pp. S263-S269, 1993.

50. S. R. Friedman, W. Wiebel, B. Jose, and L. Levin, Changing the Culture of Risk, in *Handbook on Risk of AIDS,* B. S. Brown and G. M. Beschner (eds.), Greenwood Press, Westport, Connecticut, pp. 499-516, 1993.

51. S. R. Friedman, B. Jose, A. Neaigus, and D. C. Des Jarlais, *Over-the-Counter Syringe Sales and HIV in the United States,* paper presented at the 5th International Conference on the Reduction of Drug Related Harm, Toronto, 1994.

52. C. Latkin, W. Mandell, M. Oziemkowska, D. Celentano, D. Vlahov, and M. Ensminger, *Using Social Network Analysis to Study Patterns of Drug Use among Urban Drug Users at High Risk for HIV/AIDS,* paper presented at Sunbelt 14, International Social Network Conference, New Orleans, 1994.
53. W. Wiebel, A. Jimenez, W. Johnson, L. Ouellet, J. Murray, and M. O'Brien, *Positive Effect on HIV Seroconversion of Street Outreach Intervention with IDU in Chicago, 1988-1992,* paper presented at the Ninth International Conference on AIDS, Berlin [abstract WS-C15-2], 1993.
54. S. R. Friedman, How is Racism Maintained? *Et Al, 2,* pp. 18-21, 1969.
55. P. Alexander, *Racism, Resistance, and Revolution,* Bookmarks, London, 1987.
56. P. L. Van den Berghe, *Race and Racism,* John Wiley & Sons, New York, 1967.

The Struggle for Care
among People with HIV/AIDS

CHAPTER 6

Medical Access
for Injecting Drug Users

*Russell Rockwell, Samuel R. Friedman, Jo L. Sotheran,
and Don C. Des Jarlais*

INTRODUCTION

This chapter examines access to two types of specialized medical care—drug abuse treatment and HIV testing—among injecting drug users (IDUs). IDUs are generally a medically underserved group [1]. A traditional lack of services has continued in the AIDS era, when two of their most basic new health needs are not presently being met. Despite the individual and public-health value of HIV testing, it is estimated that little more than half of this group has even been tested for this disease for which they are at great risk [2]. Further, though drug treatment has taken on an important role in preventing new infection and treating existing ones, in New York City there are drug abuse treatment slots available for less than 20 percent of the city IDU population. HIV testing is a new medical service called forth by the AIDS epidemic, of which New York City is the epicenter of infection among IDUs. Drug abuse treatment, while much older, has taken on new dimensions in response to the epidemic. Research on these services may yield valuable insights not only about a population of which relatively little is known, but also about the wider social response to the AIDS crisis.

In New York State, HIV testing is offered free and anonymously to the public. Medicaid covers methadone maintenance treatment, one of the major long-term drug abuse treatment modalities, and short-term detoxification programs, although it does not cover therapeutic communities. All providers would agree to the idea of equal access by race, and would recognize the need to provide services to the homeless, as well as those with stable residences. Their relative success in reaching IDUs who are Black, Latino, white, stably housed, and homeless, however, needs to be determined—and is the subject of this chapter.

DRUG INJECTORS
AND HEALTH SERVICES

There are an estimated 1 to 1.5 million injecting drug users in the United States, 200,000 in New York City. The national rate of HIV infection among IDUs is between about 25 and 35 percent, meaning there are 300,000–400,000 HIV-infected IDUs [3]. The rate of infection in New York City is usually estimated to be higher, about 50 percent. Thus, there may be as many as 100,000 IDUs who are HIV-positive in the city from which our data was gathered. More than 70,000 AIDS cases had been reported among IDUs in the United States by 1992, 24,208 in New York City alone, since the mid-1970s [4]. IDUs' access to HIV-related health care is critical not only for them, but for the general well-being of the communities in which they live, and public health in general. Here we look at two health-related services which are important indicators of the unmet HIV-related health-care needs of this New York City population.

DRUG TREATMENT

Drug treatment is an important health-related resource among IDUs. Studies have found enrollment in treatment, specifically long-term types of treatment such as methadone maintenance and therapeutic communities (the 2 types defined as treatment in this chapter), not only reduces drug use and injection, but has protective effects against HIV infection [5]. Though no new forms of drug abuse treatment have been developed specifically to prevent HIV infection among IDUs, many changes have been instituted in drug treatment programs in areas with a large number of HIV-positive people. These often include accessible provision of medical care for clients with HIV-related disease, and provision of education and counseling to reduce transmission from seropositive clients to sexual partners, as well as drug-related transmission from those for whom treatment is not successful [6]. These outcomes all have clear benefits not only for the individual but for the larger community and public health in general.

However, with about 40,000 treatment slots available, only about 20 percent of the approximately 200,000 IDUs in New York City are in drug treatment. Drug treatment, then, may be seen as a scarce resource. And there is little indication that health-care reform, as it is now widely debated, will address the critical problem of AIDS and IDUs through greatly expanded and innovative drug abuse treatment programs.

HIV TESTING

HIV testing is often a first necessary step into the HIV social and medical care system for those who are infected. Early detection of HIV is necessary for optimum care of those who test positive. It not only informs decisions on when or whether to use medications which may slow the onset of AIDs, or reduces the probability that not-yet-born babies will become infected, but also serves as a gateway to preventive treatment against other diseases associated with progression of HIV. Moreover, the testing process itself, in addition to detecting HIV antibody status, can be beneficial in other ways. Because testing in New York State is structured around at least two one-on-one intensive counseling sessions, including discussion of both risk behavior and risk reduction, the process may offer obvious benefits in the form of education and risk reduction even for those who test negative. Such persons may benefit in other ways from contact with testing professionals who are aware of wider social problems faced by IDUs if referrals are made for routine medical treatment, for drug treatment, or for help with problems stemming from the poverty and social isolation often associated with injecting drug use. The benefits offered by HIV testing make unequal access to it by different subgroups of IDUs a serious issue of social inequality.

In theory, New York city and state programs offer anonymous testing without charge to the client, and in that sense HIV testing is equally accessible to all. However, there are significant barriers to really equal access. Free and anonymous testing sites operate on an appointment system, and have a back-up of demand that results in appointments being set for weeks, and in some cases, months later. Further, they usually offer no on-site medical services. These arrangements are not optimum for most inner-city IDUs whose time and attention are occupied with the need to get food, shelter, and drugs, and with staying alive in often violent neighborhoods. These pressures and their lack of jobs or other routine calendar-based activities can easily lead to missed appointments. Also, while anonymous testing—or sites whose main or sole function is HIV testing—may meet the needs of many, personal familiarity with a doctor concerned about the overall long-term health of a known patient probably facilitates testing and its potential later benefits in many instances. Many inner-city minority racial/ethnic group IDUs (particularly the homeless among them) often have no pre-existing relationship to such medical care [7].

The benefits of increased access to voluntary HIV testing are not confined to the individual IDU. To the extent that the testing process is successful to some extent in reducing risk behavior, and therefore the spread of HIV, the general public health would also be served [6].

A recent National Health Interview Survey (NHIS)—representative of the U.S. population—showed that considerably less than half of a subset of those at "increased risk" for HIV infection (which included hemophiliacs, male homosexuals, and prostitutes, as well as IDUs and their sex partners), had ever been tested for the HIV virus. Among those at increased risk, there were significant racial differences in testing rates, with whites more likely to have ever been tested than Blacks. (In the study, there were no racial differences in testing rates among the groups not considered at "increased risk.") The analysis concludes with the observation that Blacks and Latinos are known to have higher rates of HIV infection, and emphasizes the importance for programs which offer testing of making continuing efforts to reach these groups [8].

This study did not survey the homeless; it was household-based, and therefore excluded that proportion of the population not living in households or those living in institutional settings. However, recent research suggests that homelessness may be related to HIV infection risk even among groups most at risk: Homeless IDUs, compared to those with homes, have a higher probability of seroconverting and becoming HIV-positive, suggesting the importance of research and HIV outreach and prevention directed toward this group [9].

Still, testing is already fairly widespread among IDUs. The first study estimating HIV testing among high-risk populations, based on national probability samples, found that 46 percent of male and 73 percent of female IDUs had ever been tested [2]. But this study—a nationwide population-based telephone survey—also excluded the homeless and thus many IDUs less likely to have been tested. As a result, its estimate of testing rates among IDUs should probably be seen as on the high end. Also, the study makes the important point that nearly a quarter of non-Medicaid federal and state funding for AIDS programs—about $119 million—was allocated for HIV testing and counseling programs alone in 1989. That HIV testing is so central to the federal government's strategy to deal with the AIDS crisis suggests the importance of establishing an equitable distribution of the service.

METHODS

This chapter draws on data from an epidemiological study of 2977 injecting drug users in New York City. Data were collected during 1990-1993 by the New York component of the World Health Organization Multi-City Study on Drug Injecting Behavior and HIV. Recruitment was from a hospital drug detoxification ward and a research storefront site, both on the Lower East Side of Manhattan.

Trained interviewers administered a structured questionnaire, with questions on demographics, including: living situation over the previous six months; prior HIV antibody testing; drug treatment history and, if not currently in treatment, whether the subject would enter it; utilization of other services; knowledge of how HIV is acquired; and HIV-related risk behavior. Racial/ethnic background was determined through self-identification by the respondents. Participants were classified as homeless if they reported living most of the time (in the previous 6 months) in the street, a shelter, or a room rented on a daily basis.

To compare receipt of HIV testing and enrollment in drug treatment, bivariate chi-squared tests were used to assess differences in HIV testing and being in drug abuse treatment among groups.

RESULTS

Sample Characteristics, Testing, and Treatment Experience

Respondents generally had a long history of intravenous drug use. They injected, on the average, more than three times a day, with nearly half having also used crack cocaine in the previous six months. Most respondents were men, were in their mid-thirties, and were unemployed. Seventy-nine percent were of minority racial/ethnic background and 26 percent were homeless (see Table 1). Latinos were less likely to be homeless than whites or Blacks (see Table 2).

Minorities, especially Blacks, were significantly more likely to have been underserved. There are significant racial/ethnic differences in having ever been

Table 1. Sample Characteristics

N	2977
Mean age (years)	36
Mean injections per month	105
Mean years injecting	17
	Percent
Use crack cocaine	48
Race/ethnicity	
White	21
Black	42
Latino	37
Women	24
Homeless	26
Employed	18
HIV+	44

Table 2. Race/Ethnicity and Homelessness ($p = .001$)

White	30%
Black	28%
Latino	20%

tested, being currently in drug treatment, or ever having been in treatment (see Table 3). However, it is difficult to isolate the impact of racial/ethnic differences because homelessness is found significantly more often among some groups, and homelessness also significantly decreases the likelihood of receiving services (see Table 4). To isolate the impact of race from that of homelessness, we looked at testing and treatment rates separately among the subsamples of people with homes, and among the homeless (see Tables 5-7). The impact of homelessness is significant only among Blacks, who are also the least medically served racial/ethnic group, regardless of whether they are homeless or not. Within the Black subsample, but not among whites or Latinos, the homeless were significantly less likely than those with homes to have ever been tested, to currently be in treatment, or to have ever been in treatment. In the case of Blacks, but not of whites or Latinos, being homeless represents an *additional* risk for being underserved.

Table 3. Access to HIV Testing and Drug Abuse Treatment
by Racial/Ethnic Group

	White (%)	Latino (%)	Black (%)	p =
Ever HIV-tested	67	60	53	.0001
Ever in drug abuse treatment	78	78	66	.0001
Currently in drug abuse treatment	41	37	24	.0001

Table 4. Access to HIV Testing and
Drug Treatment by Residential Status

IDUs Ever HIV-Tested
Homeless 54%
Not homeless 60%
p = .009

IDUs Currently in Drug Treatment
Homeless 27%
Not homeless 34%
p = .0001

IDUs Ever in Treatment
Homeless 68%
Not homeless 74%
p = .0001

Table 5. Racial Differences in HIV Testing:
Not Homeless and Homeless

| | Homelessness | |
Race/Ethnicity	Not Homeless (% tested)	Homeless (% tested)
Black	56	**45 p = 0.001**
Latino	60	58 p = 0.497
White	67	68 p = 0.826
	p = 0.001	p = 0.001

Table 6. Racial Differences in Currently Being
in Drug Treatment: Not Homeless and Homeless

| | Homelessness | |
Race/Ethnicity	Not Homeless (% currently in drug treatment)	Homeless (% currently in drug treatment)
Black	28	**15 p = .0001**
Latino	37	35 p = .528
White	41	42 p = .741
	p = .0001	p = .0001

Table 7. Racial Differences in Ever Being in
Drug Treatment: Not Homeless and Homeless

| | Homelessness | |
Race/Ethnicity	Not Homeless (% ever in treatment)	Homeless (% ever in treatment)
Black	68	**61 p = .038**
Latino	79	74 p = .130
White	79	75 p = .273
	p = .0001	p = .0001

Factors in addition to, or other than, racial/ethnic differences in access to services, or a higher degree of homelessness, or an interaction effect of the two, could help account for these findings. Examples of such factors are older age, lower injection frequency, and the use of other non-injected drugs such as crack cocaine. All of these factors could affect testing and drug treatment, and all were found significantly ($p < .05$) more frequently among Blacks in the sample. To control for these factors, as well as gender, and isolate the effects of being Black, we examined with chi-squared tests racial differences in several subsamples, dividing each into those with homes and the homeless. Thus, we analyzed sub-samples of those above and below the mean age among those with homes and the homeless; those who injected daily and those who injected less than daily among those with homes and the homeless; those who reported using crack cocaine in the last six months and those who did not among those with homes and the homeless; and finally women and men separately, among those with homes and the homeless. Race remained significant. Blacks among the homeless, and among those with homes, were significantly less likely to have been tested, to currently be in treatment, or to have ever been in treatment in each of these subsets. In most subsets, the differences between Black homeless and Blacks with homes also remained significant. (Data not shown; available from the first author).

WILLINGNESS TO ENTER TREATMENT

The mechanisms by which Blacks have come to be less likely to be in treatment currently, or to have been in treatment in the past, are unclear. This racial difference could be an outcome either of exclusion from or barriers to treatment. Increasing numbers of studies of medical care have supported this possibility among the general population [10, 11]. Alternatively, Black drug users could simply be less interested in or willing to enter treatment. To evaluate these alternatives, we looked at attitudes toward treatment among our sample.

Approximately one-half the respondents in our study were recruited from a street research storefront, the other half through a short-term treatment facility (a detoxification ward). Of the street-recruited respondents, those who reported not being currently in drug treatment were asked, "If you were offered a treatment slot (available tomorrow), would you take it?" Most would be willing to accept drug treatment: only 24 percent of this street-recruited subsample responded with an unequivocal negative. Broken down into subgroups, 22 percent of the homeless versus 25 percent of the non-homeless; 26 percent of Blacks versus 33 percent of whites and 14 percent of Latinos were unwilling to accept treatment.

To rule out of the influence of possible bad experiences among those who had previously been in treatment, we examined this question among the subgroup of those who had never been in treatment. In this subgroup, only 25 percent rejected taking a treatment slot, and rejection was not significantly related to homeless-ness. However, among those never in treatment, racial and ethnic differences were found: 30 percent of whites, 26 percent of Blacks, but only 16 percent of Latinos would refuse a treatment slot available tomorrow (see Table 8).

It is clear that Latinos are consistently less likely to say they would refuse treatment. Although it is beyond the scope of this chapter to speculate on why Latinos seem more open to treatment, we did some further analyses to rule out obvious possibilities. We controlled for drug of choice (cocaine, heroin, a mixed heroin-and-cocaine "speedball," or no preference), age, years injecting, and number of times previously in treatment. In all categories considered, Latinos were less likely to say they would refuse treatment, suggesting the need for more detailed research into cultural and structural reasons for a favorable attitude toward entering treatment.

In sum, the groups least served by treatment—Blacks and the homeless—do not appear less willing to accept it. Neither the homeless generally, nor those homeless never in treatment, appear to be less willing than others to enter treatment; neither do Blacks in general, nor those never in treatment, appear less willing than whites to enter treatment. Accordingly, a subjective factor—or some intrinsic aversion to treatment among these groups—does not seem to be a plausible explanation for their inequality of exposure to treatment. We need more research into the alternative possibility: that there are poorly understood barriers to, or exclusions from, treatment, affecting these groups disproportionately.

Table 8. Willingness to Enter Drug Treatment of Homeless and Non-Homeless, and by Racial/Ethnic Group: Previously in Treatment and Never Before in Treatment

	Percent	p
Unwilling to take a treatment slot available tomorrow (prior treatment experience)		
All	24	
Homeless	22	.328
Non-Homeless	25	
White	33	
Black	26	.0001
Latino	14	
Unwilling to take a treatment slot (those never in treatment)		
All	25	
Homeless	21	.169
Non-Homeless	27	
White	30	
Black	26	.064
Latino	16	

DISCUSSION AND CONCLUSIONS

The examination of both HIV testing and drug treatment among IDUs illustrates how multiple bases of inequality—in this case being Black and homeless—can interact, even among this already very disadvantaged IDU population. We have demonstrated consistent racial/ethnic differences in the use of HIV-related medical services among IDUs in New York City. The large number of homeless among IDUs are at a particular disadvantage in securing access to two crucial services relevant to preservation of their lives and medical well-being

On any given night, there are 24,000 people in New York City's homeless shelters [12]. Eighty-six thousand different individuals passed through the city's shelter system in 1992 alone. From 1989 through 1993, 239,425 different people, more than 3 percent of the city's population, spent some time in homeless shelters. In the same period, a similar percentage of homeless was counted in Philadelphia. The sheer volume of people who became homeless, and the similar rates in the two cities, suggest that regional, national, or even international economic problems are a factor in this new and persistent homelessness. Wages falling as housing costs rose, widespread unemployment, and cuts in welfare benefits (reflecting both ideological pressures and a long-running fiscal crisis at the local, state, and national levels), have all contributed to the number of homeless. For example, the value of the monthly rental subsidy paid by New York State to families on welfare has declined by 42 percent since 1972 while the real cost of housing has risen [13]. A large number of IDUs in this sample suffer particularly serious economic disadvantages: 26 percent are homeless, and 52 percent rely on welfare or other transfer payments. A recent study has even probed the question whether homelessness—as distinguished from poverty in general—is a cause of drug and alcohol abuse rather than the reverse, which is often assumed [14].

But among our sample, homelessness is specific in its effects on services. Blacks are significantly less likely to receive services among both those with homes and the homeless. Within the Black subsample, the homeless are significantly less likely than Blacks with homes to have received the services. In contrast, homelessness has relatively little effect on receipt of services in the white or Latino subsamples. In sum, Black homeless IDUs—as compared either to Blacks with homes or to other homeless—are a group which clearly stands out from all others in its lack of access to HIV testing and drug treatment in New York City.

Both a national health-care debate and AIDS appeared at a time of transitions in the American economy. Since AIDS and other severe health problems disproportionately affect particular groups and communities, such as IDUs, the homeless, and racial/ethnic minorities, issues of access to care are bound to grow in importance as the AIDS epidemic expands and debate over health care reform intensifies in a rapidly changing economic environment. The changing economy during the 1980s coincided, even during the several consecutive years of impressive expansion in gross national product, with a decrease in the sense of security—including affordability of medical care—previously expected by and prized by the middle class and upper working class. Along with this, an increase in the disparity between the rich and an increasingly insecure working and middle class, and between the latter and the very poor (including the burgeoning homeless population in many cities), was one of the most notable features of the economic expansion of the 1980s. These structural changes in the economy deepened just as a major new medical emergency, the AIDS epidemic, took hold across the land and moved into the inner cities, home to many of the nation's racial minorities. More attention has been paid to the health-care problems of the shaky middle class than to the particular crisis engulfing the poor and marginalized, particularly in the inner cities. We have illustrated how access to even the new medical services called forth by the AIDS epidemic can be influenced by pre-existing racial/ethnic and socioeconomic inequalities in American society. These inequalities are so deep and pervasive that they operate even within an already highly disadvantaged group.

Our data show that the racial/ethnic and resource disparities obvious in the society at large are also visible within the IDU population, an already largely marginalized group, in regard to their immediate and vital medical needs: very many are not securing basic AIDS-related services, and Blacks, particularly homeless Blacks, have the least access of all to essential AIDS services. Other studies have found some results suggestive of those presented here, including the two cited earlier, which analyzed the unequal treatment of the poor and Blacks for various diseases within the hospital setting itself [10, 11].

Many traditionally medically underserved groups are concentrated in inner-city urban areas. From an historical perspective, there is evidence that Blacks in general have not had equal access to medical care, particularly preventive medicine, and that this difference explains many of the health disadvantages of the Black population [15].

For example, a recent study discussed how Blacks, especially young Black men, are the group least likely to have access to a regular primary care physician [16]. That recent study in Baltimore examined a group of HIV-seropositive patients, for most of whom drug injection was a risk factor for AIDS. It concluded that Blacks were less likely than whites to receive AZT and drugs to prevent diseases associated with HIV. This racial difference was not explained by other demographic influences, mode of HIV transmission, health insurance coverage, greater skepticism or distrust by Blacks of the medical system, or other factors, but by unequal treatment in the primary care system which channels patients into specialized HIV care. This was shown by the finding that by the six month follow-up, after enrollment in the clinic through which the study was conducted, Blacks were no less likely than whites to be receiving medications.

We previously found, in a retrospective study of HIV testing, post-test counseling and entry into HIV-related medical treatment among HIV-positive IDUs, that being Black or being homeless were predictors of not being aware of their HIV status. This lack of access to testing and/or post-test counseling resulted in less likelihood of receiving medical attention for their illness. However, Blacks and the homeless who had been tested and received their results were no less likely than others to have received medical care for HIV [17]. That these differences are related more to access barriers, which apparently can arise at various points in the HIV care system, than to lack of desire for services is suggested by another study, in which we found that Black and Latino IDUs were less likely than white IDUs to have returned to an HIV clinic for HIV test results after having been tested. However, when we controlled for ease of access (operationalized as nearness of home to the testing clinic) the racial/ethnic differences in return rates were not significant [18].

These latter studies of the relationship of IDUs to the HIV care system suggest that IDUs' underutilization of HIV-related services is not exclusively a matter of their lack of interest in medical access or personal or social disorganization due to preoccupation with drug use. Rather, they suggest that an important role is played by barriers to access to the HIV care system. Our findings show that Black and homeless IDUs are particularly unlikely to get these needed services; but they also suggest that, in many cases, the source of the disparity can probably be identified, and reduced or eliminated by appropriate service access and delivery.

Yet, the economic restructuring of recent decades affects both the need and prospects for revision of the health care system, and the very problems the health care system is meant to treat. Recent structural changes in the economic system contribute to the spread of disease such as AIDS by leaving untouched or even increasing the poverty and poor living conditions within which it thrives. Homelessness, a phenomenon often associated with fundamental changes in the economy in recent years, has been widely debated up to the present. Its increase in U.S. cities was evident throughout the 1980s, beginning during the recession years of the early part of the decade. Even during the mid-1980s, when the gross national product was growing rapidly, homelessness persisted and remained a focus of attention and debate both in the daily press and among policy experts. While there is much disagreement on its extent and its causes, advocates for the homeless took an active part in this discussion, but organizations or social movements of the homeless did not arise to be major players in this debate. This is in contrast to many cities in Africa, Latin America, the Philippines, and Europe, where large-scale movements of homeless persons have conducted occupations of vacant housing and/or land.

This lack of mobilization by U.S. homeless may be tied to their "successful" stigmatization and to divisions fomented among them by 1) the war on drugs, 2) the related consequences of addiction on a portion of them in a stigmatizing environment, and/or 3) the efforts of social service agencies that treat homelessness and drug use as individual weaknesses rather than as public issues [19, 20].

At a time when many interest groups and constituencies in the country are politically mobilizing to influence the direction of health care reform, the consequences of a continued quiescence among this section of the nation's poor threatens to put a group with many unmet health care as well as other needs at an even greater relative disadvantage in the future.

Changes in the economy, including persistent homelessness in many major cities, interact with a public sector in constant fiscal crisis which has been resistant to funding or otherwise implementing programs to reduce racial/ethnic stratification, poverty, or homelessness. This decreases the ability of those most affected to deal with HIV infection and its consequences. And the weight of the AIDS epidemic is continuing to shift onto poor people (particularly the homeless), minorities, and drug users. Government agencies, regardless of declared fiscal constraints and sustained political pressures, if not outright opposition, are already increasingly—at least in large cities such as New York, with its large network of public hospitals and health-care clinics—becoming the health provider and insurer of last resort.

Thus, the boundaries between medicine and political economy are becoming increasingly blurred. The social and financial cost to the state of providing care for diseases which might be prevented through equitable, if not universal, provision of health services such as HIV testing and drug treatment, has the potential to turn what many perceive as normally an individual and private transaction between medical providers and patients into a much more public issue—an issue of political economy. This might increasingly prove to be the case both on the part of the state, which feels pressure to rationalize its spending, and from the perspective of political constituencies who increasingly demand inclusion of particular services in different parts of the health-care system through demand for insurance coverage, or regardless of the individual's ability to pay.

Neither of the services examined in this study is necessarily more or less "medical" than some others; the point is that characterization and categorization of them might now be viewed, for better or for worse, as questions mainly of political economy. This is so particularly if what our data illustrates—racial and socioeconomic inequalities in the utilization of new and critical health care services in the age of AIDS—is also substantially the case in other major cities.

Even if a consensus were reached that HIV testing and drug abuse treatment were just as much medical as, say, a failing heart, that still might not be sufficient to win their substantial inclusion into any new system of universal access or coverage, as they are being debated. For example, under the Clinton health reform plan, both drug treatment and mental health care were recognized as medically coverable, yet they were clearly subordinate priorities, with considerably less coverage than other illnesses. Care for AIDS—an illness with social and psychological dimensions—is widely recognized to be underfunded even now, and its complexity and cost is not likely to diminish in the near future.

In any case, this study of IDUs has shown that formally universal access or coverage may not offer all that it seems to promise. We have considered how, in the case of HIV-related care, access may be affected by racial inequalities and homelessness, both of which are exacerbated by structural shifts in the national political economy. In New York State, as we noted earlier, there already exists a system intended to provide universal access to free HIV testing. Yet, as is the case with many of today's socio-medical maladies, attempts at improving and equalizing "access" and "coverage" may be only a first step in overcoming the obstacles to actual equal provision of treatment to economically and polit- ically oppressed groups, as we have shown in the cases of Black and/or home- less IDUs.

Equal provision of drug abuse treatment may be even more difficult to provide than equal provision of HIV testing, because of the long-term nature of the service, the amount of resources required to meet the potential demand, and the scope and complexity of introducing the innovative programs necessary to meet the diversity of needs among IDUs. Also, there is widespread disdain for IDUs, and much skepticism about the value of the treatments presently available. But, it is in relationship to drug treatment that it seems most important to elicit and listen to ideas and proposals from those directly in need, a rare or nonexistent process in the present political climate.

In view of the failures of the present health-care system in regard to IDUs, it is important to recognize that demands for improvement of health care, and reduc- tions of inequalities in access, may be initiated from the affected communities themselves.

As with the homeless, IDUs' general lack of organization or political voice in the U.S. contrasts with the situations in Europe and Australia, where activities of IDUs have had an impact on public policy and on the perception of their situation. For example, in Germany, the Netherlands, and Australia, drug users' organiza- tions play an active role in HIV policy discussions, in discussions of drug policy, and in government-funded HIV prevention activities [21]. There are, however, a few notable exceptions. Street Voice in Baltimore is an organization which has addressed issues of homelessness and social welfare [22]. The formation of a North American Users' Network in March 1994, composed of drug users' organi- zations in at least six U.S. and two Canadian cities, may herald an increase in drug users' organized voice.

There are even signs of such activity among the IDUs in our study. While we have no data from our study concerning efforts at IDUs' organizing with others, 19 percent of the respondents reported volunteering, within the past twelve months, for AIDS prevention activities, or attending a demonstration or rally concerning AIDS issues, activities that might serve as a base for greater organiza- tional development. This substantial indication of social action among IDUs is at variance with prevailing stereotypes of IDUs as passive and disorganized. It also contrasts with what often seems a concerted effort to "scapegoat" drug users as the "cause" of social and economic disintegration, by which attention is drawn away from broader political-economic trends, while the situation of IDUs might be described less as the cause than as the "effect" of these trends [23].

While our illustration of the reproduction among IDUs of the general society's inequalities may not be surprising, these inequalities are hardly defensible. A good argument can be made that drug treatment and HIV testing are general social necessities that serve the interests both of those who may need them, and also the interests of many others whose lives or health may otherwise be hurt. The increased risk reduction that might result from more equal use of HIV testing, for example, might even reduce racial/ethnic differences in HIV spread, since IDUs usually inject with others of their same race/ethnicity [24]. Thus, these services should be universalized; that is, made immediately available and accessible on demand to everyone. An important element of accessibility in this context would seem to include innovative community-level outreach.

The recent politicization of health-care access in general may well intensify and broaden in the next few years, developing into an even more critical political issue. The parameters of the debate, and the scope of popular participation in it, may widen precisely because current proposals and debates may be found to be a less-than-adequate response to a crisis deeper than has yet been recognized.

For drug injectors and their communities, as for many working-class and middle-class people, aspects of "health care" can become a question of life and death. Thus, as is often the case with social crises, it raises one salient question for research and for action: will the debate and solution continue to be framed by economically and politically powerful established institutions, or will social movements—each perhaps with particular health concerns, yet generally united in the implicit demand to define the issues from the community level—reshape the debates and open possibilities for changes broader than those even being contemplated?

REFERENCES

1. A. Wartenberg, 'Into Whatever Houses I Enter': HIV and Injecting Drug Use, *Journal of the American Medical Association, 271*:2, pp. 151-152, 1994.
2. D. Berrios, N. Hurst, T. Coates, R. Stall, E. Hudes, H. Turner, R. Eversley, and J. Catania, HIV Antibody Testing among Those at Risk for Infection: The National AIDS Behavioural Surveys, *Journal of the American Medical Association, 270*:13, pp. 1576-1580, 1993.
3. D. C. Des Jarlais and S. R. Friedman, Critical Issues Regarding AIDS among Injecting Drug Users, *Bulletin of Narcotics, 45*:1, pp. 61-75, 1993.
4. D. C. Des Jarlais, S. R. Friedman, J. Sotheran, J. Wenston, M. Marmor, S. Yancovitz, B. Frank, S. Beatrice, and D. Mildvan, Continuity and Change Within an HIV Epidemic: Injecting Drug Users in New York City, 1984 through 1992, *Journal of the American Medical Association, 271*:2, pp. 121-127, 1994.
5. S. R. Friedman, D. C. Des Jarlais, and A. Neaigus, AIDS among Drug Injectors: The First Decade, in *AIDS: Etiology, Diagnosis, Treatment, and Prevention*, D. DeVita,

S. Hellman, and S. Rosenberg (eds.), J. B. Lippincott Co., Philadelphia, pp. 453-461, 1992.

6. D. C. Des Jarlais and S. R. Friedman, AIDS Prevention Programs for Injecting Drug Users, in *AIDS and Other Manifestations of HIV Infection*, G. Wormser (ed.), Raven Press, New York, pp. 645-657, 1992.

7. S. Crystal, Health Care Barriers and Utilization Patterns among Intravenous Drug Users with HIV Disease, *AIDS and Public Policy Journal*, 7:3, pp. 187-198, 1992.

8. J. Anderson, A. Hardy, K. Cahill, and S. Aral, HIV Antibody Testing and Post-Test Counseling in the United States: Data from the 1989 National Health Interview Survey, *American Journal of Public Health*, 82:11, pp. 1533-1535, 1992.

9. S. R. Friedman, B. Jose, S. Deren, A. Neaigus, and National AIDS Research Consortium, HIV Seroconversion among Street-Recruited Drug Injectors: A Preliminary Analysis, in *Problems of Drug Dependence, 1992*, NIDA Monograph 132, U.S. Department of Health and Human Services, Washington, D.C., 1993.

10. K. Khan, M. Pearson, E. Harrison, K. Desmond, W. Rogers, L. Rubenstein, R. Brook, and E. Keeler, Health Care for Black and Poor Hospitalized Medicare Patients, *Journal of the American Medical Association*, 271:15, pp. 1169-1174, 1994.

11. E. Peterson, S. Wright, J. Daley, and G. Thibault, Racial Variation in Cardiac Procedure Use and Survival Following Acute Myocardial Infarction in the Department of Veteran Affairs, *Journal of the American Medical Association*, 271:15, pp. 1175-1180, 1994.

12. D. Culhane, E. Dejowski, J. Ibanez, E. Needham, and I. Macchia, Public Shelter Admission Rates in Philadelphia and New York City, *Fannie Mae Working Paper*, pp. 1-32, 1993.

13. C. Dugger, Interview of D. Culhane, in *New York Times*, p. B4, November 16, 1993.

14. M. Winkleby, B. Rockhill, D. Jatulis, and S. Fortmann, The Medical Origins of Homelessness, *American Journal of Public Health*, 82, pp. 1394-1398, 1992.

15. S. R. Friedman, J. Sotheran, A. Abdul-Quader, B. J. Primm, D. C. Des Jarlais, P. Kleinman, C. Mauge, D. S. Goldsmith, W. El-Sadr, and R. Maslansky, The AIDS Epidemic among Blacks and Hispanics, *The Milbank Quarterly*, 65(Suppl. 2), pp. 455-499, 1987.

16. R. Moore, D. Stanton, R. Goplan, and R. Chaisson, Racial Differences in the Use of Drug Therapy for HIV Disease in an Urban Community, *New England Journal of Medicine*, 330:11, pp. 763-768, 1994.

17. J. Wenston, J. Sotheran, D. C. Des Jarlais, S. R. Friedman, and R. Rockwell, *Access to HIV-Related Treatment among Seropositive Drug Injectors in New York City*, 120th Annual Meeting, American Public Health Association, Washington, D.C., 1992.

18. R. Rockwell, J. Sotheran, J. Wenston, S. Friedman, B. Bardell, and D. C. Des Jarlais, *Geographic Proximity May Counteract Racial Barriers to Return by IDUs to an HIV Clinic on the Lower East Side (NYC) for Post-HIV-Test Counseling*, 121st Annual Meeting, American Public Health Association, San Francisco, 1993.

19. M. Fabricant and S. Burghardt, *The Welfare State Crisis and the Transformation of Social Service Work*, M. E. Sharp, New York, 1992.

20. C. W. Mills, *The Sociological Imagination*, Oxford University Press, New York, 1959.

21. S. R. Friedman, W. de Jong, and A. Wodak, Community Development as a Response to HIV among Drug Injectors, *AIDS*, 7(suppl. 1), pp. S263-S269, 1993.

22. C. Price, AIDS, Organization of Drug Users, and Public Policy, *AIDS and Public Policy Journal*, 7:3, pp. 141-144, 1992.

23. S. R. Friedman and T. P. Ward, Drug Injectors, Policy and AIDS, *International Journal of Drug Policy, 4*:4, pp. 184-189, 1993.
24. S. R. Friedman, D. C. Des Jarlais, J. Wenston, and J. Sotheran, *Stable Racial/Ethnic Differences in HIV Seroprevalence among IDUs,* First National Conference on Human Retroviruses and Related Infections, Washington, D.C., 1994.

CHAPTER 7

The Political Economy of Caregiving for People with HIV/AIDS

Anthony J. Lemelle and Charlene Harrington

In capitalist fashion, United States policy efforts to combat the growing problem of AIDS have been hierarchically directed to three major areas. The first is targeted to basic biological and clinical science research in order to identify the cause and develop a cure for the disease. The second major area is targeted to health education, prevention, and control of the spread of the disease. The third initiative is directed toward treatment of those with HIV/AIDS. This chapter questions the moral climate in which care is provided for persons with AIDS (PWAs) in the United States. Our questioning is based on the stigmatized definition of the disease in a capitalist economy hostile to universal health care. We argue that the hierarchical arrangement of addressing HIV/AIDS increasingly shifts burden of the disease to individuals in the interest of increasing corporate profit. In our view, a moral economy is characterized by reciprocity, fairness, and just taxation. In contrast, the U.S. political-economic response to the AIDS crisis is marked by an intersection of state (federal and local), corporate (insurance companies and health care industry) interests which seek the greatest profit while simultaneously shifting blame and financial responsibility for the illness onto stigmatized individuals least capable of shouldering the ordeal. The purpose of this chapter is to examine how federal policy and the insurance industry operate within the capitalist political economy to systematically discriminate against people with the HIV disease or AIDS.

In this chapter, we will raise several salient issues related to federal AIDS policy and outline the system of financing and service delivery for PLWAs. We then discuss formal treatment and service expenditures, formal long-term care and community services, and the relationship between formal and informal services. Finally, we discuss the failure of the liberal capitalist approach to AIDS care in the United States.

FEDERAL AIDS POLICY

The hierarchical arrangement of U.S. federal AIDS policy efforts can best be gleaned by national funding allocations. The federal HIV/AIDS allocations for the U.S. Public Health Service for fiscal year 1993 were $2.07 billion [1]. Of this total, 44 percent was for basic science research, 32.5 percent was for risk assessment and prevention, 20 percent was for clinical health services research and delivery (which includes Ryan White funds for health care services), and 3.5 percent was for product evaluation, research, and monitoring [1]. The President proposed a budget for 1995 of $2.7 billion for AIDS research, prevention, and other related activities (a 7% increase) [1]. These figures characterize the outcome of the national policy debate on the prioritization of spending to address the HIV/AIDS health crisis and represent a lower financial priority placed on health services research, delivery, and prevention than on basic science. These figures exclude expenditures for services by Medicare and Medicaid, which we will discuss later.

As the epidemic has grown to involve over 300,000 persons with AIDS in the United States alone, the concerns about government funding and expenditures have also escalated. The need for and use of formal and informal services by PWAs is growing rapidly, and yet the major political attention is given to work directed toward finding a cure or preventing the spread of HIV. While it is necessary to continue seeking a cure and promoting prevention, it is equally important to investigate caregiving. Even if a magic bullet is found providing a cure for AIDS, other similar diseases may be on the horizon [2].

Informal care is work provided without financial compensation. The limits of the formal services industry means that caregiving is increasingly assumed by the informal sector. The result of this development is the increasing misery among families and populations already suffering from poverty and political dis-enfranchisement and larger profits for the privileged class strata and corporations. The former Editor-in-Chief of the *New England Journal of Medicine*, Arnold S. Relman, M.D., referred to this shift as "the new medical-industrial complex" that describes a large new industry that supplies health care services for profit [3]. A major feature of the new medical-industrial complex is the rise of the ambulatory sector where for-profit hospital chains, free-standing centers for ambulatory surgery, and diagnosis-related groups (particularly "imaging centers" that provide investor-owned magnetic resonance imagers and computerized tomography scanners) have become the norm rather than the exception [3].

What the new medical-industrial complex means for HIV/AIDS is the creation of a new sector of profiteering that works in conjunction with the cultural anxieties associated with risk groups [4]. In this way the moral, religious, and political codes of the society intersect to produce over-determined images of both the normality and deviance [5]. Through the state ideological apparatuses that include churches, the educational system, television, and the publishing medium, persons with HIV/AIDS are reproduced as stigmatized groups [6]. Simultaneously, they are increasingly relegated to out-of-sight positions by the organization of the ambulatory care technologies of the new medical-industrial complex. Late capitalism's relationship to PWAs is one that reproduces shunning of its victims at the same time that great profit is extracted from their conditions.

SYSTEM OF FINANCING AND SERVICE DELIVERY

The U.S. health care system is largely a privately operated and managed system with growing federal support. In 1995, the United States spent $977.5 billion on formal health care services. Of the total services, 43 percent was paid by government and 34 percent by private insurers. Individuals paid 18 percent of the cost directly out-of-pocket and 3 percent were from other sources [7]. Individuals and companies paid $353 billion in insurance premiums in 1994 [7].

There are about 1,500 private health insurance companies and health plans in the United States. These companies are largely (92%) profit-making companies [8]. The health insurance companies are consolidating into larger companies in an effort to cover larger populations and to have a national network of services [9]. This movement is designed to maximize revenues, profit, and growth. Health insurance plans continue to be profitable [10].

To maximize profit, insurance companies have an elaborate system to reduce coverage, add charges, or deny coverage. Risk rating is a common practice in which higher rates are charged for those individuals with higher risks for illness and where major and even minor health problems can be excluded from coverage [11]. Since HIV/AIDS is a potentially high cost illness, individuals with HIV/AIDS have been a particular target for exclusion by companies. Redlining or exclusion of entire groups of workers or companies has also been common. For example, workers in beauty parlors, restaurants, and other groups whom insurance companies consider to be a high risk have been excluded [11].

The regulation of the health insurance industry by states has been historically ineffective because of the complexity of practices, the political lobbying efforts by the insurance industry, and ineffective state regulatory mechanisms. It is the halfway competitive market and the ineffective regulation which have fueled the rapid growth in health care expenditures [12]. Renewed efforts at the federal level for regulation of insurance practices as a part of national health care reform could bring about needed changes in eliminating these practices which not only exclude those who need coverage the most but make health insurance unaffordable for many.

In spite of the efforts of private insurance companies to eliminate or reduce their coverage of HIV/AIDS, many companies do have substantial enrollments of HIV/AIDS patients. Little is known about the specific insurance coverage problems individuals with HIV are experiencing. As we will show, the literature documents that having insurance is a critical factor in having access to formal care services, and this is even more important for those persons with HIV/AIDS.

Medicare pays for an important part of care for the disabled. The Medicare rules, however, require that individuals with disabilities (including those related to HIV/AIDS) must have the disability for twenty-four months before they are eligible for health care services under the Social Security Disability Insurance program. Thus, only a small proportion of those with HIV/AIDS are eligible for Medicare coverage. Medicare is estimated to pay 1 to 2 percent of the total direct medical expenditures for PWAs or $385 million in FY 1993 [13]. Medicare expenditures, however, are expected to increase as new medical technologies and drugs enable PWAs to survive the twenty-four month waiting period [13].

Medicaid is designed as the major health care payer for those who are poor or on low incomes [7]. Medicaid eligibility is tied to eligibility for the Aid to Families with Dependent Children or Supplemental Security Income (SSI) benefits. SSI is designed to provide cash payments for those who are poor and aged, blind, or disabled. Since Medicaid is a joint federal and state program which is administered by states, the states have some discretion in their rules regarding eligibility for coverage. Thirty-six states have programs for the medically needy including those who spend down their other financial resources and become Medicaid eligible by virtue of their medical costs. Most single and childless adults with AIDS or a severe HIV-related illness who qualify for Medicaid do so because they meet the disability standard of the SSI program. Other states have no such programs available. In 1991, 33 percent of women and 54 percent of men aged nineteen to forty-four who were poor in the United States were not covered by Medicaid because of restrictive state eligibility policies [14].

Nevertheless, the Medicaid program is the largest single payer of direct medical care services for those with HIV/AIDS. Medicaid covers costs associated with 40 percent of all persons with AIDS and an estimated 25 percent of all national HIV/AIDS expenditures [13]. In FY 1993, the federal and state Medicaid HIV/AIDS expenditures were estimated to be $2.51 billion. In spite of these increasing costs to Medicaid, the expenditures for AIDS are only 1.5 percent of all Medicaid expenditures [13].

The state Medicaid programs have established special optional benefits and waiver programs for home- and community-based services for persons with HIV/AIDS. These optional services may include case management, hospice services, and other services. In 1992, eight state Medicaid programs had case management for PWAs, thirty-five state Medicaid programs offered hospice care services, fifteen states had home and community-based programs for PWAs, and all states offered coverage for AIDS and AIDS-related drugs [13].

Even though Medicaid services for those with HIV/AIDS are improving, the federal government is shifting responsibility for care from the federal to state and local governments. Rice reports that 5 percent of the nation's urban public hospitals are treating more than 50 percent of PWAs [15]. This suggests that private hospitals may be discriminating against PWAs. Although the Health Care Finance Administration, a federal agency, has pledged to enforce federal laws against discrimination by providers against Medicare and Medicaid eligible people with HIV/AIDS, this is a difficult area to monitor and enforce [15].

The current private and public health insurance system in the United States left an estimated forty million individuals (16% of the population) with no health insurance coverage in 1991 [14]. These uninsured individuals have dramatically reduced access to health care services. Poor access to services has been found to be related to poor health status [16]. Persons with HIV/AIDS are likely to be uninsured; about 25 percent of all AIDS patients have no insurance, either public or private [15].

FORMAL TREATMENT AND SERVICE EXPENDITURES

The utilization and cost of medical and health care for PWAs and those infected with HIV disease have dramatically increased. Because HIV/AIDS is a progressively debilitating disease, individuals with infections generally require a wide range of formal and informal services [17]. The most expensive and common formal services used by PWAs are hospital and physician services.

In 1992, the lifetime cost of treating a person with HIV from the time of infection until death was estimated to be approximately $119,000 [18]. The estimated cost of care from HIV infection until the development of AIDS is $50,000. The estimated cost from AIDS development until death is approximately $60,000. These costs include formal care in hospitals, clinics, and physician services. They omit the cost of informal care.

Recent studies of HIV/AIDS show a shift of utilization and costs from hospital care to outpatient care and rapidly growing costs associated with the use of drugs such as AZT [19-21]. Even though costs decrease with the shift away from hospitalization and toward outpatient care, the median survival for HIV/AIDS has increased so that the estimated lifetime costs continue to increase [21]. Estimates are that the costs of treating all people with HIV will increase 13 to 15 percent each year between 1992 and 1995, and that the cumulative costs of treating all persons with HIV will increase to $15 billion in 1995 [22].

Using utilization data from several studies Hellinger estimates that the average PWA has 1.6 hospitalizations annually at an average cost of $28,700 in 1992 [22]. He estimates that outpatient care constitutes 25 percent of the total average costs of care or $9,600 in 1992, of which $3,660 is for outpatient or physician visits, $420 for long-term care costs, $1,460 for home care, and $4,060 for outpatient drugs. Thus, the average medical costs for a person with AIDS was $38,300 for

7.5 months or $5,100 per month in 1992 [22]. Few individuals could afford to pay such catastrophic costs out-of-pocket without insurance. Those with AIDS and no private insurance can quickly spend all their income and become dependent upon Medicaid.

Utilization of formal health care services is closely associated with health insurance coverage. A recent study of PWAs recruited from outpatient AIDS clinics and community service organizations found that only 30 percent had private insurance, 29 percent had no insurance, and 41 percent were covered by some form of public health insurance [23]. Those who had private insurance (47%) were less likely to use clinics for their care than those with public insurance (95%). Those without insurance were less likely to have been hospitalized and had shorter lengths of stay when they were hospitalized [23]. White males who do not use intravenous drugs have higher rates of outpatient use, while nonwhite, female, intravenous drug users have higher rates of emergency room use [24]. One recent study shows a marked shift from private health insurance coverage for AIDS hospitalized patients toward Medicaid coverage in both New York and California [25]. Older adults have experienced this for years, and an already strained system will now experience additional financial difficulties [26].

Utilization and cost differences for HIV/AIDS are also strongly associated with geographical region of the country. New York consistently shows higher hospital use and services and lower outpatient use and services than California [27]. In New York, outpatient costs were estimated to be 18 percent of the total AIDS costs, compared to 27 percent in California [18].

Utilization patterns for formal health care services have traditionally varied based on the demographics of the population. Andrews and colleagues, for example, found significant differences in service utilization by age, gender, injection drug use status (IDUs), and Medicaid eligibility [27]. Multivariate analyses suggested these differences were largely attributed to diagnosis and income level. Another recent study showed that IDUs with AIDS have longer lengths of hospital stay and higher hospital costs than non-IDU AIDS patients [28]. Merzel and his colleagues also documented differences in utilization patterns for IDUs with HIV [29]. Severity of illness is another obvious factor which affects utilization. One study of hospital utilization showed that more severely ill AIDS patients have longer stays, higher costs, and account for more of the variance than gender, race, and drug use [30].

Utilization of services is also associated with gender differences. A recent study found that male IDUs with AIDS were twenty times more likely to be hospitalized than their female counterparts [20]. Male IDUs with AIDS received $9,180 more in hospital services than women IDUs with AIDS [20]. Women are much more likely than men to have been infected by intravenous drug use, heterosexual contact, and through transfusions of blood. Women were not systematically sought to participate in drug trials and most of the AIDS community services and formal long-term care targeted white men [20]. These findings suggest discriminatory practices that could adversely affect the outcomes of care for women with AIDS.

FORMAL LONG-TERM CARE AND COMMUNITY SERVICES

Long-term care services can include: home care, hospice, day care, homemaker services, case management, and a variety of other support services. Long-term care and community services can be categorized into the following types: 1) nursing and personal assistance services, 2) management of personal affairs, and 3) psychological services. Housing is also of critical importance for those who are ill, along with skilled nursing care and residential care [31]. Although the number of community-based services for PWAs appears to be increasing, few studies have examined their use [32]. Most utilization studies have focused on hospital and medical services [32]. These services may be provided either in the home or in other community settings.

Little is known about the utilization patterns for community-based services. Some studies have described the growing importance of community-based services and the need to examine such programs [33]. Such programs include home care, hospice, social services, counseling, transportation, planning and care coordination, food and meals, legal and financial support, and many other services in the community and in the home [32-34]. As Crystal points out, the current long-term care system which was designed primarily for the elderly may not be well prepared to meet the needs of younger PWAs who often have more intensive needs of nursing and other patient care services [35].

The availability of such services in a community is also an important factor in examining utilization of services. Arno and Hughes described the differences in community responses and service availability for the AIDS epidemic between New York and San Francisco [36]. Socioeconomic status, race, IDU, crack, and alcohol abuse indicated difference in community response and service availability. Harrington and her associates found differences in availability of services between San Francisco and Los Angeles [37]. Income differences, history of drug use, and family organization were associated with differences in the availability of services.

PWAs from low socioeconomic groups are of the greatest concern, because they are less likely to be employed, have lower incomes (by definition), have less education, and are more likely to be poor and eligible for Medicaid. One study of PWAs recently found that those with a history of IDU, crack, or alcohol use had fewer housekeeping services, but used more home delivered meals, food bank services, emergency financial services, and transportation services [37]. Use of these services may primarily reflect income differences between the kind of drug use groups. Also, those with a history of drug use have lower incomes and thus are more likely to be eligible for formal food and emergency services. Those without a drug history may be better able to purchase the basic food and housekeeping services that they require.

In addition, the utilization patterns for PWAs who were organized in more traditional family groups seemed similar to the utilization patterns of the PWAs who had a history of drug use within the traditional family sample. This contrasted with PWAs who were organized in lesbian and gay family groups. It is not surprising that those with IDU, crack, or alcohol problems would have different service needs than those without a history of substance abuse [37]. These kinds of differences are often overlooked in a health care system such as that in the United States where generally the highest priority is given to the reduction of service delivery costs.

One study of social support and mental health services for men with HIV infection found that Black men were less likely to be open about their sexuality with their primary social support network [38]. Nonetheless, the Black men reported that they found the social support to be more positive than did the white men. Another recent study of the condemnation of homosexuality in the Black community found that African Americans were more homophobic than whites [39]. The authors constructed a homophobia scale where responses ranged from acceptance, moral condemnation, to desire to inflict violence on lesbians and gays. The authors showed that the intolerant attitudes about sexuality strongly correlated with the perception of Black women that there is a diminishing pool of healthy, date-able, and marriage-able Black men. This may partly explain why Black men are more reticent about discussing their sexuality to primary social support groups. Important ethnic or cultural differences could be affecting utilization patterns [38].

The needs of PWAs from various social and economic groups for formal home and community-based services are similar. A wide range of services are needed and used, and these vary by the types of problems PWAs experience [32]. As PWAs continue to live longer, the process of treatment shifts to a chronic illness regimen which may include periods when acute illness occur [32]. Those with chronic illness rely more heavily on community-based and long-term care services than those with acute illness. In general, providing care for the chronically ill is concerned more with assistance for activities of daily living than upon treatments for specific types of illness. Dependence on assistance with activities of daily living is the most predominant treatment characteristic of PWAs. However, individual needs for assistance often vary dramatically. As Benjamin notes, developing a continuum of care services for those with chronic illness involved accommodating three elements: "(1) clients with enduring, or recurring and complex problems; (2) a comprehensive array of health, mental health, personal care, and social services; and (3) an integrating mechanism (e.g., case management) for monitoring needs, arranging access to services, and coordinating care over time" [32]. Community care can be viewed as services which complement hospital and medical services, rather than as a substitute for such services [32].

RELATIONSHIP BETWEEN
FORMAL AND INFORMAL SERVICES

Although a number of studies have documented the importance of informal caregiving for the elderly and for PWAs [40], little is known about the relationship between formal and informal services [41]. A more intensive examination of the use of formal services and their relationship with informal caregivers is needed.

In the AIDS crisis, traditional caregiving roles in the society are being challenged. For example, Schiller found that in health services research about the utilization by and financing of health services for PWAs, women kin as caregivers virtually disappear and the sacrifices made by women kin become socially invisible [42]. Women's roles became subsumed under the rubric "community care." These findings are important because caring has been traditionally defined as woman's work and has been institutionalized within the family structure. Schiller contrasted the health services perspective with the lived realities of caregiving by women kin as documented in data from a "needs assessment" of PWAs which was conducted by the New Jersey Department of Health. She concluded that the disregarding of women's caregiving is part of larger hegemonic processes that maintain concealed structures of domination.

Another aspect of the structural relationship between informal and formal caregiving is the number of women PWAs who have died leaving orphaned children. Since women usually perform the unpaid caregiving role for children in society, AIDS results in disrupting other normative caregiving tasks. Michaels and Levine estimated the number of motherless youth orphaned by AIDS in the United States [43]. They reported that by the end of 1995, maternal deaths caused by the HIV/AIDS epidemic will have orphaned an estimated 24,600 children and 21,000 adolescents. They estimate that unless the course of the disease changes dramatically, by the year 2000 the number of motherless children and adolescents will exceed 80,000. Michaels and Levine reported an increasing proportion of mothers who die from all causes in the United States are dying from AIDS. In 1991, an estimated 13 percent of children and 9 percent of adolescents whose mothers died did so from AIDS. By 1995, the proportions will surpass 17 percent of children and 12 percent of adolescents. Most of these motherless children will come from poor communities of color. Moreover, these families are disproportionately without fathers who might normally be available to serve as the substitute parents.

Of course, one of the problems confronting policy-makers is the regional nature of the way that institutions interface and form relationships to contend with the AIDS crisis. The collection of data about the epidemic is confounded even more by the fact that within regions there are ethnic and other group features, like regional illicit drug use practices, which need attention when collecting and organizing scientific knowledge about the relationship between formal and informal caregiving. Samuel R. Friedman and his colleagues examined how AIDS researchers have produced and reproduced a discriminatory knowledge of the

AIDS epidemic which primarily focuses on issues related to white gay males [44]. They point out that researchers from differing groups may have been systematically excluded from professional role opportunities under the management of standard scientific practices. They add "that the social position of the observer affects what is observed and how it is interpreted" [44, p. 459].

Coordination problems among hospital, primary care, and community-based services for PWAs have been identified as problematic [45]. Bennett studied some of the organizational and managerial issues related by the HIV/AIDS epidemic [46]. He examined organizational processes and responses and revealed the importance of the way coordination problems are addressed. He found that successful and efficient problem solving was based on the local prevalence of the issue, the existing infrastructure for addressing the problem, the number of high status individuals who join the issue, and the organization of political action around the issue. As more agencies are involved with care, there is an identified need for greater coordination to avoid inappropriate, discriminatory (particularly racist and sexist practices), and/or duplicative services [47, 48].

INFORMAL SERVICES AND CAREGIVING

There are many different informal caregivers for PWAs: those cared for by partners, lovers, and friends and those cared for by traditional relatives who are kin, parents, siblings, or spouses [49, 50]. Informal caregiving has always been important to individuals who are ill. In a national survey of the elderly, of two million elderly with limitations in activities of daily living, 1.8 million had informal caregivers [51]. In a national survey of informal caregivers for a sub-sample of these elderly, less than 10 percent of caregivers reported the use of paid services and those caregivers who used formal care were caring for individuals who were severely disabled [51].

Who Are the Caregivers?

Little is known about the HIV/AIDS caregivers, although the characteristics are somewhat similar to the characteristics of PWAs. Overall, there are many sociodemographic differences between PWAs and their caregivers.

Allers reports on a survey of PWAs registered with a community organization in Atlanta and found that primary caregivers were friends (32%), lovers or spouse (20%), parent or grandparent (30%), sibling (8%), or no caregiver (10%) [52]. It was not surprising that as PWAs lose their financial and physical resources, they become dependent on others. The older adults who were parents or grandparents were found to be providing important care to PWAs and some PWAs thus become residents of senior public housing by default [52]. Of course, the issue of financial spend down is an issue related to class status. Groups who were always poor or physically challenged will not experience the increase of dependency in the same way as groups who were privileged at the onset of the disease [53].

In a study of 487 AIDS caregivers in San Francisco and Los Angeles, the caregivers were primarily white (78%), mean age was thirty-nine, male (89%), lovers or partners (54%), and living with the PWA (70%) [50]. In a companion sample of 170 traditional family caregivers, 60 percent were white, mean age was forty-five, male (18%), partner or spouse (35%), and living with PWA (72%) [37]. The sampling of caregivers remains a significant problem. To date the samples are not systematically representative of the population of caregivers of PWAs in the United States.

Bonuck found that in the AIDS epidemic, caregiving practice stretches beyond the traditional concept of kin to a broader view of family [49]. At the cultural level, AIDS has challenged the notions of who is a family member and what functions as a family. In addition, Bonuck reported that the AIDS crisis reshaped both language and behaviors about family and resulted in various family types emerging in the AIDS community. All of the family types shared role reconfiguration, both financial and social, when contrasted with traditional family roles. This does not mean that the reshaping of family organization is caused by AIDS per se. Rather, the PWAs are from groups that typically represent healthy adults where children and the elderly are usually the care recipients. With the AIDS crisis, the typical family structure is reversed when the generation that "should be" caregivers become care recipients.

What Do They Do?

Formal services for PWAs are supplemented by informal services provided by partners/lovers, family members, and friends. Informal caregivers often serve as the primary advocates for and managers of care for PWAs. They frequently facilitate access to and coordination of formal community-based support services. Additionally, informal caregivers provide companionship, run errands, buy and prepare food, and do housework for PWAs. Often, they must intervene in family disputes which arise from changes in typical family role behaviors, financial conflicts, stigma associated with the disease, and the assignment of blame. Caregivers are pulled into an experience of waiting for the death of a friend or loved one; they are therefore required to provide emotional balance to the social network of the PWA.

What are the Needs of the Caregivers?

The stress on caregivers of PWAs has been described by a number of studies that are discussed here. Fundamentally, the needs of caregivers of PWAs are similar to the needs of caregivers generally, but AIDS caregivers are associated with greater stigma. Pearlin and his colleagues noted multiple sources of stress in AIDS caregiving [54]. These include stress in the caregiving role itself because of its extensive time and energy requirements. Conflicts between roles of care-giving, work, and other social roles can be problematic. Also, role conflict can develop as can conflicts in relationships with friends. Contacts between caregivers and PWAs can also be problematic. It is possible for conflicts to develop between family members and caregivers. In fact, the stress of caregiving may result in conflict between the caregiver and her/his family and/or between the PWA's family and the caregiver. Interpsychic processes, identification, and attendant life strains can also be a source of strain [54]. The experience of having multiple losses leads to serious grief and bereavement issues [55]. Guinan and his colleagues found volunteer caregivers experience problems of "emotional overload, lack of support, and lack of training" [56]. Offsetting rewards were important to these caregivers.

Brown and Powell-Cope described the experience of AIDS family caregiving using the method of grounded theory where they approached the subject without a theoretical perspective but allowed the categories of their study to emerge from the interviews [57]. They studied fifty-three AIDS caregivers including lovers, spouses, parents of either adults or children with AIDS, siblings, and friends. They found the basic psychological problem of "uncertainty" was the core category for the analysis of the presentation of stress in caregivers. The uncertainty is consis-tently found in five stressful subcategories: 1) managing and being managed by illness, 2) living with loss and dying, 3) renegotiating the relationship, 4) going public, and 5) containing the spread of HIV.

In another article, Powell-Cope and Brown used the method of grounded theory to report the fears associated with AIDS they observed in their study [58]. AIDS invokes fears of contagion, disability, and fierce death. In addition, the authors reported that the condition of HIV/AIDS elicits "virtual morality." The virtual morality are the commonly held negative beliefs about drug abuse, presumed perverse sexual behavior, and identity. They view these moral categories as socially constructed claims-making. The authors reported the analytical category of "going public" as a consistent pattern with the caregivers they studied. Going public is when caregivers let others know that they are giving care to a PWA. The caregivers had to negotiate the proper persons and audiences to tell of their AIDS caregiver status which resulted in them devising approaches for communicating information. The caregivers had to consider the risks and benefits of telling others of their roles as caregivers.

Powell-Cope and Brown determined that AIDS caregivers were obligated to share the stigma of AIDS and become socially discredited as are the PWAs for whom they care [58]. Caregivers need ways to cope with the tremendous personal suffering experienced by caregiving associated with the stigma of AIDS. In Powell-Cope and Brown's study, such suffering was reported by caregivers as forms of rejection, loss of friends, and general harassment. The authors suggested that any effective AIDS education efforts should include recognizing and resolv-ing the suffering of AIDS caregivers.

Costs of Informal Caregiving

In a study of labor and cost in AIDS family caregiving, the cost of care for PWAs were calculated and showed that care provided by family or other social support network members is economic as well as social [59]. The authors sampled fifty-three self-identified primary caregivers of PWAs. The caregivers reported an average of five hours each week of housework performed specifically for the PWA. Caregivers spent an average of 8.5 hours a day performing personal care tasks for each PWA. Three of the most common activities reported were providing companionship, running errands, and performing food/meal-related activities. When Ward and Brown looked at gender comparisons they found that women caregivers performed more hours of housework than men but that both provided similar types of personal care for similar numbers of hours [59].

Ward and Brown concluded through market valuation computations that the value of a day's caregiving work was estimated to be $43.78. The annual value of unpaid care, including housework, for one PWA was calculated to be $25,858.

A recent study of the care of persons with dementia found that unpaid labor accounted for 71 percent of the family care costs and cash expenditures were only 29 percent of the total costs (which averaged $4,564 for 3 months or $18,256 per year) [60]. The total care costs increased substantially with each additional dependency in activities of daily living [60]. The indirect caregiving costs for AIDS have not been calculated. If the indirect costs for AIDS care was 2.5 times the direct costs (using the Alzheimers' estimates), then the direct costs of AIDS would need to be multiplied by 2.5 times to estimate total direct and indirect caregiving costs.

Most cost of illness studies take into account the productivity losses caused by an illness. Recent estimates of the productivity losses due to lifetime earnings, premature deaths, and lost productivity for AIDS in the United States for 1990 were calculated by Rice to be $17.6 million [15]. In addition, future studies which examine the loss of caregiver productivity are needed. These losses are a major part of overall cost estimates for AIDS.

DISCUSSION

What is suggested by our chapter is the intersection of state, corporate, and health care interests in the reproduction of capitalist profits which sacrifices caregiving for PWAs. The United States is unique among capitalist countries in that the health care system is significantly more capitalized; the fact that the United States is the only nation aside from South Africa in the industrialized world without a universal health care system makes caregiving for AIDS in the United States a consequentially different structure from what it is in other industrialized countries. As we have indicated, it means that caregiving is subject to consider-ably more private governance of those who are in the privileged strata. Because those individuals are in corporations rather than operating from positions in the state, there is not even the pressure of the noblesse oblige to provide care, rather it is simply private maximization of profit.

Another aspect laid opened in our chapter is the attempt to universalize care needs of victims of HIV/AIDS at the expense of group needs. The AIDS research and prevention industry reproduce existing social inequalities by directing most spending, treatment, formal caregiving to white males. The needs of other groups based on race, class, gender, or regional drug use practices have received little attention. The function of the one-size-fits-all approach to care is the reduction of treatment cost. Moreover, there is the ideological function of medicine that hierarchically cast medical doctors as miracle workers; as AIDS increasingly becomes a chronic rather than an acute condition, doctors with such ideological orientations will surely avoid AIDS patients who require therapies of chronicity.

The reproduction of the stigma associated with AIDS is of paramount importance for the reproduction of privilege in terms of class, gender, and race. By relegating the victims of AIDS to the category of "Other" with moral deficiencies, it makes the idea of overlooking their medical caregiving needs more palatable to a nation ostensibly committed to promoting the general welfare of life and liberty. After all, according to the current ideological conventions, PWAs have no one to blame but themselves for their illness. As the ideological logic goes, in general, AIDS is a matter of individual behavior which is unrelated to larger societal structures. If the "Other" would behave as do white heterosexual males, there would be no need for caregiving.

AIDS is not only stigmatized, but expensive. In the context of a capitalist society with no strong tradition of socialized medicine, it is an uphill battle to get caregiving recognized as legitimate. The ideological narrative of the ruling class and its professional managerial stratum regarding AIDS and caregiving is comparable to the ruling class narrative regarding work and welfare. People should earn money through meritorious rewards in a neutral labor market. Such thinking reasons that individual character and behaviors with respect to competence and effort, results in acquiring the most competitive positions with high salaries in the labor market. As the thinking goes, good health like good work is a matter of individual character and responsibility. But, all work is not paid work. When an individual becomes infected with AIDS, eventually they cannot work; they need care. But AIDS, like welfare, is not a legitimate condition. Therefore, the claim for care according to the dominant ideological logic is understood as illegitimate.

Added to the ideological narrative prevailing in the United States around the AIDS crisis is the organization of work. Much of the health care provision is non-paid or low-paid work, what the economists refer to as work in the secondary labor market. Typically, women's work is understood as non-paid and low-paid work. AIDS further challenges the dominant class's conception women's work, since a disproportionate number of men are found providing care for PWAs. But the stigma of homosexuality results in the feminization of gay men's status, of PWAs, and their caregivers. Therefore, the caregiving work is masked behind the structure of dominance which reproduces race, class, gender, and health differences as "Otherness."

ACKNOWLEDGMENTS

The authors are grateful to Vasilikie Demos, Joel Eisinger, Kenneth Ferraro, and Linda Mitteness for their comments on an earlier draft of this chapter. This research was partially funded by grant NIA T32 AG00045 from U.C. San Francisco, Division of Medical Anthropology and Institute for Health and Aging.

REFERENCES

1. Consortium of Social Science Associations, FY 1995 Budgets for Social and Behavioral Science Research, *COSSA Washington Update, 13*:4, pp. 1-33, 1994.
2. D. L. Selden, Just When You Thought It was Safe to Go Back in the Water . . . , in *The Lesbian and Gay Studies Reader,* H. Abelove, M. A. Barale, and D. M. Halperin (eds.), Routledge, New York, pp. 221-223, 1993.
3. R. Relman, The Health Care Industry: Where Is It Taking Us? in *The Nation's Health,* P. R. Lee and C. L. Estes (eds.), Jones and Bartlett, Boston, pp. 67-75, 1994.
4. C. Patton, *Inventing AIDS,* Routledge, New York, 1990.
5. D. Wippen, Science Fictions: Making of a Medical Model for AIDS, *Radical America, 20*:6, pp. 39-53, 1987.
6. S. Watney, *Policing Desire: Pornography, AIDS and the Media,* University of Minnesota Press, Minneapolis, 1987.
7. S. T. Burner and D. R. Waldo, National Health Expenditures, Projections, 1994-2005, *Health Care Financing Review, 16*:4, pp. 221-242, 1995.
8. B. H. Gray, *The Profit Motive,* Harvard University Press, Boston, 1991.
9. C. L. Estes, C. Harrington, and S. Davis, The Medical-Industrial Complex, in *Health Policy and Nursing: Crisis and Reform in the U.S. Health Care Delivery System,* C. Harrington and C. L. Estes (eds.), Jones and Bartlett, Boston, pp. 54-69, 1994.
10. C. T. Geer, Insurance, in *Forbes,* pp. 166-167, January 4, 1993.
11. D. W. Light, The Practice and Ethics of Risk-Rated Health Insurance, *Journal of the American Medical Association, 267*:18, pp. 2503-2508, 1992.
12. S. H. Altman and M. A. Rodwin, Halfway Competitive Markets and Ineffective Regulation: The American Health Care System, *Journal of Health Politics, Policy and Law, 13*:2, pp. 323-339, 1988.
13. E. M. Howell and P. Pine, Overview of the HCFA Study of Cost and Utilization of AIDS Services in California and New York, *Journal of Acquired Immune Deficiency Syndromes, 4*:10, pp. 1010-1014, 1991.
14. K. R. Levit, G. L. Olin, and S. W. Letsch, Americans' Health Insurance Coverage, 1980-91, *Health Care Financing Review, 14*:1, pp. 31-57, 1992.
15. D. P. Rice, Ethics and Equity in U.S. Health Care: The Data, *International Journal of Health Services, 21*:4, pp. 637-651, 1991.

16. T. A. LaVeist, Segregation, Poverty and Empowerment: Health Consequences for African Americans, *The Milbank Quarterly, 71*:1, pp. 41-65, 1993.
17. L. Katoff, Community-Based Services for People with AIDS, *Primary Care: Clinics in Office Practice, 19*:1, pp. 231-243, 1992.
18. F. J. Hellinger, The Lifetime Cost of Treating a Person with HIV, *Journal of American Medical Association, 270*:4, pp. 474-478, 1993.
19. C. L. Bennett, M. Cvitanic, and A. Pascal, The Costs of AIDS in Los Angeles, *Journal of Acquired Immune Deficiency Syndromes, 4*:2, pp. 197-203, 1991.
20. F. J. Hellinger, The Use of Health Services by Women with HIV Infection, *Health Services Research, 25*:5, pp. 543-561, 1993.
21. G. R. Seage, III, S. Landers, G. A. Lamb, and A. M. Epstein, Effect of Changing Patterns of Care and Duration of Survival on the Cost of Treating the Acquired Immunodeficiency Syndrome (AIDS), *American Journal of Public Health, 80*:7, pp. 835-839, 1990.
22. F. J. Hellinger, Forecasts of the Costs of Medical Care for Persons with HIV: 1992-1995, *Inquiry, 29*, pp. 356-365, Fall 1992.
23. J. A. Fleishman and V. Mor, Insurance Status among People with AIDS: Relationships with Sociodemographic Characteristics and Service Use, *Inquiry, 30*:2, pp. 180-188, 1993.
24. V. Mor, J. A. Fleishman, M. Dresser, and J. Piette, Variation in Health Service Use among HIV-Infected Patients, *Medical Care, 30*:1, pp. 17-29, 1992.
25. J. Green and P. S. Arno, The 'Medicalization' of AIDS, Trends in the Financing of HIV-Related Medical Care, *Journal of American Medical Association, 264*:10, pp. 1261-1266, 1990.
26. The National Commission on Acquired Immune Deficiency Syndrome, *American Living with AIDS: Transforming Anger, Fear, and Indifference into Action*, U.S. Government Printing Office, Washington, D.C., 1991.
27. R. M. Andrews, M. A. Keyes, T. R. Fanning, and K. W. Kizer, Lifetime Medicaid Service Utilization and Expenditures for AIDS in New York and California, *Journal of Acquired Immune Deficiency Syndromes, 4*:10, pp. 1046-1058, 1991.
28. G. R. Seage, III, T. Hertz, V. E. Stone, and A. M. Epstein, The Effects of Intravenous Drug Use and Gender on the Cost of Hospitalization for Patients with AIDS, *Journal of Acquired Immune Deficiency Syndromes, 6*:7, pp. 831-839, 1993.
29. C. Merzel, S. Crystal, and U. Sambamoorthi, New Jersey's Medicaid Waiver for Acquired Immunodeficiency Syndrome, *Health Care Financing Review, 13*:3, pp. 27-44, 1992.
30. J. V. Kelly, J. K. Ball, and B. J. Turner, Duration and Costs of AIDS Hospitalizations in New York: Variations by Patient Severity of Illness and Hospital Type, *Medical Care, 27*:12, pp. 1085-1098, 1989.
31. L. Beresford, Alternative Outpatient Settings of Care for People with AIDS, *Quality Review Bulletin, 15*:1, pp. 9-16, 1989.
32. A. E. Benjamin, Continuum of Care for HIV Illness, *Medical Care Review, 46*:4, pp. 411-437, 1989.
33. P. S. Arno, The Nonprofit Sector's Response to the AIDS Epidemic: Community-Based Services in San Francisco, *American Journal of Public Health, 76*:11, pp. 1325-1330, 1986.
34. S. Crystal, C. Merzel, and C. Kurland, Home Care of HIV Illness, *Family and Community Health, 13*, pp. 29-37, 1990.
35. S. Crystal, The Impact of AIDS on Services for the Elderly: New Demands and Economic Consequences, *Generations, 13*, pp. 23-27, 1989.

36. P. S. Amo and R. G. Hughes, Local Policy Responses to the AIDS Epidemic: New York and San Francisco, *New York State Journal of Medicine, 87*, pp. 264-272, 1987.
37. C. Harrington, L. Wardlaw, S. Chang, L. Ibrahim, L. I. Pearlin, J. Mullan, and A. Lemelle, *Utilization of Community-Based Support Services: A Comparison of Familial and Non-Familial Caregivers to Persons with AIDS*, paper presented to American Public Health Association Annual Meeting, San Francisco, California, 1993.
38. D. G. Ostrow, R. E. D. Whitaker, K. Frasier, C. Cohen, J. Wan, C. Frank, and E. Fisher, Racial Differences in Social Support and Mental Health in Men with HIV Infection: A Pilot Study, *AIDS Care, 3*:1, pp. 55-62, 1991.
39. F. A. Ernst, R. A. Francis, H. Nevels, and C. A. Lemeh, Condemnation of Homosexuality in Black Community: A Gender-Specific Phenomenon? *Archives of Sexual Behavior, 20*:6, pp. 609-614, 1991.
40. L. I. Pearlin, J. T. Mullan, S. J. Semple, and M. M. Skaff, Caregiving and the Stress Process: An Overview of Concepts and Their Measures, *The Gerontologist, 30*:5, pp. 583-594, 1990.
41. J. T. Mullan, Barriers to the Use of Formal Services among Alzheimer's Caregivers, in *Caregiving Systems: Informal and Formal Helpers*, S. H. Zarit, L. I. Pearlin, and K. W. Schaie (eds.), Lawrence Erlbaum Associates, Hillsdale, New Jersey, pp. 241-260, 1993.
42. N. G. Schiller, The Invisible Woman: Caregiving and the Construction of AIDS Health Services, *Culture, Medicine and Psychiatry, 17*:4, pp. 487-512, 1993.
43. D. Michaels and C. Levine, Estimates of the Number of Motherless Youth Orphaned by AIDS in the U.S., *Journal of American Medical Association, 268*:24, pp. 3456-3461, 1992.
44. S. R. Friedman, J. L. Sotheran, A. Abdul-Quaderr, B. J. Primm, D. C. Des Jarlais, P. Kleinman, C. Mauge, D. S. Goldsmith, W. El-Sadr, and R. Maslansky, The AIDS Epidemic among Blacks and Hispanics, in *Health Policies and Black Americans*, D. P. Willis (ed.), Transaction, New Brunswick, pp. 455-499, 1989.
45. S. Layzell and M. McCarthy, Community-Based Health Services for People with HIV/AIDS: A Review from a Health Service Perspective, *AIDS Care, 4*:2, pp. 203-215, 1992.
46. C. Bennett, HIV/AIDS Some Organizational and Managerial Issues, *Health and Manpower Management, 19*:3, pp. 25-28, 1993.
47. S. Layzell and M. McCarthy, Finding Policies for HIV and AIDS: Time for Change, *British Medical Journal, 307*:6900, pp. 367-369, 1993.
48. K. A. Elder-Tabrizy, R. J. Wolitski, F. Rhodes, and J. G. Baker, AIDS and Competing Health Concerns of Blacks, Hispanics and Whites, *Journal of Community Health, 16*:1, pp. 11-21, 1991.
49. K. A. Bonuck, AIDS and Families: Cultural, Psychosocial, and Functional Impacts, *Social Work in Health Care, 18*:2, pp. 75-89, 1993.
50. L. I. Pearlin, J. T. Mullan, C. S. Aneshensel, L. Wardlaw, and C. Harrington, The Structure and Functions of AIDS Caregiving Relationships, *Psychosocial Rehabilitation Journal, 17*:4, pp. 51-67, 1994.
51. R. Stone, G. L. Cafferata, and J. Sangl, Caregivers of the Frail Elderly: A National Profile, *The Gerontologist, 27*:5, pp. 616-626, 1987.
52. C. T. Allers, AIDS and the Older Adult, *The Gerontologist, 30*:3, pp. 405-407, 1990.
53. N. el-Bassel and R. F. Schilling, Drug Use and Sexual Behavior of Indigent African American Men, *Public Health Reports, 106*:5, pp. 586-590, 1991.

54. L. I. Pearlin, S. J. Semple, and H. Turner, The Stress of AIDS Care Giving: A Preliminary Overview of the Issues, *Death Studies, 12*:5/6, pp. 501-517, 1988.
55. R. Biller and S. Rice, Experiencing Multiple Loss of Persons with AIDS: Grief and Bereavement Issues, *Health and Social Work, 15*:4, pp. 283-290, 1990.
56. J. J. Guinan, L. W. McCallum, L. Painter, J. Dykes, and J. Gold, Stressors and Rewards of Being an AIDS Emotional-Support Volunteer: A Scale for Use by Care-Givers for People with AIDS, *AIDS Care, 3*:2, pp. 137-150, 1991.
57. M. A. Brown and G. M. Powell-Cope, AIDS Family Caregiving: Transitions through Uncertainty, *Nursing Research, 40*:6, pp. 338-345, 1991.
58. G. M. Powell-Cope and M. A. Brown, Going Public as an AIDS Family Caregiver, *Social Science and Medicine, 34*:5, pp. 571-580, 1992.
59. D. Ward and M. A. Brown, Labor and Cost in AIDS Family Caregiving, *Western Journal of Nursing Research, 16*:1, pp. 10-22 and discussion pp. 23-25, 1994.
60. M. Stommel, C. E. Collins, and B. A. Given, The Costs of Family Contributions to the Care of Persons with Dementia, *The Gerontologist, 34*:2, pp. 199-205, 1994.

SECTION IV

AIDS in the Third World

CHAPTER 8

The Political Ecology of AIDS in Africa

Meredeth Turshen

This chapter reviews recent developments in the spread of AIDS in the context of the changing political economy of Africa. It situates AIDS among current health problems and the financial straits of African health service delivery systems; it looks particularly at the service problems arising from the 1987 and 1993 World Bank recommendations for the privatization of health care [1, 2]. Privatization entails the use of government policies to shift provision and financing from the public to the private sector. Recommendations for reduced government spending on social services form part of the Bank's loan package; aid is conditional on the adoption of specified budget reforms.

In 1987, the World Bank recommended that medical treatment be offered privately. The Bank's 1993 World Development Report, which focuses on the health sector, modifies that position. Noting that the market has failed to respond to the needs of the indigent, the Bank now proposes that the poorer countries of Africa and Asia use the public sector to provide an essential "clinical" package that emphasizes maternal and child health, family planning, and case management of sexually transmitted diseases. This two-tiered strategy—curative medicine for the rich in Europe and North America and public health for poor Africans and Asians—raises issues of unequal social relations across national, class, racial, ethnic, and gender lines, as well as the role of the Bank's power in shaping social events and social conditions.

The World Bank's strategy for privatizing medical treatment is to turn government services over to church missions and other nongovernmental organizations

(NGOs), a strategy that undermines the state's ability to provide care for its historically underserved citizens. In African countries with no prior management experience of an NGO sector, competing NGOs duplicate services and waste scarce resources. This chapter explores the consequences of privatization for AIDS prevention and the treatment of Africans with AIDS.

THE SPREAD OF AIDS IN AFRICA

As of June 30, 1995, forty-seven nations reported 415,595 cases of AIDS to the Regional Office for Africa of the World Health Organization (WHO) [3]. That figure is cumulative from 1979, and its compilation is contrary to the usual public health practice of reporting new cases of disease and death annually. Figures for the single year 1993 (the latest year for which complete data are available) are much lower, 81,738 cases [3]. These statistics should be read against estimates of 100 million clinical cases of malaria in Africa each year and more than 1 million deaths, mainly among children under five years old [4], and 1.7 million new cases of tuberculosis and 871,000 deaths [5]. WHO does not report the number of deaths from AIDS, which is included in the cumulative case data. If the ratio of cases to deaths is the same in Africa as it is in the United States (about 63% of Americans with AIDS have died), then we may estimate that 217,753 deaths occurred over a period of fifteen years; this estimate may be too low because little treatment exists in Africa for AIDS patients and because mortality from AIDS has an inverse relation to socioeconomic status. Even so, this figure represents a small fraction of all deaths in Africa; AIDS is not yet a major cause of death on the continent.[1]

The cumulative AIDS case figure for the African continent represents 34 percent of the world total. The United States continues to report the majority of AIDS cases, 38 percent of the world total [3]. A major disparity exists between the number of AIDS cases reported by African governments and WHO's estimate of cumulative HIV incidence (that is, all estimated HIV infections since the onset of the epidemic in the late 1970s): WHO estimates that eleven million adults were infected with HIV in sub-Saharan Africa in mid-1995 [3]. Unfortunately, WHO does not reveal the methods used to calculate this number, so we do not know the assumptions on which it is based (and we have seen New York City officials halve their estimates, though presumably statistics are more accurate in the United States). Rather than the number of cases being under-reported, some authors suggest that over-reporting is at least as likely because of

---

[1] Because the database for the most recent analyses of mortality by cause of death is from 1985 [6], AIDS does not figure as a major cause of death anywhere in Africa. Mathematical models, such as that used by the U.S. Bureau of the Census to characterize a "typical" African HIV epidemic over twenty-five years, predict dramatic increases in adult mortality and a population growth rate that falls from 2.8 to 2.2 percent per year [7].

the high number of false positives in HIV testing under African conditions [8]. Also, given the shift of scarce resources into AIDS control, many chronically under-funded African public health services are claiming they need AIDS donations, even if they report few cases (as in Nigeria). In other words, these numbers are highly political.

Although almost every African country reports a few cases of AIDS, most cases are clustered in the area surrounding Lake Victoria that covers Burundi, Kenya, Rwanda, Tanzania, Uganda, and Zaire: as of 1993, these six countries accounted for almost half of cumulative cases [3]. From this epicenter, the virus spread south to Malawi, Zambia, and Zimbabwe. A second cluster has appeared in the west African states of Côte d'Ivoire and Ghana; scientists believe that a different strain of the virus, HIV-2, causes AIDS in west Africa [9, p. 2]. East and west African nations share a common feature, the type of AIDS transmission that WHO calls Pattern II, which is caused predominantly by heterosexual intercourse (in contrast to Pattern I industrial countries, where AIDS affects mainly homosexuals and IV drug users) [9, pp. 4-6]. These designations are at the center of heated controversy over the role of unsterile needles and syringes in spreading AIDS through African health clinics [10]. The implications of such labeling for health policy are discussed below.

Falling living standards, deteriorating health conditions, and shrinking access to health care justify concern over an AIDS epidemic in Africa. Table 1 gives several indicators of death, disease, and health care in selected countries of sub-Saharan Africa. The most striking statistic is median age at death, which is typically under five years in Africa and over seventy-five years in Europe. The link between poverty and HIV is not widely researched; one study from Uganda found that both male and female heads of the poorest households were most likely to be HIV positive [11]. The burden of AIDS seems to fall more heavily on poor households.

Despite decades of international assistance, poverty is increasing in Africa. The United Nations Development Programme estimates that Africa's share of the world's poor will rise from 30 percent to 40 percent by the year 2000, overtaking Asia [12, p. 23]. More than half the continent's population will live below the poverty line at the end of this decade.[2] Poor women increasingly outnumber poor men. The gender-sensitive Human Development Index (HDI) finds that the female HDI is only half the male HDI in Kenya, the only African country for which data are available [13, p. 16]. The Human Development Index, developed by the United Nations Development Programme, measures female and male estimates of life expectancy, adult literacy, mean years of schooling, and wage rates.

---

[2] Fifteen countries—Benin, Botswana, Burundi, Chad, Kenya, Lesotho, Malawi, Rwanda, Sierra Leone, Somalia, Sudan, Swaziland, Tanzania, Zaire, and Zambia—report that between 50 and 85 percent of their rural populations live in absolute poverty (data for the period 1977-1989 [13, p. 171]).

Table 1. Death, Disease, and Health Services in Selected African Countries

Country	Median Age at Death 1990	Annual Incidence Rate of Tuberculosis per 100,000 Pop., 1990	Population per Doctor 1990	Hospital Beds per 1,000 Pop. 1985-90	% Population with Access to		
					Health Services 1987-90	Safe Water 1988-90	Sanitation 1988-90
Angola	3	225	17,750	1.2	24	38	22
Burkina Faso	4	289	57,330	0.3	70	67	10
Cen. Afr. Rep.	15	139	23,510	0.9	13	12	20
Cote d'Ivoire	10	196	—	0.8	60	83	36
Ghana	7	222	20,460	1.5	76	56	30
Malawi	4	173	11,340	1.6	80	53	—
Nigeria	7	222	6,420	1.4	67	46	13
Mozambique	2	189	37,970	0.9	30	22	19
Senegal	15	166	13,970	0.8	40	53	—
Tanzania	5	140	24,990	1.1	93	52	77
Zambia	11	345	7,150	—	75	59	55
Zimbabwe	26	267	7,180	2.1	71	36	42
Established Market Economies	75	20	630	8.3	—	—	—

Source: UNDP, *Human Development Report 1993*, Oxford University Press, New York, pp. 158-159, 1993; World Bank, *World Development Report 1993*, Oxford University Press, New York, pp. 200-201, 206, 208, 292-293, 1993.

The number of HIV-infected women is far greater in Pattern II than in Pattern I countries; and in Africa, where medical facilities and support services are inadequate, the responsibility of caring for relatives with AIDS and for the orphans of relatives dead of AIDS falls heavily on women [14-16]. The alleged role of commercial sex work in the transmission of HIV in Pattern II countries has added to the burdens of African women. McFadden notes the widespread belief that sexually transmitted diseases, including AIDS, are caused by women: "the sex-worker is the most obvious scapegoat of such superstitions" [14, p. 160]. As a result, Ankrah notes, when a woman contracts AIDS, she is likely to be sent back to her relatives or to be abandoned [15].

AIDS AND THE CHANGING POLITICAL ECONOMY

The political economy of Africa changed dramatically as economic reforms designed by the World Bank [17] failed to resolve the debt crisis in Africa [18]. Economic instability has caused more workers to migrate in search of work, disrupting family life and increasing the behaviors associated with the spread of HIV. In several countries, economic instability has led to political instability, creating further disruption and dislocation. Reduced access to health, education, and other social services, a consequence of the privatization of public services and part of structural adjustment programs, has considerably increased poverty and the hardships of the poor (see Table 2) [19]. The World Bank has adopted these policies even though it knows that "the free play of market forces can generate levels of poverty that are socially unacceptable" [20, p. 258].

The debt crisis, the current recession, and structural adjustment programs aggravate the transmission, spread, and control of HIV infection, as has been shown in several parts of Africa [21, 22]. Schoepf et al. point out that disease epidemics generally erupt in times of crisis, and they elaborate on the relation between economic turmoil, widespread unemployment, intense competition in the crowded informal sector, the feminization of poverty, women's low status in society, and the spread of HIV in Zaire:

> Like so many other diseases produced by socioeconomic and political conditions, AIDS is a disease of development and underdevelopment. The virus is a biological event, the effects of which are magnified by the conditions of urbanization in African societies, distorted development, and the current world economic crisis [21, p. 201].

Sanders and Sambo maintain that the population at risk of AIDS is increased directly by urban migration, poverty, women's powerlessness, and prostitution, and indirectly through a decrease in health care provision [22]. This is the political ecology of AIDS—the social and economic context of the spread of HIV/AIDS in Africa.

Table 2. Central Government Expenditures: Selected African and Industrial Countries, 1972 and 1990

Country[a]	Population Millions Mid-1990	GNP p.c. $ 1990	Total Health Expenditure p.c. $ 1990	Percent of Total Expenditures							
				Health		Housing, Social Security, Welfare		Education		Defense	
				1972	1990	1972	1990	1972	1990	1972	1990
Tanzania	24.5	110	4	7.2	—	2.1	—	17.3	—	11.9	—
Malawi	8.5	200	11	5.5	7.4	5.8	3.2	15.8	8.8	3.1	4.5
Nigeria	115.5	290	9	3.6	—	0.8	—	3.6	—	40.2	—
Burkina Faso	9.0	330	24	8.2	—	6.6	—	20.6	—	11.5	—
Ghana	14.9	390	14	6.3	9.0	4.1	11.9	20.1	25.7	7.9	2.3
Zambia	8.1	420	14	7.4	7.4	1.3	2.0	19.0	8.6	0.0	0.0
Lesotho	1.8	530	—	8.0	7.4	6.5	2.4	19.5	15.2	0.9	9.9
Zimbabwe	9.8	640	42	—	7.6	—	3.9	—	23.4	—	16.5
Botswana	1.3	2,040	—	6.0	4.8	21.7	10.6	10.0	20.2	0.0	11.6
Namibia	1.8	—	—	—	11.1	—	15.0	—	20.8	—	5.5
UK	57.4	16,100	1,039	12.2	14.6	26.5	34.8	2.6	3.2	16.7	12.2
Italy	57.7	16,830	1,426	13.5	11.3	44.8	38.6	16.1	8.3	6.3	3.6
Australia	17.1	17,000	1,331	7.0	12.8	20.3	29.7	4.2	6.8	14.2	8.5
Netherlands	14.9	17,320	1,500	12.1	11.7	38.1	42.3	15.2	10.8	6.8	5.0
Austria	7.7	19,060	1,711	10.1	12.9	53.8	48.2	10.2	9.2	3.3	2.5
Canada	26.5	20,790	1,945	7.6	5.5	35.3	37.0	3.5	2.9	7.6	7.3
USA	250.0	21,790	2,763	8.6	13.5	35.3	28.2	3.2	1.7	32.2	22.6

[a]Ranked in ascending order of GNP per capita.
Source: World Bank, *World Development Report 1992*, Oxford University Press, New York, pp. 218-219, 238-239, 1992.

Medical commentators implicate prostitution in the spread of HIV, and several authors describe the circumstances of the rise in commercial sex work in Africa [21-25]. Jochelson, Mothibeli, and Leger interviewed workers on the South African mines about the impact of the migrant labor system on heterosexual relationships, assessing the implications for the future transmission of HIV [23]. They describe how the migrant labor system in southern Africa creates a market for prostitution in South African mining towns:

> Migrants' frequent and lengthy absences from their homes disrupt their familial and stable sexual relationships. In a lonely and hostile environment and separated for long periods from their wives, some migrants may seek sexual relationships with women in nearby towns. Migrancy also subjects marriages to great strain, and divorce or abandonment deprives women of economic support. With access to few opportunities on the labor market, some women may choose prostitution as the only means of economic survival [23, p. 157].

Parpart found the same circumstances in the rise of prostitution on the Zambian copperbelt [24], and White described a similar development of commercial sex work catering to migrant workers in Nairobi [25]. Schoepf et al. also observed women turning to commercial sex work to make ends meet [21].

In the same vein, Bassett and Mhloyi explore the history of social and economic influences on culture in relation to the current spread of AIDS [16]. They trace the present pattern of family dissolution—wives left to head households in rural areas, while husbands live with multiple partners in urban areas—back to the colonial transformation of Zimbabwean society and economy. The traditional culture was patriarchal, conformed to a patrilineal system of inheritance, and limited women's entitlements. Under colonial rule, some of these sexist traditions were reinforced and other, more protective, customs were undermined: for example, colonial law reduced women to perpetual minority status, reinforcing patriarchy, and European expropriation meant that women were no longer awarded land in their own right, undermining women's entitlements. Tax obligations forced men to leave home and seek wages, creating a cycle of male labor migration, which in turn fostered new patterns of sexual relations and left wives dependent on absent husbands. Like Sanders and Sambo, Bassett and Mhloyi see women's powerlessness as related to prostitution and thus to the spread of AIDS.

Migration to search for work is not the only cause of population move-ments around the continent. Armies have been fighting in Angola, Chad, Liberia, Rwanda, Sierra Leone, Somalia, Sudan, and the Western Sahara, displacing and breaking up families. Political violence has health consequences for civilians as well as soldiers, and women and children are the majority of civilians. War, civil unrest, assassination, rape, and torture cause death, disability, and psychological stress [26]. These are high-risk settings for the sexual transmission of disease, settings in which individual behavioral choices are nil or controlled. The spread of

HIV may be linked to political violence through rape, prostitution, and the contamination of blood samples: the link is the soldiers themselves, many of whom test positive for HIV [27]. Indirectly, violence also takes a toll in the destruction of health services and decreased food production and distribution, which may result in malnutrition and increased susceptibility to disease [26].

The political economy changed in the 1980s because so many African countries accepted the austerity measures prescribed by the World Bank, which required reduced public expenditures in the health sector. Even where public spending was already low, real disbursements per person dropped. In Madagascar, expenditures fell 24 percent in the period 1977 to 1985; they fell 14 percent in Central African Republic between 1982 and 1991, and by 13 percent in Zaire between 1980 and 1987 [28, p. 34]. In Senegal, a reduction in the proportion of expenditure on health in the state budget led to shortages of supplies in hospitals and public health centers, the introduction of payment for consultations and medical care even for the destitute, and a freeze on the recruitment of doctors [29, pp. 131-132]. In Zambia, the real value of the budget for pharmaceuticals in 1986 was one-fourth of that in 1983 [30, p. 34]. Some third world governments virtually abandoned their historic role in the health sector, and many African governments retreated from their commitment to free health care [30, p. 38]. Most countries accepted various forms of international aid to help balance state health budgets. These external sources of funds amounted to more than 50 percent in Mozambique [30, p. 38] and to 80 to 90 percent of total health sector investments in other countries [28, p. 35].

One result of these cutbacks is the noticeable deterioration of services [31]. According to Jespersen, a "disproportionate decline in non-wage recurrent expenditure (for items such as maintenance, drugs, and other consumables) led to a deterioration in the quality and quantity of health care services that was far greater than would have been expected on the basis of the monetary value of the expenditure cuts" [32, p. 37]. Women were especially affected as measured, for example, by declining numbers of births in public maternities [33, p. 621]. The general decline in health care affects all people with AIDS; anecdotal evidence suggests that many health services do not admit the sick because they feel they can do nothing for them [15, p. 976]. For mothers and their infants, the lack of maternity care is doubly grave as HIV can be transmitted in utero and during childbirth.

PRIVATIZING HEALTH CARE

In 1987, the World Bank noted the general deterioration of financial resources in developing countries, which it attributed to the slowdown in economic activity and, in some areas, to drought. Specifically, the Bank observed that diminished resources were available for government financing of health care, which it attributed to rapid population growth [1, p. 15]. To increase resources, the Bank recommended privatization in the following forms: First, in order to recover costs, governments were to charge users of state health facilities, especially consumers of drugs and curative care, on a fee-for-service basis. The Bank reasoned that by making the "rich" pay for curative care, governments would have more money to spend on community services and public health care for the poor. This reasoning is faulty on a number of grounds. Personal health services are needed by rich and poor alike; if anything, the poor are more often ill and need more services. Further, because free preventive measures or routine screening for the early detection of disease are rarely available to them, poor people tend to present for treatment later in the course of an illness and require more intensive care. The dichotomy between preventive and curative is specious in dealing with diseases such as tuberculosis, which require both treatment to reduce pools of infection and immunization to protect infants and children. In general, the health conditions common in poverty require this combined approach.

Second, to enable users to pay, governments were to promote various third-party insurance schemes, including sickness funds and social security systems. Third, to reduce demand for free public care, governments were to foster private facilities and donors were to invest in upgrading private hospitals and clinics to make them more attractive. Fourth, the Bank advised governments to decentralize planning, budgeting, and purchasing for state health services. It also suggested that governments use market incentives to motivate staff and to allocate resources [1, pp. 3-7].

The Bank's recommendations were universal—that is, they were applied throughout the world, regardless of a country's specific historical, social, political, or economic situation (including variations in the leading causes of death and availability of health services), and without reference to sex, age, and race or ethnic composition of national populations. The Bank made the same recommendations in Africa where, it acknowledges, health resources (especially personnel and skilled facilities) are fewer and levels of poverty higher than elsewhere in the third world. Social services have been worsening since the early 1970s in Uganda in terms of declining physical capacity, reduced professional labor time, misappropriation of supplies, and deterioration in institutional and moral support [34, p. 101]. Despite civil war and reports of 45,000 cases of AIDS, which have increased the need for public services, the IMF and the Bank welcomed dramatic shifts from public to private health facilities on grounds of allocative efficiency and cost effectiveness. But, according to Banugire, "there is no evidence that the widespread breakdown in public social services had promoted greater access to reliable health services, or more effective alternative delivery systems" [34, p. 102]. Instead, all over the country there is evidence of decline in visits to public health centers.

Many privatization schemes are based on economists' assumptions that they can treat the health sector in the same way as urban transport or telecommunications. Market conditions are not the same because problems of imperfect information are more pervasive in the health sector than in others. As a result, private markets are unable to furnish complete coverage against the risks of sickness and disability, or are unable to furnish insurance at affordable prices, excluding the most needy from the insurance market [20, p. 258]. In addition, the unique relationship between physician and patient offers scope for supplier-induced demand. Problems of cost inflation arise through the combination of a strong profit motive and opportunities for providers to determine the level of services supplied, as in the provision of unnecessary care, the overuse of surgery, and the excessive provision of drugs.

The recommendation to privatize health care delivery in Africa is surprising because government allocation generally accounts for less of total spending on health care in Africa than in Europe where the strategy might make sense. In Zimbabwe and South Africa, for example, government outlays account for 52 to 57 percent of health spending, respectively, whereas in Sweden and Norway, the public sector accounts for 90 and 95 percent of health expenditures [2, pp. 210-211].[3] In other words, African households already bear a substantial share of national expenditures on health.

The privatization of health care affects people with AIDS directly by reducing the services available for treatment of the many diseases associated with the syndrome. Two World Bank policy recommendations account for this outcome: first, the Bank advises governments to cut back on public health services, and second, the Bank advises health providers in both public and private sectors to restrict care to those conditions for which low-cost responses of proven efficacy are available [2, p. 59]. Privatization and fee-for-service schemes such as "user charges" also affect AIDS treatment by raising the cost of health care, forcing many families to choose between medicine for an AIDS patient and food for the household [15, p. 973]. Finally, privatization impairs African governments' ability to respond to AIDS as a public health issue by limiting state intervention to the provision of selected services, which seems to design to check population growth rather than control disease.

AIDS CONTROL
AND POPULATION CONTROL

For low-income countries, the Bank recommends that governments provide an essential "clinical" package, which consists of perinatal and delivery care, family planning services, management of the sick child, treatment of tuberculosis, and case management of sexually transmitted diseases. "Clinical" in this context means services provided in a health clinic by nurses and midwives, not physicians.

---

[3] World Bank figures for the public sector include external aid in the government's share of total spending on health, which inflates the real numbers for Africa. For example, in 1991 the Mozambican government's share of public expenditure on health was 5 percent; the donor community financed 95 percent of the budget [35, p. 3].

A close analysis of the provisions in this package suggests that population control is the ulterior motive. Sick children are the main beneficiaries of this package because World Bank economists assume that families will limit the number of births only after child mortality falls; the underlying motive, then, is family size limitation [36, p. 108]. The treatment of tuberculosis is included, again to save child lives, presumably because BCG vaccination of children is not effective without the simultaneous treatment of infectious adults to reduce the pool of contagion. The inclusion of tuberculosis may also be related to fears that AIDS is causing the number of TB cases to rise; many new cases of TB are found to be HIV positive. AIDS prevention also motivates the inclusion of clinics for case management of sexually transmitted diseases; STDs are thought to accelerate the spread of HIV [7]. The term "case management" suggests finding and notifying the sexual contacts of patients, which is the classic public health approach to venereal disease [7]. Presumably the contacts will be tested for HIV, but no provision is made for the treatment of people with AIDS, which is what African women say is their greatest need [15].

The Bank's population analysts do not believe that AIDS will have a major impact on African mortality; despite WHO's gloomy forecasts, the Bank predicts that the AIDS epidemic will not result in negative population growth, even in the next century [37, p. xxxvii]. Indeed, growth in the 1990s is expected to exceed the rate for 1975-90, and the population of Africa will be larger than that of the Americas or Europe in the year 2000. Lowering the crude birth rate is a major objective. With contraceptive prevalence a low 5 percent in most African countries, the Bank's emphasis on family planning services in the essential package is not surprising. But analysis suggests that the reduction of population growth in Africa is the main purpose of this package; the Bank seems to have made family planning the new, reductionist version of primary health care.

The Bank gave as one of its four reasons for lending in health that its presence in the health sector would enable it to pressure governments to control population growth [38, p. 8]. The Bank has always held that rapid population growth slows development. Its calculations are simple: between 1970 and 1982 sub-Saharan GDP grew at 3 percent per year, roughly the same pace as population, "so that there was virtually no improvement in per capita incomes for the region as a whole" [39, p. 1]. Sustainable development in the health field apparently means population control.

IMPLICATIONS FOR AIDS POLICY

Other approaches contextualize AIDS and differ quite markedly from the World Bank's strategy. For example, the Committee on Women, Population and the Environment and the International Women's Health Coalition have issued statements, prepared for the decennial world population conference held in Cairo in

September 1994, which ask for broad reproductive health services that include safe, voluntary contraception and abortion, infertility services, care in pregnancy and birth, and the prevention and treatment of sexually transmitted diseases including HIV and AIDS.

The portrayal of AIDS in Africa as mainly a sexually transmitted disease exposes women to victimization and justifies a health assistance policy limited to health education and condom distribution, combined with HIV testing as a means of monitoring the spread of infection. This vertical approach dominates the foreign aid policy of the U.S. government, which has allocated $400 million to AIDS control through WHO and USAID for the five-year period 1991-1995 [40]. Women are being blamed for the spread of AIDS in Africa, even though clinical hypotheses about the role of prostitution in the transmission of HIV cannot be proved by epidemiological studies of the clients of STD clinics, which are usually offered as evidence [41]. A recent report from Rwanda is typical of the literature: it imputes HIV infection in men to previous heterosexual relationships with "free women" who have multiple partners [42], although the probability of this source could not be estimated from the data available through the study. African women are angry at being stigmatized as prostitutes, blamed for transmitting HIV to men, for having "unprotected" sex, for getting pregnant, and for passing HIV to their infants [16].

One way to shift the focus from women to the social and economic context of the syndrome is to designate AIDS as an environmental disease, much as we understand diarrheal disease to be related to poverty and an unsanitary environment. This designation would call attention to high-risk settings for the transmission of HIV/AIDS such as political violence and the conditions of labor migrants. It would entail a different health policy, one that calls for the modernization of sanitation (the recent rise in cholera attests to this glaring need) and investment in the prevention and treatment of common infections, including malaria, tuberculosis, and sexually transmitted diseases. Treatment of people with AIDS implies financial aid to comprehensive public health systems, not vertical programs or fragmented private services. Recognition that AIDS is an environmental disease would also call for new solutions to malnutrition, which undermines the body's resistance to disease.

Because AIDS is still primarily an urban disease, an environmental approach would entail plans to accommodate rural-urban migration, which has increased under the pressure of austerity measures and structural adjustment programs. African cities are now growing at the rapid rate of 6 percent per year; in twelve countries more than 50 percent of the urban population lives in the country's largest city [39, p. 10]. Urban planning is needed to design housing, water supplies, sanitation, and transportation, as well as health care.

A broad environmental approach would address the underlying determinants of the spread of HIV—for example, the structures of underdevelopment that created the need to migrate in search of work and in the process destroyed the social and familial networks that had protected people from some types of disease experience. For example, social sanctions, which regulated the lives of the young, effectively protected girls from sexually transmitted diseases before marriage. Today women recognize the failure of alternative networks in urban areas to protect young girls, in particular, from the sexual exploitation that is the stigma of AIDS. They do not, however, advocate a return to traditional institutions of patriarchal domination [15, 16].

An environmentally oriented AIDS policy would reexamine certain development strategies that are proving detrimental to health. The tourist industry, sponsored by national governments and encouraged by international agencies as a solution to underdevelopment, has (in some cases, intentionally) promoted prostitution throughout east Asia; the spread of AIDS in several countries is a byproduct of sex tourism [43]. There has been almost no comparable research on the links between tourism, prostitution, and the spread of AIDS in Africa.

CONCLUSIONS

This chapter reviewed the spread of AIDS in the context of the political economy of Africa, which changed dramatically over the 1980s as economic reforms designed by the World Bank and the International Monetary Fund failed to resolve the debt crisis. Economic instability caused more workers to migrate in search of work, disrupting family life and increasing the behaviors associated with the spread of HIV. In several countries, economic instability led to political instability, creating further disruption and dislocation of the population. Reduced access to health, education, and other social services, a consequence of the privatization of public services and part of structural adjustment programs, considerably increased poverty and the hardships of the poor; it created a crisis for AIDS patients and their families.

In recommending the privatization of health services the World Bank fails to examine the interface between public and private sectors or the impact of privatization on the quality of public care and the geographical distribution of services. The Bank continues to promote policies that assume expansion of the private sector is compatible with the public provision of essential clinical services for the poor and does not shrink the public sector by draining limited trained personnel and other resources. It seems that the Bank ignores the lessons of a decade of primary health care experiments which show that reform of the tertiary system of urban teaching and referral hospitals is critical for success in rural areas.

The World Bank's importance in the health sector should not be underestimated; it extends far beyond the Bank's loan program, which totaled $3.4 billion for loans to population, health, and nutrition projects between 1980 and 1993 [44, p. 168]. In contrast, WHO relies increasingly on voluntary funds, which shifts program planning from the secretariat to a handful of donors and weakens the region structure of the organization [45, p. 136]. Voluntary contributions account for almost all of the budget for the WHO Global Programme on AIDS. The World Bank's health policies are now more influential than those of WHO and inform much of the current practice of many other donors [46, p. 141]. World Bank and International Monetary Fund economic reforms have brought about a shift of provision from the state to nongovernmental organizations—directly, by encouraging donor financial support for NGOs, and indirectly, by squeezing state resources and obliging consumers to patronize the private sector [18, p. 16].

The International Monetary Fund and the World Bank should take responsibility for the part austerity measures and structural adjustment programs have played in the spread of HIV in Africa [47]. These "development" strategies have reduced social spending for health, education, and welfare services, have lowered living standards, reduced real wages, increased unemployment, and aggravated malnutrition. Despite abundant evidence of policy failures in Africa [32, 46, 48], the World Bank continues to deny that its policies have had these effects [49].

ACKNOWLEDGMENTS

I wish to acknowledge gratefully a grant from the Rutgers University Research Council, which enabled me to collect the data for this chapter, and a Faculty Academic Study Program award, which gave me the time to write it.

REFERENCES

1. World Bank, *Financing Health Services in Developing Countries: An Agenda for Reform*, The World Bank, Washington, D.C., 1987.
2. World Bank, *World Development Report 1993*, The World Bank, Washington, D.C., 1993.
3. World Health Organization, *The Current Global Situation of the HIV/AIDS Pandemic*, WHO Global Programme on AIDS, Geneva, July 3, 1995.
4. J. Nájera, B. H. Liese, and J. Hammer, Malaria, in *Disease Control Priorities in Developing Countries*, D. T. Jamison et al. (eds.), Oxford University Press for the World Bank, New York, 1993.
5. C. Murray, K. Styblo, and A. Rouillon, Tuberculosis, in *Disease Control Priorities in Developing Countries*, D. T. Jamison et al. (eds.), Oxford University Press for the World Bank, New York, 1993.
6. A. D. Lopez, Causes of Death in Industrial and Developing Countries: Estimates for 1985-1990, in *Disease Control Priorities in Developing Countries*, D. T. Jamison et al. (eds.), Oxford University Press for the World Bank, New York, 1993.
7. M. Over and P. Piot, HIV Infection and Sexually Transmitted Diseases, in *Disease Control Priorities in Developing Countries*, D. T. Jamison et al. (eds.), Oxford University Press for the World Bank, New York, 1993.
8. *New African*, pp. 8-11, December 1993.
9. World Health Organization, *Current and Future Dimensions of the HIV/AIDS Pandemic*, WHO/GPA/SFI/90.2 Rev. 1, WHO, Geneva, 1990.
10. R. M. Packard and P. Epstein, Epidemiologists, Social Scientists, and the Structure of Medical Research on AIDS in Africa, *Social Science and Medicine, 33*:7, pp. 771-794, 1991.

11. J. A. Seeley et al., Socioeconomic Status, Gender, and Risk of HIV-1 Infection in a Rural Community in South West Uganda, *M.A.O.*, *8*:1, pp. 78-89, 1994.
12. United Nations Development Programme, *Human Development Report 1991*, Oxford University Press, New York, 1991.
13. United Nations Development Programme, *Human Development Report 1993*, Oxford University Press, New York, 1993.
14. P. McFadden, Sex, Sexuality and the Problems of AIDS in Africa, in *Gender in Southern Africa: Conceptual and Theoretical Issues*, R. Meena (ed.), SAPES, Harare, 1992.
15. E. M. Ankrah, AIDS and the Social Side of Health, *Social Science and Medicine*, *32*:9, pp. 967-980, 1991.
16. M. T. Bassett and M. Mhloyi, Women and AIDS in Zimbabwe: The Making of an Epidemic, *International Journal of Health Services*, *21*:1, pp. 143-156, 1991.
17. World Bank, *Accelerated Development in Sub-Saharan Africa: An Agenda for Action*, The World Bank, Washington, D.C., 1981.
18. C. Stoneman, The World Bank: Some Lessons for South Africa, *Review of African Political Economy*, *58*, pp. 87-98, 1993.
19. P. Gibbon, Introduction: Economic Reform and Social Change in Africa, in *Social Change and Economic Reform in Africa*, P. Gibbon (ed.), Nordiska Afrikainstitutet, Uppsala, 1993.
20. G. A. Cornia and J. deJong, Policies for the Revitalisation of Human Resources Development, in *Africa's Recovery in the 1990s: From Stagnation and Adjustment to Human Development*, G. A. Cornia, R. van der Hoeven, and T. Mkandawire (eds.), St. Martin's Press, New York, 1992.
21. B. G. Schoepf et al., Gender, Power, and Risk of AIDS in Zaire, in *Women and Health in Africa*, M. Turshen (ed.), Africa World Press, Trenton, pp. 187-203, 1991.
22. D. Sanders and A. Sambo, AIDS in Africa: The Implications of Economic Recession and Structural Adjustment, *Health Policy and Planning*, *6*:2, pp. 157-165, 1991.
23. K. Jochelson, M. Mothibeli, and J.-P. Leger, Human Immunodeficiency Virus and Migrant Labor in South Africa, *International Journal of Health Services*, *21*:1, pp. 157-173, 1991.
24. J. L. Parpart, Sexuality and Power on the Zambian Copperbelt: 1926-1964, in *Patriarchy and Class: African Women in the Home and the Workforce*, S. B. Stichter and J. L. Parpart (eds.), Westview Press, Boulder, pp. 115-138, 1988.
25. L. White, Domestic Labor in a Colonial City: Prostitution in Nairobi, 1900-1952, in *Patriarchy and Class: African Women in the Home and the Workforce*, S. B. Stichter and J. L. Parpart (eds.), Westview Press, Boulder, pp. 139-160, 1988.
26. A. Zwi and A. Ugalde, Towards an Epidemiology of Political Violence in the Third World, *Social Science and Medicine*, *28*:7, pp. 633-642, 1989.
27. M. Baldo and A. J. Cabral, Low Intensity Wars and Social Determination of the HIV Transmission: The Search for a New Paradigm to Guide Research and Control of the HIV-AIDS Pandemic, in *Action on AIDS in Southern Africa: Maputo Conference on Health in Transition in Southern Africa April 1990*, Z. Stein and A. Zwi (eds.), Committee on Health in South Africa, New York, n.d.
28. M.-O. Waty, Etat des lieux sur la crise du financement des services de santé en Afrique: quelles perspectives pour le financement communautaire? in *Argent et Santé: expériences de financement communautaire en Afrique*, Centre International de l'Enfance, Paris, 1993.
29. A. Bathily, Senegal's Structural Adjustment Programme and its Economic and Social Effects: The Political Economy of Regression, in *The IMF, the World Bank, and the*

African Debt: The Social and Political Impact, B. Onimode (ed.), Zed Books, London, 1989.

30. F. Stewart, S. Lall, and S. Wangwe, Alternative Development Strategies: An Overview, in *Alternative Development Strategies in SubSaharan Africa*, F. Stewart, S. Lall, and S. Wangwe (eds.), St. Martin's Press, New York, 1992.

31. Editorial. Structural Adjustment and Health in Africa, *Lancet, 335*, p. 885, 1990.

32. E. Jespersen, External Shocks, Adjustment Policies and Economic and Social Performance, in *Africa's Recovery in the 1990s: From Stagnation and Adjustment to Human Development*, G. A. Cornia, R. van der Hoeven, and T. Mkandawire (eds.), St. Martin's Press, New York, 1992.

33. O. Ogbu and M. Gallagher, Public Expenditures and Health Care in Africa, *Social Science and Medicine, 34*:6, pp. 615-624, 1992.

34. F. R. Banugire, Employment, Incomes, Basic Needs and Structural Adjustment Policy in Uganda, 1980-87, in *The IMF, the World Bank, and the African Debt: The Social and Political Impact*, B. Onimode (ed.), Zed Books, London, 1989.

35. E. Kazilimani, Mozambique—From Destruction to Development: The Health Sector, *WIPHN News, 14*, Winter 1993.

36. World Bank, *World Development Report 1984*, The World Bank, Washington, D.C., 1984.

37. E. Bos, P. W. Stephens, M. T. Vu, and R. A. Bulatao, African Region Population Projections: 1990-91 Edition, *World Bank Working Papers 598*, Washington, D.C., 1991.

38. World Bank, *Health Sector Policy Paper*, The World Bank, Washington, D.C., 1980.

39. World Bank, *Population Growth and Policies in Sub-Saharan Africa*, The World Bank, Washington, D.C., 1986.

40. M. Turshen, Does U.S.A.I.D. Aid People with AIDS in Africa? *Covert Action Information Bulletin, 39*, pp. 31-34, 1991-1992.

41. See the references in P. Piot and M. Laga, Genital Ulcers, Other Sexually Transmitted Diseases, and the Sexual Transmission of HIV, *British Medical Journal, 298*, pp. 623-624, 1989.

42. S. Allen et al., Human Immunodeficiency Virus Infection in Urban Rwanda, *Journal of the American Medical Association, 266*:12, pp. 1657-1663, 1991.

43. M. Maurer, *Tourisme, Prostitution, SIDA*, Editions l'Harmattan, Paris, 1992.

44. World Bank, *The World Bank Annual Report 1993*, The World Bank, Washington, D.C., 1993.

45. G. Walt, *Health Policy: An Introduction to Process and Power*, Zed Press, London, 1994.

46. A. Hoogvelt, D. Phillips, and P. Taylor, The World Bank and Africa: A Case of Mistaken Identity, *Review of African Political Economy, 54*, pp. 92-96, 1992.

47. P. Lurie, P. Hintzen, and R. A. Loew, Socioeconomic Obstacles to HIV Prevention and Treatment in Developing Countries; the Roles of the International Monetary Fund and the World Bank, *AIDS, 9*:6, pp. 539-546, 1995.

48. T. Mkandawire, Crisis and Adjustment in Sub-Saharan Africa, in *The IMF and the South: The Social Impact of Crisis and Adjustment*, D. Ghai (ed.), Zed Books, London, 1991.

49. World Bank, *Adjustment in Africa: Reforms, Results and the Road Ahead*, World Bank, Washington, D.C., 1994.

CHAPTER 9

More Than Money For Your Labor. Migration and the Political Economy of AIDS in Lesotho

Nancy Romero-Daza and David Himmelgreen

The health and well-being of a population are intrinsically related to the wider socioeconomic and political conditions under which its members live. Nowhere is this better illustrated than in communities that are dependent on more powerful ones. Lesotho, a small country in southern Africa, epitomizes such dependency. A variety of geographic, economic, and political factors make this independent kingdom an enclave of its powerful neighbor: South Africa. This chapter explores the way in which the long history of oppression and exploitation by South Africa, and the resulting system of labor migration combine to place Lesotho at a very high risk for the uncontrollable spread of AIDS.

Lesotho, located in the Maluti Mountain Range, is completely surrounded by the Republic of South Africa (Figure 1), and encompasses an area of 11,716 square miles [1, 2]. Decades of conflict and uneasy cooperation with its neighbor relegated Lesotho and its people (the Basotho) to some of the most arid and infertile areas in the region. It is estimated that at present less than 10 percent of the land is suited for agriculture [2-4]. Excessive overgrazing, difficulties in large-scale irrigation, and inadequate agricultural technology further contribute to extensive depletion of the soil [5, 6], and result in an almost nonexistent agricultural base. The impoverished environment, pressing population growth at 2.63 percent [2], and the absence of significant national industries combine to make

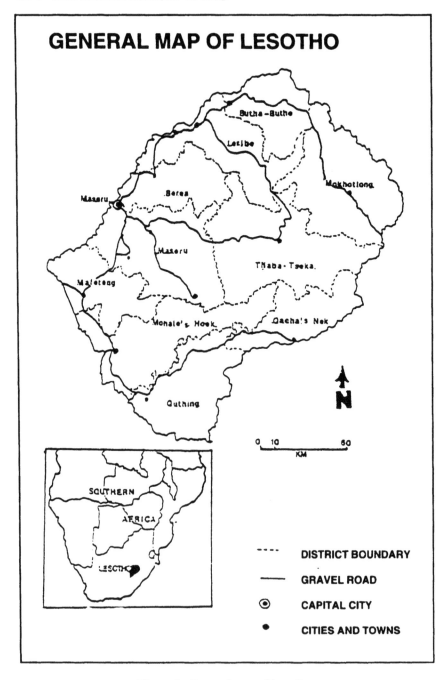

Figure 1. General map of Lesotho.

Lesotho one of the poorest countries in the world [7, 8], with an estimated 57 percent of its population living below the poverty level [9].

Like many other countries in the southern region of Africa, Lesotho has been forced into a system of labor migration controlled by the Republic of South Africa. While this system clearly serves the capitalist interests of South Africa by providing cheap labor for the exploitation of gold and diamond mines, it has been detrimental to the labor reserves, which find themselves at the mercy of their powerful employer. Lesotho derives its main revenue from labor migration [10, 11], in which close to 60 percent of the male workforce is involved [2, 5, 6, 9, 12, 13]. Because of its role as a labor reserve, and its lack of natural resources and industry, Lesotho is heavily dependent on South Africa for its economic survival. Thus, as Gay et al. explain:

> Lesotho cannot be taken as an economic entity, even though it has political independence. It has been an inseparable part of the larger Southern African economy ever since the discovery of gold mines and diamonds . . . Basotho overworked what little soil they still had in the 19th century to feed these [South African mining] industries, and then gave their labor to produce wealth for the South African owners. In return they received little but the privilege to return home to exhausted and infertile fields [3, p. 4].

Although primarily economic in nature, the continuous migration of men in and out of Lesotho has effects that go far beyond the economic sphere and permeate every aspect of Basotho life. The separation of families for extended periods of time places economic and emotional burdens on women, weakens family cohesion, and very often leads to the establishment of extramarital relations on the part of both partners. Further, the isolation of men in single sex hostels may increase their involvement with sex workers and with homosexual partners. In a setting where sexually transmitted diseases (STDs) are rampant, and where health care facilities are insufficient to deal with background infections that may compromise the immune system, all these factors significantly increase the risk of infection with HIV. While this risk applies to the population at large, it is especially severe for the inhabitants of rural areas which contribute most of the manpower for the South African mining companies. This chapter examines such risk in the District of Mokhotlong, one of the poorest and most isolated rural regions of the country.

A BRIEF HISTORY OF LABOR MIGRATION

The system of labor migration on which so many southern African economies depend, is the direct result of and the most effective vehicle for the domination and exploitation of African nationals by the white South African minority. As Magubane explains, the racial inequality on which the system is built finds its roots in the British colonial legacy [14]. Ideologies of white racial superiority combined with the desire for economic expansion were used to justify the social, economic, and political exploitation of Blacks. Through measures such as the appropriation of lands from Black nationals, the forced resettlement into home-lands, the imposition of taxes, and the passing of laws that severely restricted their economic options and forced Blacks to seek employment in the mines [15], the system of institutionalized racism that fuels the mining industry in South Africa was set into motion.

REGULATION OF MIGRANT LABOR

Concomitant with labor migration is the continuous separation of families for long periods of time. This forced separation stems from the establishment of regulations to control the influx of Black Africans into what were deemed white South African areas during the time of white government rule and the apartheid years. The first of such laws, the Black Urban Areas Act established in 1923, stipulated that Blacks could only remain in white areas for purposes of employ-ment [3, 14]. Only Blacks who had worked for the same employer for an uninter-rupted period of ten years were eligible for permanent residency in their areas of work. Since most mining companies limited work contracts to a period of one or two years, this Act effectively prevented most laborers, both South African and foreign, from settling permanently in the proximity of their work areas. The forced movement of miners between their homelands and their places of work is highly advantageous for the mining companies which do not have to provide benefits such as social security, or the right to unionize to their transient workers. In addition, the short-term contracts allow for the constant replenishing of the labor pool with healthy and strong workers to increase productivity, while the sick or injured are forced to return to their homelands. In order to ensure the unlimited availability of inexpensive labor, the native reserves or Bantustans were kept in a state of turmoil and subjugation which resulted in overcrowding, poverty, unemployment, and lack of basic sanitary and health services. Under these cir-cumstances, and faced with increasing taxation by the national government, most males are forced into the exploitative system of migration in which they spend most of their productive years.

Of all African countries, Lesotho is the most dependent on external labor migration [6, 16, 17]. Migrant labor of Basotho into South Africa dates back to the early 1860s with the opening of the first diamond mines in Kimberly, in the Cape Colony [3, 18, 19]. The early years of diamond exploitation were highly beneficial for Lesotho's agriculture, as wheat production and export to South Africa reached their peak. At this point Lesotho was considered the "bread basket" of southern Africa [20]. However, in the 1880s, severe droughts, epidemics, and economic depression took their toll on agricultural production. After a brief recovery, which coincided with the gold mining fever in South Africa, heavy taxes imposed on Basotho grains by the Transvaal and the Orange Free State, and competition from

America and Australia for South African markets brought Lesotho's agricultural prosperity to an end. The worsening economic situation was compounded by the rinderpest outbreak of 1896 that killed 90 percent of the cattle in Lesotho [3, 5, 6, 17, 21]. These unfavorable conditions set the stage for the pattern of massive migration and economic dependency of Lesotho on South Africa.

The establishment of border posts in 1963 between South Africa and Lesotho was the beginning of a tight control over the migration of Lesotho nationals. By virtue of the Black Laws Amendment Act of 1963, labor regulations made it illegal for Basotho (or any other African foreigners) to enter South Africa with the purpose of looking for employment [3]. Rather, a request for entry into the country had to be accompanied by a labor contract issued in Lesotho by The Employment Bureau of Africa (TEBA), a labor recruitment agency that represents South African mining companies. Additional regulations stipulated that after one or two years, a foreign migrant had to return to his home country to reapply for employment through TEBA [5, 11, 22].

Migration of family members was made impossible by laws that prohibited foreign migrants to own or rent living quarters in South Africa, and by specific regulations passed in 1963 that prohibited the employment of foreign women. About 10 percent of the migrant force is made up of women, most of whom are illegally employed, especially as domestic workers [5, 13, 21]. At present it is estimated that the average Basotho migrant spends around 35 percent of his working life away from home, with extreme cases (30% of the workers) spending up to 60 percent of their productive years in the mines [1]. Interviews carried out from 1991 into 1992 with 195 women in the isolated northeastern district of Mokhotlong in Lesotho [23, 24] reveal the negative impact such extended separations have on interpersonal relations. As expressed by one of the women,

> People who are apart are the ones that fight the most. You try really hard to survive by yourself and do the best for your children, but when the man comes back home he doesn't like anything that has been done. He immediately assumes that if anything bad happens it's the wife's responsibility. Sometimes they don't even send money home, but they want everything to be perfect when they come back from the mines.

MIGRANT LABOR AND THE NATIONAL ECONOMY

The contribution of migrant labor to the national economy is reflected by the fact that the total revenue from migrant work is substantially higher than Lesotho's gross domestic product [5, 25, 26]. In order to ensure the flow of migrant revenues into the country, a system of deferred payment was institutionalized in 1975. By law, between 60 and 90 percent of each migrant's salary is paid directly to the Lesotho government and deposited in national bank accounts from which workers receive their payments. In addition, miners can arrange for a portion of their salaries to be sent directly to their families in rural areas. In spite of these regulations, only a small proportion of rural households directly benefit from migrant income, since only about 10 percent of the workers make arrangements for remittances to be sent home [2] and many spend a major part of their wages in their place of employment, thus fueling the South African economy. Moreover, by virtue of its geographic location, South Africa has de facto control over Lesotho's national borders, and exerts political and economic power over its land-locked neighbor. For example, in 1986, in response to political and social unrest in Lesotho, South Africa closed the borders between the two countries. This action, which hastened the overthrow of Prime Minister Jonathan's government by the military, effectively isolated Lesotho from the rest of the world and severely affected the national economy as the flow of goods from and to Lesotho was halted. South Africa serves its economic needs by restricting Lesotho's access to outside markets, and by exporting its products to Lesotho. The flooding of Lesotho markets with South African goods, especially food and clothing, ensures the flow of migrant revenue back into South Africa [27] and undermines efforts to create small industries in the country.

While the mass exodus of labor into South Africa has helped to bolster the standard of living for a segment of society, it also has been detrimental to the internal economy, since many of the most skilled workers have left in search of a better life. Additionally, the recession in South Africa during the late 1980s and early 1990s, which resulted from worldwide sanctions and a depressed gold market, led to the repatriation of thousands of Basotho miners. The lack of employment opportunities in Lesotho has contributed to rising crime, homelessness, and political restlessness.

LABOR MIGRATION AND AIDS

The deleterious effects of labor migration on the general health and well-being of migrant workers are well recognized. The sub-standard conditions into which migrants are forced to live and work in the mines have led to the spread of diseases such as tuberculosis, measles, gonorrhea, and syphilis, and to high morbidity and mortality rates resulting from work-related accidents. In addition, high levels of stress, alcoholism, and mental illness are often found among migrant workers [11, 14, 25, 28-31]. As Doyal states,

> the structure of the labor system created not only the environmental conditions in which disease proliferates but also the ideal mechanisms for its widespread dissemination beyond the immediate labor areas [29, p. 111].

The validity of the above observation is apparent when analyzing the central role played by migrant labor in the spread of AIDS in Africa, where rising rates of infection are identified along the major labor migration routes [32-37]. As Shannon demonstrates, the spread of HIV infection in central Africa coincides with the route of the Trans-African Highway across Kenya, Uganda, Rwanda, northern Zaire, Central African Republic, Cameroon, and Nigeria [38, p. 27].

MULTIPLE SEXUAL PARTNERS

The separation of men from their permanent sexual partners for extended periods of time often leads to their involvement with sex workers in the mining areas, and to the establishment of secondary households either in South Africa or in the regions around the national borders [15, 27, 39, 40]. Participation in sexual relations with multiple partners greatly increases the risk for infection with sexually transmitted diseases, including AIDS for both migrants and their casual partners. However, an equally or even higher risk is posed to populations in rural areas from which most of the manpower comes [40-43]. Upon their return home, migrant laborers expose their spouses and other sexual partners to the infections they may have acquired in their places of work [28], and they, in turn, may spread them to their future partners. As one of our informants explained,

> When they are away, but also when they are [home], men sleep around. They always do that, they even bring diseases to their wives, all those things they get from their girlfriends.

A progression pattern in the transmission of HIV infection and AIDS from the mines to urban centers in the labor reserve countries, and from these to the rural areas has been already identified in Africa [28, 31, 44]. Thus, it is clear that, as Keller states: "in a migrant society AIDS commutes" [45, p. 4a] posing a serious threat to the population at large. A surveillance study carried out in South Africa found that migrant men were 7.3 times more likely to be infected with the HIV virus than were non-migrants [46]. Similarly, members of migrant families who had changed their residence during the previous twelve months were three times as likely to be infected as were permanent settlers in the area.

HOMOSEXUALITY

The housing system of single sex hostels characteristic of labor migration in South Africa also has implications for the spread of HIV infection. Although in many African communities the existence of homosexuality is denied [33, 47, 48], its occurrence cannot be dismissed [49-54]. In fact, homosexual behavior is believed to be common in the segregated compounds in which workers live in the South African mines [14, 22, 25, 55]. Although the extent of this practice is yet to be determined, homosexual activity appears to play an important role in increasing the risk of HIV infection among miners and their heterosexual partners.

INFECTION RATE AMONG MINERS

In 1988 the rate of HIV infection among miners working in South Africa was estimated at .06 percent, comprising about 2000 cases, with an approximate doubling period of eight months [22]. Most of the infections are found among foreigners who make up 40 percent of the total mining force [55]. For example, in 1987 infection rates were estimated at 3.8 percent among miners from Malawi, and at 17.8 percent for those Malawian workers suffering from STDs [56].

The reaction of the South African mining companies to the growing epidemic has been in keeping with existing policies by which sick employees are repatriated to their countries of origin or to their homelands [57]. The South African Department of National Health and Population Development started the repatriation of AIDS sufferers in the late 1980s [56]. In addition, in 1987, amendments made to the Aliens Act of 1937 made it illegal for an employer to hire an HIV positive foreigner [22, p. 36], and regulations were established to allow mining companies to test all prospective workers [56, 57]. Most likely, this will result in discriminatory practices that limit employment opportunities for individuals from countries with high incidence rates. Although the National Union of Mine Workers proclaims that HIV sero-positivity should not be a basis for dismissal of employees [58], in effect the mining companies can practice what Seripe terms "passive repatriation" [57, p. 102] by denying the renewal of work contracts to HIV positive individuals.

There are no recent data on the prevalence of HIV infection among miners from Lesotho. However, a study carried out in 1986 by the South African Chamber of Mines showed a prevalence of HIV infection in the Basotho miner population of .09 percent or about one individual per 1,000 miners [2, 59]. This rate is considerably higher than that of .02 percent among blood donors in 1987. The rate of infection among this latter group rose to .14 percent in 1989, and to 1.46 percent in 1991 [47, p. 5]. It is safe to assume that similar, if not higher, increases might have occurred among the migrant population.

THE IMPACT OF
MIGRANT LABOR ON WOMEN

The constant migration of Basotho men out of the country is reflected in the skewed demographic composition of the population with a 93/100 male to female ratio [2]. With so many men away from their households for most of the year, the responsibility for the survival of the entire family falls almost exclusively on women. Women are in charge of agricultural production, which although minimal, provides some basic support. In addition, since the land is not privately owned, but rather allocated to households by chiefs, agricultural work ensures the right of the family to live on it [6].

Women whose families do not own rights to fields often work other people's fields in exchange for food and a small portion of the produce. Further, in order to complement the negligible income obtained from agriculture, women often engage in intensive manual labor in the construction of roads for which they receive basic food staples. Other income-generating activities include the selling of vegetables, fruit, prepared food, and articles of clothing in the village markets [2, 6]. An even more important source of income for many women in the rural areas is the brewing of sorghum beer (joala), which, when sold to migrant workers visiting from the mines, helps to distribute migrant wages to women in rural areas [2]. At the national level it is estimated that the sale of home-made beer constitutes a major source of income for over 34 percent of rural households [2]. However, while most of these economic activities are demanding in terms of time and labor, they usually do not generate enough income to meet the basic needs of women and their dependents.

The hardship of the economic situation is further accentuated by women's legal status in Basotho society. Regardless of her age, a woman is considered a "perpetual minor" [2, p. 161] under the control of her father, husband, or eldest son. Thus, women are granted little or no decision-making power in financial matters, do not have a right to own property, and have limited access to credit [2, 6]. In addition, although at the national level the educational status of women is higher than that of men at all school levels, job opportunities for women in the formal sector are usually limited to low-level positions [2, p. 158].

SEX AS A SOURCE OF INCOME

Although migrant labor constitutes the major source of revenue for the country at large, only a small proportion of migrant wages directly benefits the rural families left behind. In the Mokhotlong study sample, over 30 percent of the women whose husbands were involved in migrant labor in South Africa, reported not having received any remittances for several years [23, 24]. It is in fact quite common for the wife not to know the whereabouts of her husband, as men often do not return home and fail to maintain any kind of connection with their families. Further, as illustrated by the following comment, the economic situation of the household often deteriorates even more when men return home.

> when my husband comes home from the mines sometimes he brings money but sometimes he doesn't and so there is one more person in the house but there is not enough food for all of us.

Considering the disadvantageous economic and social circumstances under which Basotho women live, it is not surprising to find that in Lesotho, as in other African countries [28, 60, 61] women often involve themselves in sexual relationships with multiple partners, in what Ankrah calls the "prostitution of poverty" [39]. This phenomenon, known in Sesotho (Lesotho's language) as "Bonyatsi," involves the exchange of sex not only for money, but also—and perhaps more frequently—for basic necessities such as food, clothing, and furniture for women and their dependent children. The transfer of these goods from men to women needs not be immediate, and is usually done over a long period of time. More importantly, "Bonyatsi" usually implies long-term relationships which may extend for years or even decades.

Bonyatsi, as defined above, is highly common in Lesotho [2, 50, 62, 63], especially in rural areas where economic opportunities are more scarce. Bonyatsi extramarital relations often involve migrants, and thus "provide one of the routes along which migrants' wage earnings [are] diffused within rural communities in Lesotho" [63, p 147]. As Spiegel notes, men usually get involved with women whose husbands are absent working in South Africa, or have already returned home from the mines and find themselves sick or unemployed [63]. As the following excerpt shows, quite often such relations offer the only source of support for women,

> [Bonyatsi] is something that helps us survive. If you don't have money you go to a man and get some, then you go to another man and get more, and so on, when they come home from the mines they bring money for their girlfriends . . . so you can survive.

THE FUTURE OF "BONYATSI"

As discussed previously, for a variety of social and economic reasons, Bonyatsi relations have become an integral component of the lives of rural women in the district of Mokhotlong. In addition, as 20 percent of the women interviewed stated, the existence of cultural norms such as post-partum sex taboos contributes to the practice of sex with multiple partners. Sex during the post-partum period is believed to result in the contamination of breast milk by semen, which in turn causes "Senyeha," a debilitating and often fatal childhood disease characterized by weight loss, severe diarrhea, lack of appetite, and failure to thrive. Since children are generally breast-fed for two to three years, it is not uncommon for men to establish extramarital relations during this period of time. As one of the respondents stated:

> You are not supposed to sleep with men when you are breast-feeding your child . . . since you can't satisfy your husband, sometimes he goes sleeping around and you can do nothing about it.

While, in general, Bonyatsi relations are not openly condoned, neither do they appear to be assigned the negative connotations of prostitution. More importantly, respondents believe that the practice is very likely to continue indefinitely. In fact, over 83 percent of the women interviewed in our study believe that the practice of Bonyatsi will increase in the near future. The worsening economic situation is by far the number one reason cited for this increase:

In the past [Bonyatsi] wasn't as common because everyone had enough resources to survive, but now food and everything else from the shop is very expensive, people have many problems and they need their boyfriends' money and support.

The growing number of women who have been deserted by their husbands and who, therefore, find themselves living without any economic support, was also mentioned as a major contributing factor for the continuation of Bonyatsi. In addition, the increasing involvement of adolescents who find in these relations a way to provide money for their families is believed to perpetuate this practice.

HEALTH IMPLICATIONS OF BONYATSI

The close relation between the continuous mobilization of men in and out of the rural areas of Mokhotlong and the associated practice of Bonyatsi illustrates the way in which cultural and political economic factors intertwine to place an entire population at great risk of infection with HIV. Faced with very limited economic opportunities in a nation in which agriculture endeavors are not sufficient for basic subsistence, and in which national industries are almost nonexistent, Basotho men are forced into the pool of disenfranchised African Blacks who sell their labor to serve the capitalist interests of the South African mining companies. Laws that prohibit the workers' permanent migration and keep them away from their families for long periods of time, lead to their involvement in sexual relations with prostitutes and other sexual partners. Prevented from legal migration into South Africa, women left behind in Lesotho's rural areas have little option for survival other than providing sex to returning miners from which they receive monetary and material support.

A "ways and means" model can be used to show the interrelationship between culture and political economy in Lesotho [58]. Bonyatsi as a cultural pattern is maintained by the wider population economy because it serves as a means for economic survival. The capitalist and racist policies of the old South Africa have literally drained Lesotho of its power by forcing its most important resource—its people—into the system of migrant labor. The dissolution of family and the lack of economic opportunity within Lesotho will continue to perpetuate Bonyatsi in spite of the clear health risks. Short-term survival, having enough food on the table, surely outweighs the risk of AIDS which to many is amorphous and too far down the road to worry about.

The risk of HIV infection is especially accentuated by the rampant spread of sexually transmitted diseases, especially gonorrhea and syphilis, which constitute the most common outpatient condition for adults in the country as well as in the District of Mokhotlong [47, 48]. The high incidence of STDs, coupled with insufficient and inadequate medical facilities for their treatment, offers a fertile ground for the epidemic. While the actual numbers of diagnosed cases in the country are still low in comparison to other areas in Africa, this should not be taken to suggest low infection rates. Since the lack of technological and financial resources precludes the generalized screening of blood, it is not possible to determine exact rates of infection in the area. Considering the sky-rocketing increase in HIV cases in South Africa [64], with the latest figures showing an increment from 5,000 in 1990 to over 1.8 million as of July 1995 [65], it is very possible that similar patterns could have taken place in Lesotho. In light of the continuous flow of potentially infected men in and out of Lesotho, it is safe to assume that a considerable proportion of the sexually active population in the country may already have been exposed to HIV and may themselves be infected.

STRATEGIES FOR CHANGE

The very existence of Bonyatsi is deeply embedded in the prevailing social and economic conditions in which the population lives. Thus, as several authors have emphasized when describing similar situations in other African settings [37, 61, 66-69], the practice cannot be modified unless the underlying factors that make it necessary are changed.

Economic Alternatives for Women, Cutting Dependence on "Bonyatsi"

Of utmost importance is the provision of viable economic alternatives for women, in order to diminish their dependence on sexual relations with multiple partners [28, 37, 53, 60, 69-71]. At present, ecological and technological restrictions preclude any major improvements in agricultural activities involving the major crops grown in the country (e.g., maize, sorghum). However, an alternative would be the strengthening of already existing programs to increase women's involvement in gardening. Although many households already grow their own vegetables, the continued development of communal gardens for those women who do not own their own needs to be encouraged. If possible, these programs should encourage the growing of products such as fruit and vegetables not only for domestic consumption, but also for sale in local markets.

The Lesotho National Council of Women (LNCW), a nongovernmental organization, has as its main objective the improvement of women's economic potential [2]. In rural areas such as Mokhotlong the activities of this Council need to be further emphasized. The establishment of women's organizations to create and regulate income-generating activities open to women of different economic backgrounds must be given priority. Such activities may include the production of clothing and handicrafts, as well as the raising and sale of small animals such as poultry and rabbits.

In light of the reported increase in the involvement of adolescent girls in "Bonyatsi" relations, programs that target this specific group must be developed.

Special training courses should be included in the high school curriculum to provide students with practical skills that allow them to participate in income-generating activities.

At a more general level, changes are necessary in the regulations that restrict women's access to credit and loans. In addition, regulations that prevent women from taking major decisions unless they secure their husbands' authorization need to be abolished. Such changes would provide women with more autonomy to undertake small businesses, either by themselves or in association with other women.

Finally, considering the extent of women's responsibilities, it must be kept in mind that problems with time allocation often impose a barrier to women's economic activities. Therefore, whenever possible, affordable (or if possible, free) child care services need to be provided to facilitate women's involvement in small industries, which will, in turn, lessen dependency on exchanges of sex for money or goods.

Education Strategies

As Konotey-Ahulu states when discussing AIDS programs in Africa, due to the limited budgets with which most African governments operate, efforts should be diverted from serological studies that try to determine the sero-prevalence of HIV infection among specific (and non-representative) groups, and concentrated on education and culturally appropriate prevention campaigns for the general population [72]. In Lesotho, there is an urgent need to educate the general public on the nature, causes, symptoms, prevention, and consequences of STDs in general, and of AIDS in particular. In order to maximize the probability of success of such efforts, they have to be designed in accordance not only with the economic and political reality of the community, but also with the prevalent cultural and social norms [73]. For example, cultural norms that preclude the discussion of sexual matters between parents and their children in Mokhotlong should be respected. Therefore, in as far as possible, educational efforts geared toward adolescents should involve adults other than parents as disseminators of AIDS information.

Our research in Mokhotlong demonstrates that while women already have some basic knowledge about AIDS, they also have misconceptions about its prevention [23, 24]. Of special interest is the fact that 5 percent of the women interviewed believe family planning methods other than condoms (e.g., IUDs, depoprovera) to be effective in preventing AIDS. As expressed by one of the women:

> To prevent [AIDS] you should go to LPPA [Lesotho Planned Parenthood Association], they will insert a loop inside you and then AIDS won't pass to your blood.

Extensive efforts need to be made to increase existing knowledge, and especially to dissipate misconceptions about the cause and prevention of the disease.

AIDS education can be delivered as part of the existing family planning services provided by the local government hospital. However, such efforts need to be combined with broader strategies that provide information to a wider range of women, especially to those for whom hospital services are not easily accessible. Our research showed that most women acquire knowledge about AIDS from their peers, a fact that can be used as the basis for educational programs. Since economic resources are limited, a possible strategy would be the training of core groups of influential women from different regions of the district who would in turn be responsible for disseminating information about AIDS to other women in their villages. The training activities could be incorporated as part of the scheduled visits of medical personnel to village health posts in distant areas of the district. As De Bruyn reports, similar approaches have been initiated in South Africa and advocated in Zimbabwe in which, based on cultural norms of respect for elders, older women are being trained to serve not only as care providers for HIV-infected patients, but also as counselors and educators [53]. While up to now there are no data available on the effectiveness of such approaches, they appear to be promising both in terms of cost-effectiveness and cultural sensitivity.

Condom Promotion

There is no doubt that the use of condoms as an AIDS preventive measure needs to be promoted. However, in order to be effective, such campaigns must be framed in the general context of gender relations in Africa, where women's lower status and powerlessness vis-à-vis men prevent them from protecting themselves against possible infection. Unlike commercial sex workers who can organize and demand that their clients use prophylactics, women who participate in Bonyatsi behavior do not generally have such power with either their husbands or their lovers [37, 41, 44, 61, 70, 74-76]. It is therefore necessary to specifically target the male population in efforts to increase condom use. Considering the importance African men place on having a large number of children, Ulin [44] suggests that campaigns that promote the use of condoms minimize their contraceptive effect. A special challenge for these campaigns is to overcome attitudes such as the association of condoms with promiscuity and prostitution, which also have been reported in other settings [53, 66, 77] and which, as the following excerpt demonstrates, presents a major barrier for the use of condoms in rural Lesotho,

> If you want to be in good terms with your boyfriend or husband, you should never even mention condoms. They don't like that, even if you just try to talk about condoms with men they immediately think you are a prostitute.

One possible strategy to increase the acceptance of condoms by both men and women would be to emphasize their role as a protection against "senyeha," which, as described above, can be lethal for breast-feeding children. In a society that places high value on children this emphasis on the use of condoms to protect their health may very well translate into higher rates of condom use among rural women who are breast-feeding. The stress given to this positive aspect of condoms, may in turn contribute to counter the negative associations of condoms with prostitution and promiscuity.

Considering the active participation of men in migrant labor, AIDS educational campaigns should be established in collaboration with the South African mining companies. Miners already receive AIDS information, condoms, and health services in their places of work [55]. However, the mining industry and its major recruiting agent, TEBA, should undertake special AIDS campaigns for prospective workers in their country of origin. Such an approach would be beneficial to workers as well as to the mining companies in their efforts to curtail the spread of AIDS among their workforce.

CHANGING THE SYSTEM OF LABOR MIGRATION TO CONTROL AIDS

In order to better control the spread of HIV infection and AIDS in Africa, it is necessary to implement changes in the system of migrant labor on which so many national economies depend. Of utmost importance is the improvement of the social and economic conditions that facilitate the spread of the disease. Central to such improvement is the adoption of measures that allow for the settlement of families in the proximity of work areas [22, 46, 78]. With the abolition of pass laws and other recent developments in post-apartheid South Africa, the provision of family housing, and the concomitant reduction in the number of single-sex hostels may become common in the near future [22, 27]. The preservation of families may, in turn result in a reduction in commercial sex, and thus, in a decrease in the spread of sexually transmitted diseases [22, 74]. However, significant improvements in public sanitation, health care services, and schooling for newly relocated families, and especially in economic alternatives for women must accompany such changes.

Changes in housing conditions also are necessary to improve the general health (both physical and mental) of foreign migrants to whom family housing would not apply. Health care programs and education campaigns must be specifically designed to address the needs of foreign migrant workers whose separation from wives and stable partners will, in all likelihood, continue to promote the establishment of relations with sex workers and casual partners. Special emphasis should be given to the problem posed by the high prevalence of sexually transmitted diseases. Preventive and curative services for both sex workers and their clients, and an adequate provision of condoms are two especially important measures that need to be emphasized in order to attempt to control the spread of AIDS among these sectors of the population [55, 78].

CONCLUSION

In this chapter we suggest that the spread of AIDS from South Africa into Lesotho is directly tied to the political economy of the region, where a long history of mass labor migration and subjugation places Lesotho in a perpetual state of economic dependency. Although this dependency has improved the standard of living of individual Basotho miners, it has not been overly beneficial to the national economy. Today Lesotho's agricultural base is rapidly eroding, there is little industrial infrastructure, and economic aid from Western governments and NGOs is shrinking.

Lesotho's future looks even more grim as the AIDS epidemic belt extends its grip into southern Africa. Labor migration, coupled with highly restrictive and racist immigration regulations of the past, resulted in the forced separation of families and the promotion of practices such as Bonyatsi. These in turn have provided a highly viable route for the back-and-forth transmission of HIV between the two countries. The spread of AIDS in Lesotho has an impact not only in the major urban areas but also in the hinterlands where many young men have been recruited to work in South African mines.

Even though at present South Africa is facing a monumental challenge in dealing with its own epidemic [64], it has the responsibility of helping Lesotho and other economic enclaves from which it has derived so much economic benefit. However, Lesotho also bears a responsibility and should play a critical role in making sure that HIV/AIDS prevention efforts are effective and spread out throughout the country. As in other developing countries, there is inequality in the distribution of resources within Lesotho, with the lion's share going to the capital city of Maseru and other district centers. As a result, economic opportunities and health care resources are insufficient and inadequate for those in the lower stratum of society, especially in isolated rural areas such as Mokhotlong [79]. This situation cannot continue if prevention efforts are to succeed. Finally, in developing effective AIDS prevention efforts, great care must be taken to encourage and foster empowerment of those individuals, families, and communities affected by the epidemic [73]. Without such empowerment and the concomitant change in social inequalities, efforts to stem the rising tide of AIDS in Lesotho will be futile and short-lived.

REFERENCES

1. D. Ambrose, *The Guide to Lesotho*, Johannesburg, Winchester Press, 1976.
2. Ministry of Planning, Economic and Manpower Development, *The Situation of Women and Children in Lesotho*, Government of Lesotho, Maseru, Lesotho, 1991.
3. J. Gay et al., *Poverty in Lesotho: A Mapping Exercise*, Food Management Unit, Government of Lesotho, Maseru, Lesotho, 1990.
4. C. Gautier et al., *Lesotho, A Review of Commerce and Industry*, Rockhaven Press, Maseru, Lesotho, 1989.

5. C. Murray, *Families Divided, the Impact of Migrant Labour in Lesotho,* Cambridge University Press, Cambridge, 1981.
6. J. Gay, *Basotho Women's Options: A Study of Marital Careers in Rural Lesotho,* Ph.D. dissertation, University of Cambridge, 1980.
7. Editorial, *Africa Insight, 15,* pp. 132-135, 1985.
8. S. D. Turner, *Sesotho Farming: The Condition and Prospects of Agriculture in the Lowlands and Foothills of Lesotho,* unpublished Ph.D. thesis, University of London School of Oriental and African Studies, 1978.
9. S. Saenz de Tejada, *Food Consumption and Its Relation to Production, a Survey in Lesotho,* unpublished paper, Maseru, Lesotho, 1989.
10. J. Cobbe, Consequences for Lesotho of Changing South African Labour Demand, *African Affairs, 85,* pp. 23-48, 1986.
11. S. Stitcher, *African Society Today: Migrant Laborers,* Cambridge University Press, Cambridge, 1985.
12. D. Schwager, *Lesotho,* Schwager Publications, Maseru, Lesotho, 1986.
13. J. C. Plath, Labor Migration in Southern Africa and Agricultural Development: Some Lessons from Lesotho, *Journal of Developing Areas, 21,* pp. 159-175, 1987.
14. B. M. Magubane, *The Political Economy of Race and Class in South Africa,* Monthly Review Press, New York and London, 1979.
15. C. De Bee, *The South African Disease. Apartheid Health and Health Services,* Africa World Press, Inc., Trenton, New Jersey, 1984.
16. Bureau of Statistics, *Incomes, Expenditure, and Consumption of Basotho Households. Main Results from the Household Budget Survey 1986/87,* Maseru, Lesotho, 1988.
17. J. Gay, *Women and Development in Lesotho,* Instructional Materials Resource Center, Maseru, Lesotho, 1982.
18. B. Sanson, *Traditional Economic Systems in the Bantu Speaking Peoples of Southern Africa,* D. Hammond-Tooke (ed.), Rutledge & Kegan Paul, London, 1974.
19. High Commission of the Kingdom of Lesotho, *Lesotho Facts and Figures,* Ottawa, Canada, 1985.
20. R. Palmer et al., *The Roots of Rural Poverty in Central and Southern Africa,* Heinemann, London, 1977.
21. O. Gish, Economic Dependency, Health Services, and Health: The Case of Lesotho, *Journal of Health Politics, Policy, and Law, 64,* pp. 762-779, 1982.
22. A. Jooma, *Migrancy After Influx Control,* South African Institute of Race Relations, Braamfontein, South Africa, 1991.
23. N. Romero-Daza, *Migrant Labor, Multiple Sexual Partners, and Sexually Transmitted Diseases in Rural Lesotho,* Ph.D. dissertation, Department of Anthropology, State University of New York at Buffalo, 1993.
24. N. Romero-Daza, Multiple Sexual Partners, Migrant Labor and the Makings for an Epidemic: Knowledge and Beliefs about AIDS among Women in Highland Lesotho, *Human Organization, 53,* pp. 192-211, 1994.
25. F. Wilson, *Migrant Labor in South Africa,* The South African Council of Churches, Johannesburg, 1972.
26. World Health Organization and Ministry of Health, *Health For All Evaluation Report,* World Health Organization, Maseru, Lesotho, 1990.
27. J. Harker et al., *Beyond Apartheid Human Resources for a New South Africa,* The Commonwealth Secretarial, Marlborough House, London, 1991.
28. M. T. Bassett and M. Mhloyi, Women and AIDS in Zimbabwe: The Making of an Epidemic, *International Journal of Health Services, 21,* p. 143, 1991.
29. L. Doyal, *The Political Economy of Health,* South End Press, Boston, Massachusetts, 1981.

30. M. H. Dawson, AIDS in Africa, Historical Roots, in *AIDS in Africa: The Social and Policy Impact*, N. Miller and R. C. Rockwell (eds.), The Edwin Mellen Press, Lewiston, New York, pp. 57-69, 1988.
31. C. Hunt, Migrant Labor and Sexually Transmitted Disease: AIDS in Africa, *Journal of Health and Social Behavior, 30*, pp. 353-373, 1989.
32. T. Conover, Trucking Through the AIDS Belt, *The New Yorker, 69*, pp. 56-60, 1993.
33. D. B. Hrdy, Cultural Practices Contributing to the Transmission of Human Immuno-deficiency Virus in Africa, in *The Heterosexual Transmission of AIDS in Africa*, D. Koch-Weser and H. Vanderschmidt (eds.), Abt Books, Cambridge, Massachusetts, pp. 255-265, 1988.
34. M. Lewis Renaud, "We Are All in It Together": AIDS Prevention in Urban Senegal, *Practicing Anthropology, 15*, pp. 25-29, 1993.
35. C. Obbo, HIV Transmission Through Social and Geographical Networks in Uganda, *Social Science and Medicine, 36*, pp. 949-955, 1993.
36. S. Schear, AIDS in Africa, *Dissent*, pp. 397-398, Summer 1992.
37. B. G. Schoepf, Comment on R. Packard and P. Epstein, *Social Science and Medicine, 33*, pp. 791-793, 1991.
38. G. W. Shannon, AIDS: A Search for Origins, in *AIDS and the Social Sciences, Common Thread*, R. Ulack and W. F. Skinner (eds.), The University of Kentucky Press, Lexington, Kentucky, pp. 8-29, 1991.
39. E. M. Ankrah, AIDS, Methodological Problems in Studying Its Prevention and Spread, *Social Science and Medicine, 29*, pp. 265-276, 1989.
40. R. Packard and P. Epstein, Epidemiologists, Social Scientists, and the Structure of Medical Research on AIDS in Africa, *Social Science and Medicine, 33*, pp. 771-794, 1991.
41. D. A. Feldman, Comment and R. Packard and P. Epstein, Epidemiologists, Social Scientists, and the Structure of Medical Research on AIDS in Africa, *Social Science and Medicine, 33*, pp. 783-785, 1991.
42. C. Haq, Data on AIDS in Africa: An Assessment, in *AIDS in Africa: The Social and Policy Impact*, N. Miller and R. C. Rockwell (eds.), The Edwin Mellen Press, Lewiston, New York, pp. 9-29, 1988.
43. B. Torrey et al., Epidemiology of HIV and AIDS in Africa: Emerging Issues and Social Implications, in *AIDS in Africa: The Social and Policy Impact*, N. Miller and R. C. Rockwell (eds.), The Edwin Mellen Press, Lewiston, New York, pp. 31-54, 1988.
44. P. R. Ulin, African Women and AIDS: Negotiating Behavioral Change, *Social Science and Medicine, 34*, pp. 63-73, 1992.
45. B. Keller, As Isolation of Racism Eases South Africa Confronts AIDS, *New York Times*, pp. 1A and 4A, March 16, 1993.
46. Q. Abdool Karim et al., Sero-Prevalence of HIV Infection in Rural South Africa, *AIDS, 6*, pp. 1535-1539, 1992.
47. S. Lazzari and M. Lekometsa, *Epidemiological Report on HIV/AIDS Status in Lesotho as at 31 December 1991*, Lazzari and Lekometsa, Maseru, Lesotho, 1992.
48. R. J. Biggar, The AIDS Problem in Africa, in *The Heterosexual Transmission of AIDS in Africa*, D. Koch-Weser and H. Vanderschmidt (eds.), Abt Books, Cambridge, Massachusetts, pp. 3-7, 1988.
49. P. J. Imperato, The Epidemiology of the Acquired Immunodeficiency Syndrome in Africa, in *The Heterosexual Transmission of AIDS in Africa*, D. Koch-Weser and H. Vanderschmidt (eds.), Abt Books, Cambridge, Massachusetts, pp. 134-137, 1988.
50. R. Schumacher et al., *Sexually Transmitted Diseases, Family Planning, and Condoms*, Mokhotlong Health Service Area, Mokhotlong, Lesotho, 1990.

51. H. Standing, AIDS, Conceptual and Methodological Issues in Researching Sexual Behavior in Sub-Saharan Africa, *Social Science and Medicine, 345,* pp. 475-483, 1992.
52. T. Quinn et al., AIDS in Africa, an Epidemiological Paradigm, in *The Heterosexual Transmission of AIDS in Africa,* D. Koch-Wesser and H. Vanderschmidt (eds.), Abt Books, Cambridge, Massachusetts, pp. 7-16, 1988.
53. M. De Bruyn, Women and AIDS in Developing Countries, *Social Science and Medicine, 34,* pp. 249-262, 1992.
54. D. Brokensha, Overview: Social Factors in the Transmission and Control of African AIDS, in *AIDS in Africa: The Social and Policy Impact,* N. Miller and R. C. Rockwell (eds.), The Edwin Mellen Press, Lewiston, New York, pp. 167-173, 1988.
55. C. B. Ijsselmuiden et al., Knowledge, Beliefs, and Practices among Black Goldminers Relating to the Transmission of Human Immunodeficiency Virus and Other Sexually Transmitted Diseases, *South African Medical Journal, 78,* pp. 520-523, 1992.
56. A. Zwi et al., HIV and AIDS in South Africa—Towards an Appropriate Public Health Response, in *Action on AIDS in Southern Africa. Maputo Conference on Health in Transition in Southern Africa,* Z. Stein and A. Zwi (eds.), Committee for Health in Southern Africa, New York, pp. 48-61, 1991.
57. B. Seripe, AIDS, Issues and Policies for Workers and Unions, in *Action on AIDS in Southern Africa. Maputo Conference on Health in Transition in Southern Africa,* Z. Stein and A. Zwi (eds.), Committee for Health in Southern Africa, New York, pp. 98-106, 1991.
58. M. Singer, personal communication, 1995.
59. C. T. Moorosi, Update on AIDS and HIV infection in Lesotho, *Lesotho Epidemiological Bulletin, 5,* pp. 53-55, 1990.
60. B. G. Schoepf et al., AIDS and Society in Central Africa: A View from Zaire, in *The Heterosexual Transmission of AIDS in Africa,* D. Koch-Weser and H. Vanderschmidt (eds.), Abt Books, Cambridge, Massachusetts, pp. 265-280, 1988.
61. B. G. Schoepf, Ethical, Methodological, and Political Issues of AIDS Research in Southern Africa, *Social Science and Medicine, 33,* pp. 749-763, 1991.
62. D. Hall and G. Malahlela, *Health and Family Planning Services in Lesotho, the People's Perspective,* Hall and Malahlela, Maseru, Lesotho, 1989.
63. A. D. Spiegel, Polygyny as Myth: Towards Understanding Extramarital Relations in Lesotho, in *Tradition and Transition in Southern Africa,* A. D. Spiegel and P. A. McAllister (eds.), Witwatersrand University Press, Johannesburg, pp. 145-166, 1991.
64. V. Van der Vliet, Apartheid and the Politics of AIDS, in *Global AIDS Policy,* D. Feldman (ed.), Bergin and Garvey, Westport, Connecticut, pp. 107-128, 1994.
65. *The Hartford Courant,* p. A7, Sunday, July 23, 1995.
66. B. G. Schoepf, AIDS, Sex, and Condoms: African Healers and the Reinvention of Tradition in Zaire, *Medical Anthropology, 14,* pp. 225-242, 1992.
67. M. Novicki, Interview: Fighting the AIDS Epidemic, Dr. Peter Lamptey, *Africa Report,* pp. 27-29, July-August 1992.
68. J. W. McGrath et al., Cultural Determinants of Sexual Risk Behavior for AIDS among Baganda Women, *Medical Anthropology Quarterly, 6,* pp. 153-161, 1992.
69. N. Krieger and G. Margo, Women and AIDS: Introduction, *International Journal of Health Services, 21,* pp. 127-129, 1991.
70. South African Medical Journal, Editorial, AIDS in South Africa, Into the Second Decade, *South African Medical Journal, 81,* pp. 55-56, 1992.
71. P. Piot and M. Laga, Current Approaches to Sexually Transmitted Disease Control in Developing Countries, in *Research Issues in Human Behavior and Sexually*

Transmitted Diseases in the AIDS Era, J. N. Wasserheit, S. O. Aral, and K. K. Holmes (eds.), American Society for Microbiology, Washington, D.C., pp. 281-295, 1991.

72. F. Konotey-Ahulu, Clinical Epidemiology, not Seroepidemiology, is the Answer to Africa's AIDS Problem, in *The Heterosexual Transmission of AIDS in Africa,* D. Koch-Weser and H. Vanderschmidt (eds.), Abt Books, Cambridge, Massachusetts, pp. 192-197, 1988.

73. R. Bolton and M. Singer, Introduction: Rethinking HIV Prevention: Critical Assessments of the Content and Delivery of AIDS Risk-Reduction Messages, *Medical Anthropology, 14,* pp. 139-143, 1992.

74. K. K. Holmes and S. O. Aral, Behavioral Interventions in Developing Countries, in *Research Issues in Human Behavior and Sexually Transmitted Diseases in the AIDS Era,* J. N. Wasserheit, S. O. Aral, and K. K. Holmes (eds.), American Society for Microbiology, Washington, D.C., pp. 318-344, 1991.

75. I. F. Newman et al., Epidemiological and Ethnographic Methods for Research in High Risk Behavior: Integrated Approaches to Acceptability and Intervention, in *Research Issues in Human Behavior and Sexually Transmitted Diseases in the AIDS Era,* J. N. Wasserheit, S. O. Aral, and K. K. Holmes (eds.), American Society for Microbiology, Washington, D. C., pp. 258-266, 1991.

76. G. Seidel, The Competing Discourses of HIV/AIDS in Sub-Saharan Africa: Discourses of Right and Empowerment vs Discourses of Control and Exclusion, *Social Science and Medicine, 36,* pp. 175-194, 1993.

77. J. C. Caldwell et al., Under Reaction to AIDS in Sub-Saharan Africa, *Social Science and Medicine, 34,* pp. 1169-1182, 1992.

78. E. Van de Walle, The Social Impact of AIDS in Sub-Saharan Africa, *Milbank Quarterly, 68*(suppl. 1), pp. 10-32, 1992.

79. D. Himmelgreen, *Coping in a Highly Seasonal Environment: A Household Study of Changing Nutritional Status, Health, and Diet among Women and Children from Highland Lesotho,* Ph.D. dissertation, Department of Anthropology, State University of New York at Buffalo, 1993.

CHAPTER 10

Political Economy and Cultural Logics of HIV/AIDS among the Hmong in Northern Thailand

Patricia V. Symonds

INTRODUCTION

Minorities around the world are especially vulnerable to the human immuno-deficiency virus (HIV) because of their cultural, political, and economic subor-dination to dominant cultures. This study focuses on one such group, the Hmong, who live in the northern hills of Thailand. As is typical of ethnic minorities, the Hmong are often uninformed or misinformed about modes of transmission and means of protection against this devastating infection. This is due in part to the fact that there is an inadequate supply of information in languages and forms they readily understand. Moreover, the problems of most minorities do not merely involve language but also are entrenched in their relative powerlessness in politi-cal economy and culture. Poverty, lack of adequate primary health care and medicine, as well as chronic malnutrition are daily battles in the lives of many minority peoples. The situation is especially severe for minority peoples living in Third World nations because their struggle for survival is further aggravated by racism and discrimination embodied in more powerful majority populations' perception of them as the "Other." This frequently means they are treated as second class citizens [1-3]. Because subordinated groups face a considerably different situation than dominant populations, they require a revised set of assumptions about how to combat the spread of the HIV virus. These assumptions must include ethnicity, sexuality, and gender relations and should be more flexible about the ways in which health care education should be phrased and conducted [4].

Any HIV/AIDS prevention strategy will logically tend to gravitate toward an analysis of sexual activity and intravenous drug use, these being the major pathways of HIV transmission. But economic, political, and cultural contexts surrounding sexuality and the reasons behind injection drug use often are not included in research agendas.[1] Programs are often blindly applied to people, irrespective of their utility to that group [4]. Such programming has dire consequences for minorities. Often treated as outsiders—not as "us"—excludes them from feeling as though they are part of a cooperative educational strategy for prevention, treatment, and care. The acquired immunodeficiency syndrome (AIDS) is a global problem which does not ignore "isolated" groups considered to be on the fringe; in fact the disease is a local manifestation of the epidemic confronting the major population. The fringe is not separate from the majority, as the global, national, and micro worlds all interact and coexist. As such, information and treatment of HIV must be global in reach but local in its methods of outreach. As Brooke Schoepf has argued, the adequate research strategy for the social epidemiology of HIV/AIDS is one which includes linkages between macro-level political economy, cultural logics, and social interactions [5].

HIV/AIDS IN THAILAND: CONNECTIONS BETWEEN THE MACRO AND MICRO WORLDS

In the past few years HIV/AIDS has exploded in Asian countries, and by the year 2000 it is predicted that 42 percent of the infected population of the world will be Asians.[2] In Thailand, at the epicenter of this exploding epidemic, the Ministry of Public Health's AIDS Division predicts two to four million HIV-1 infected individuals and 350,000~650,000 AIDS cases by the end of this century [6]. These figures are indeed staggering. Investigative reports and research point to three issues that contribute to the growth of infection among Asian populations: the magnitude of HIV seropositivity, the enormity of the commercial sex industry, and the prevalence of intravenous drug use [7]. Most report on majority lowland ethnic Thai populations as being the most vulnerable. These reports seldom refer to interethnic groups within Thailand or in the neighboring border countries, nor have they adequately examined the sexual cultures of the peoples living at the nation's fringe [8]. This chapter will alleviate to some extent such vast oversights

---

[1] These issues are not only problematic from the viewpoint of research agendas conducted but often funding is not forthcoming for issues which include applied types of research. Also local economic and political usages do not always coincide with government funding intentions.

[2] While this number in statistical form is correct it must be remembered that 50 percent of the world's population lives in Asia.

by focusing on data collected during my many visits to Northern Thailand to conduct fieldwork among people primarily living in "Flower Village" and more recently (1994-95) in sixteen other villages in the north. It is important to consider the historical changes which have occurred over the last decades. Severe political and economic changes have rendered non-Thai upland minorities increasingly dependent on lowland markets for their livelihood. Forced eradication of the poppy crop, leading to crop replacements and loss of traditional modes of trade and land use, have led to cultural changes. In some cases, these changes have included behavioral shifts from opium smoking to injection drug use and brothel visits by minority men.

The area of Thailand with the highest known incidence of HIV seropositivity and AIDS is the North and particularly the provinces of Chiang Mai and Chiang Rai. It is in these two provinces that the largest groups of minority hilltribe populations reside in scattered villages. These ethnic groups, newly involved in valley-oriented economic development, are at high risk for HIV, as they struggle to participate in the cash economy with dependence on the market system and wage labor. These changes also lead to loss of social and cultural controls within villages. In addition to their status within Thailand as a peripheral minority, the Hmong live in the "Golden Triangle" where Laos, Myanmar (Burma), and Thailand meet. Opium cultivation and use in this area are extensive. Many villages are located on the smuggling routes for trafficking in commodities such as gold, weapons, and drugs from refineries on the borders with Myanmar (Burma). Political oppression in neighboring countries also fuels illegal cross-border migration among peoples who share kinship, linguistic, and cultural connections. Young ethnic women from the Shan States of Myanmar (Burma) cross over these border regions into the far north of Thailand in great numbers and many become involved in the Thai commercial sex industry. Some are sold as prostitutes and are kept against their will by force [9]. Others have decided to earn money to make the lives of their parents easier during their old age. Even when given information about the dangers of HIV, these girls, often only in their early teen years, ignore the obvious health consequences and state they will "sacrifice themselves to help their families." These women, along with hilltribe women, are perceived as young, virginal, and sexually exotic. As the HIV epidemic has taken hold in urban areas of the country, they have become considered more desirable as commercial sex workers. Thus it is clear that many complex political and cultural factors are at work which contribute to HIV risk among minority populations in Thailand.

The primary focus of this chapter is one of the six upland minorities in Thailand, the Hmong (Meo, Miao),[3] and their increasing vulnerability to the HIV/AIDS

---

[3] In this chapter I adopt the ethnonym used by the Hmong themselves in Thailand. Hmong are called Meo in Thailand and Miao in China. There are several other tribal minorities in Thailand. The most common of these are the Karen, Lisu, Lahu, Mien (Yao), and the Akha. Along with the Hmong, they form about 1 percent of Thailand's national population of some fifty-five million.

epidemic. I intend to provide a description and analysis of HIV risk among the Hmong by linking history, political economy, and culture [1-3]. In 1993-95 collaborative medical anthropological research was conducted in minority villages in the north of Thailand. The major aim of the research was to discover how Hmong and two other tribal peoples of the Golden Triangle area, the Akha and the Lisu, fit the HIV/AIDS epidemic into their view of the world. The further goal of the project was to foster effective AIDS prevention among these three hill tribes. The research team, which consisted of four anthropologists, each of whom was competent in one of the tribal languages, was joined by two Thai physicians. The interests of the team, then, reflected the view that disease, including HIV/AIDS, is both a biological and sociocultural phenomenon and that prevention must therefore involve not only medical intervention but social—rather than individual— change. As Bolton and Singer point out, while the goal of prevention efforts is to reduce risk-taking by individuals, the processes whereby that goal is accomplished are necessarily social, as they occur within specific cultural contexts [10, p. 2]. Although political and economic factors contribute to a better understanding of the causes underlying tribal minority vulnerability to the deadly HIV virus, from the point of view of prevention, it is also important to consider the cultures of the tribal people themselves.

Field research in 1993-95 expanded upon my earlier investigation of Hmong medical anthropology and gender relations which was conducted in 1987-88 [11]. This research with the anthropological perspective is crucial to understanding the meanings of complex issues as it draws upon prolonged intensive research methods such as participant observation, individual in-depth interviews, and group discussions in local languages. These forms of inquiry afford the outsider a way to enter into the different cultural world and provide insight into issues of gender, power relations, sexuality—and the values and taboos which surround it, as well as conceptions of disease and contagion. By increasing communication and understanding, anthropologists can facilitate local empowerment [12]. An emphasis on the Hmong world view, and their changing perceptions triggered by community, national, and international development, is important because it is in terms of cultural logics that people act upon their situations and evaluate the relative risks they face in their daily lives.

WHO ARE THE HMONG?

The Hmong, Miao/Yao speaking people,[4] are an ethnic minority who began to move out of southwestern China into Laos, Burma, and Vietnam from the

---

[4] Hmong and Mien (Miao/Yao) speak linguistically related languages from this family. Linguistics are not in agreement on the genetic roots of this language family. In Thailand there are two mutually intelligible types of the Miao language spoken, Green and White Hmong.

seventeenth century. Within the last hundred years, migration from those countries flowed into northern Thailand, where some 91,500 Hmong now live [13]. They have settled in the mountainous areas of these countries and have for years practiced swidden agriculture as one of their main forms of livelihood. Among other crops, they cultivate dry rice and the opium poppy. Swidden agriculture was successful in the past, as Hmong had access to sufficient land to allow restoration of soil fertility through fallowing. The swidden system, however, has been undermined by recent changes including population increase and the cultivation of cash crops. Hmong value large families for practical and cosmological reasons; more mouths to feed require more land. This factor, along with the growing tendency for land occupation by large development projects, has meant a lack of primary-forest for cultivation and the introduction of alternative market crops, which have affected the patterns of Hmong livelihood. More recently, many of the Hmong communities have relocated to lowland areas. While some have been forced by the government to relocate, others have joined Christian communities, and some of the youth have moved to the valleys to attend schools or universities. Others, unable to subsist by means of village farming engage in construction work, cook in restaurants, and participate in other economy driven wage labor.

Hmong descent is patrilineal; Hmong clans (xeem) are patrilineal exogamous surname groups which inhabit a wide geographical distribution ranging from China to Southeast Asia. Although clan members cannot trace links genealogically, they presume affiliation through a putative ancestor. Clan affiliation is the major basis of social identity and interaction. This means that a Hmong person can count on members of her/his clan or affinal clan for assistance, especially in times of need or if s/he is away from the home village. Clan membership also defines who one can or cannot marry. Within clans, members share specific customary types of behavior, particularly those concerned with rituals, which maintain and confirm identities.

Although clan membership defines a person's identity, it is within a household that daily interaction takes place. Residence is viri-patrilocal. In other words, most goods, privileges, and mutual obligations are passed from one male to another in the household. Hmong clans and patrilineages are unstratified, however, within the lineage, age and gender define an individual's social position: young pay homage and respect to elders, and women are subservient to men. For example, young men rely on their elders for bride price silver to obtain a wife, and older women command respect and obedience from young daughters-in-law. These specific cultural issues, especially with regard to the position of women in Hmong households and the larger society will be discussed further, as they have shown to have significant impact on the transmission pattern of HIV/AIDS.

Even though the Hmong have carved out a space for themselves in the north of Thailand where they have lived for over a century, they have remained largely on the periphery of the dominant Thai political and economic sectors. Today, economic, political, and social realities—such as integration of the Hmong into the Thai state, development, and global pressures for the cessation of opium poppy cultivation—necessitate changes in patterns of Hmong livelihood. They have also brought changes in their cultural norms. These changes have led some people to heroin use, to consumption of alcohol in other than ritual contexts, and to visit brothels in the valley towns. These practices also have influenced their increased vulnerability to HIV/AIDS as the epidemic has exploded in Thailand.

HMONG AND THE POPPY

In approximately the eighth century A.D., the opium poppy (*papaver som-niferum*) was first introduced into China by Arab traders. At that time, and for centuries thereafter, it was used primarily for medicinal purposes rather than as an abusive drug [14-16]. In the eighteenth century the British East India Company, seeking appropriate goods to exchange with the Chinese for tea, silk, and other desirable imports, began to use opium as a barter currency. This led to abuse of opium on a large scale in China, and despite attempts by the government to forbid importation of the substance, the British, for reasons of trade, and with tremendous violence, were able to force its acceptance. In response, the Chinese legalized the importation, cultivation, and production of the poppy in 1858 and imposed corresponding taxes. Eventually, Chinese poppy cultivation exceeded imports, and around the year 1883, Hmong in China began to cultivate the poppy themselves as their principle cash crop [14, pp. 171-173; 15].

In the highland areas of Southeast Asia to which Hmong migrated, they also cultivated poppy for sale. In British Burma and French Laos, colonial governments imported opium from China and India and discouraged internal growth, thereby contributing to a brisk black market in the hills as cultivation continued [15, 17, 18]. French taxation led to revolts by the Hmong, and opium production again increased [19]. During the Vietnam war, when the Hmong were used by the United States as a "secret army" in Laos, trade in opium continued, and was encouraged and even endorsed by the West [17].

In Thailand, opium was legally imported until 1947 when the Thai government sanctioned its production in the northern highlands [17, p. 233]. Production did not increase notably until the end of the Second World War, and even then, less was produced in Thailand than in other counties of the Golden Triangle. In 1949, the new Communist government attempted to stop opium cultivation and trade in China. Many Hmong crossed the southern borders of China into Laos, Burma, and eventually Thailand to continue poppy cultivation, and, according to Cohen, did so to evade Communist control [20]. The opium poppy crop became the mainstay of the Hmong economy in Thailand and has remained so, even though the Thai government, due to external political pressure, made it illegal in 1958.

GROWING OPIUM

The growing and harvesting of the poppy crop is labor intensive, time consuming, and backbreaking work. Seeds are planted around September in the "sweet" soil located high in the mountainous regions. In November, and again in December, the plants are thinned and weeded. This is extremely difficult and physically arduous work because it requires bending to the ground and digging up the small plants to relocate them in more spacious areas. Although I have seen men participate in these tasks, most of the work is done by women and older children. Another labor intensive period is during the harvesting of the poppy sap. Women rise early and walk to the fields, which are filled with the colorful and beautiful poppy blossoms. As the petals fall and reveal the egg-shaped seed bulbs they begin to incise the poppy heads. Many women work for a whole day in the hot sunshine slicing hundreds of these pods to release the milky poppy sap. They return early the next morning in order to scrape the congealed sap from each of the pods and wrap it in poppy petals. It is then transported back to the village and air dried until it becomes a brown gummy substance. This raw opium can be ingested orally or prepared for smoking. Some of it will be shaped into small bricks and wrapped into banana leaves or pieces of rice paper for storage. From there it is sometimes buried in the earth, or alternatively prepared for sale to the Yunnnanese "Haw," who have long been involved with Hmong in the trade and marketing of opium [14].

While brothers and their wives work together in the cultivation of rice and other crops, the poppy crop can belong to individual families or to individual women. In the research site I observed, old widowed women addicted to the substance worked a whole rai (0.4 acre) of these poppies alone in order to support their addiction and to buy rice and other staple goods. I have seen Hmong employ other tribal people to work in the poppy fields (under careful circumstances so that the poppy sap will not be stolen), and yet I have seldom seen them employ others in the rice fields.

USES AND ABUSES OF OPIUM BY THE HMONG

Opium has never been simply an illegal, addictive, abusive drug for the Hmong in Thailand; it was and continues to be socially and culturally valued in many different contexts. One of the advantages of opium is that it is lightweight and easy to transport. Formerly, and still today, Yunnanese "Haw" traders visit Hmong villages in Thailand in order to obtain the processed poppy sap which they market in the valley. In the past they brought with them material goods which the Hmong needed, such as cooking utensils, salt, cloth, and silk threads and needles. The foodstuffs were used for household cooking chores, but the other more specialized items were used by women to sew and embroider the beautiful, intricately detailed clothing typical of Hmong men and women.[5] Trading opium was also one of the ways women obtained cash of their own to buy things for themselves and for their children. In exchange for these goods, the Hmong used as their "money" opium sap. Needless to say, traders gave much less than they received in this barter trade.

Another important use for the substance was that it was used medicinally by a group of people who had little access to biomedical health care. There were no roads for transportation other than horses, and this usually meant walking for a day or two to reach the valley doctor—if one could pay for it, of course. Health was then, and is now, a matter-of-fact category of knowledge and behavior for Hmong. Like religion and economy, it is embedded in an undifferentiated and complex dynamic lived world. Pain itself is a very important aspect of the Hmong lived life. The Hmong live in communities where sanitation is at a minimum, water is impure due to poor storage, and food is so scarce that there is often not enough to eat. Meat is valued as the main source of protein, but it is usually eaten only at ritual occasions when pigs or chickens are sacrificed. In such cases it is believed that the animals' souls are exchanged for the souls of sick human beings which have fled to the spirit world. Pains caused by intestinal and respiratory problems, menstrual cramps, dental caries, and severe wounds inflicted with sharp farming implements can be "treated" by applying salve made from the poppy sap, or smoking or ingesting the analgesic *yeeb* (opium). For many years it was thought to be the only recourse for relief of stomach ulcers, asthma, rheumatism, and symptoms of malaria, which are all symptoms present in the hill population [21].

The poppy was also used as a vegetable. When the plant was young and growing profusely, mothers occasionally cut some of the small poppy buds and their delicate leaves and cooked them to serve as a special treat with rice. After harvesting, some of the light brown poppy seed was fried and ground into a paste and mixed with sticky rice. The rice cakes were then toasted on the open fire and eaten. Unplanted seeds were also ground into oil for cooking purposes. Poppy sap was also exchanged for silver bars, to be used for brideprice or "*nqe mis nqe hmov*":[6] money for breast milk and food fed to the girl through her early life. These silver bars, paid by the wife-takers to the wife-givers, were not only exchanged for the woman but for her capacity to produce children and ensure the continuation of the patriline. This is considered extremely important by the Hmong, and the significance is reflected in their high birthrates, one of the highest in all of Thailand [22].

---

[5] Formerly, Hmong women grew hemp and wove it into cloth which they dyed with indigo. Most now purchase cloth.

[6] Silver bars come from China and Burma. Sometimes they are made from melted silver coins from India.

Courting games for Hmong take place at the important holiday period of the New Year. Young women dress in finery they have embroidered over the past year. Young men wear clothing embroidered by their sisters and mothers. Of this highly decorated and exquisite clothing, the *sev* or aprons worn by young women over their clothing to cover the front and back of their bodies, is most significant. These finely made aprons signal that a young girl is ready for marriage. That is, she has reached menarche and is fertile. The aprons cover her sexuality and at the same time call attention to it [11]. Young women, who are carefully protected until marriage, stay in their villages and wait for young male travelers from other villages who have arrived to begin the process of looking for an appropriate wife. If he finds a suitable young woman, the male youth will then return to his home village and discuss his choice with his father and other family members. Negotiations regarding bride price and suitability of the union are carried out by male go-betweens who travel to the young woman's village to debate or confirm the match.

In matters of love, opium is well-known as a poison. In the village where I conducted research in 1987-88, a young man and woman decided they would like to marry each other. Upon discussions between families it was concluded that this was not a suitable match. The young man left with his family and returned to his home village. The young woman went to the rice field and committed suicide by ingesting raw opium. A few years earlier in the same research site, a woman with six children had committed suicide in the same fashion. I was told by my inform-ants that ingesting opium for suicidal purposes was quick and easy, and they all knew of women and men in other villages who had killed themselves from the despair of being forbidden to marry or other unhappiness in their lives.

In addition to the uses outlined above, the poppy crop was an important component in the active, dynamic, and competitive prestige economy that was, and to an extent still is, an integral part of Hmong culture. This was manifested in requests for blessing which took the form of feasting. Blessing itself is a request to the ancestors and other spirits for fertility [23]. Fertility of one's fields assures food, rice, and other food crops, and poppy is the most obvious and trustworthy currency of the hills. Fertility of one's animals, fed by the fertility of the fields, assures that one can sacrifice offerings to the spirits in return for fertility of the humans in one's lineage. This all leads to wealth, and by supplying food, rice, and sacrificial animals for one's feasts it surely leads the way to power, repute, prestige, and self-esteem. Wealth assures that one can obtain the most prestigious wife for a son, which in turn is partially dependent on one's daughter being considered a valuable woman, well cared for and trained to be a good, fertile Hmong wife. This continuing flow of blessing(s) calls for exchange and reciprocity between/among individuals, generations, genders, households, and lineages; and these relations are what the dynamics of Hmong social life revolve around and what assures cultural well-being.

Formerly, Hmong social controls were involved in the abuse of opium for pleasurable smoking. Although some people became addicted as a result of illness [24], it was mainly older men and a few older women who consumed the pipe as addiction. When a younger man became addicted to opium, it caused great hardship for his family. His wife and children had to bear the brunt of his lack of energy for work. In Hmong terms, he became *"mob nkeeg,"* or lazy. For older men, however, smoking was a social event and the pipe was often shared with an older visiting relative as a way of showing regard for the individual. On one occasion, upon the death of an elderly opium-addicted man, I saw a plug of opium and his pipe placed in the coffin before it was tied shut. This was described as a gift and sign of respect from his son. Its purpose was purely functional: so that on the long journey from this world to the next, he would be able to smoke it if the need to do so should arise. The vast and various uses of poppy, from economic trading to pure pleasure, underscore the wide range of cultural sanctifications of the poppy in the social sphere of Hmong practices and customs; as such, any new adaptations and uses of the poppy tend to signal the changing nature of social and economic relations in Hmong daily life.

CHANGES IN THE LIVES OF THE HMONG

Although lowlanders and hilltribes in Thailand have always been involved in commercial and political practices, they have experienced different environmental, social, and cultural boundaries. When the Hmong began to move into Thai territory, from 1840-1870 [25, 26], they brought with them a self-sustaining pattern of life. They moved into the far northern forested hills where they could continue this life style, which was much different from the life style typical of Thai peoples from the lowland areas. Among other farming methods, Thais practiced wet rice cultivation in fairly fixed land locations. Hmong have been swidden farmers, practicing slash-and-burn methods to produce dry rice in fields owned by usufruct. They foraged in the jungle for food and medicine, and hunted the wild animals that were then quite plentiful.

Differences in belief mirror and reinforce differences in social relations. Lowlanders are Buddhists; Hmong worship ancestors, spirits, and Gods of the Sky. Although some Hmong have become Buddhists, it has not been a popular change for many. The differences in practices and beliefs are considered unbridgeable. Buddhist cremate their dead. Hmong believe a good life for the living is dependent on burying the dead in a place deemed appropriate by geomancy, where water and mountains meet. This shows respect for one's ancestors who, in turn, will assure future wealth and health for their descendants. Thai Buddhists strive to reach nirvana, an end to the cycle of life when transmigration of souls will terminate and there will be no more reincarnation. Hmong believe in a continuous and never ending cycle of birth and rebirth. Thai rely on hierarchy and patron-client ties for trade and protection; Hmong rely on power and repute among clans, households, and individuals.

Despite their difficult life, Hmong had control over their livelihood and enjoyed cultural autonomy. They were not part of the lowland principalities, nor were they ruled by the courts and political powers of the valley. The Hmong respected the valley people as "other" than themselves and the lowlanders thought of the hill or forest dwellers as "primitive" and "backwards": they considered the forest to be dangerous, the abode of evil spirits [27]. Lowlanders were not aware that the Hmong, too, thought of the forest areas as dangerous and in need of special care in everyday living situations. There were no roads out of the hills and Hmong often spent days walking out to valley markets. The state society of the valley and the non-state Hmong lived autonomous lives, although never totally separate.

During the twentieth century, European and Japanese colonization of surrounding countries influenced the Thai polity. Formation of the Thai nation-state, capitalist penetration, and modernization altered relations between Thais and minority peoples in the direction of political centralization, and the involvement of Hmong in the capitalist economic system. The stated goal of these changes is "national integration" which is supposed to benefit the highland people and to make them good Thai citizens. But, as McKinnon has shown, there is a difference between stated policy and effective action [28].

The Thai government established the Border Patrol Police (BPP) in 1953 to maintain security in remote mountainous border regions. The BPP was also involved in setting up the first schools in hilltribe villages to teach the Thai language to young people. In 1959, the National Hill Tribes Welfare Committee was established by the Thai government to assist Hmong and other hill tribes to change their agricultural life styles from slash-and-burn to sedentary cultivation, to promote crop substitution and eliminate opium poppy cultivation [16, 19]. In 1971, a joint program in the hills, co-sponsored by the United Nations and the Thai government, was established as the United Nations Programme for Drug Abuse Control in Thailand (UNPDAC). While this program has been responsible for educational programs, road building, and health care of tribal people, its primary goal has been crop replacement—that is, the eradication of the poppy crop [29]. The United States has invested heavily in this kind of program and much of the funding has gone to the Thai military. In 1992, the United States supplied US$1,870,000 to Thai narcotics law enforcement and US$1,100,000 to narcotic crops control [30]. What began as a border security program has expanded to drug eradication and rehabilitation programs.

The Hmong are one example of those who have been stereotyped as subversive and a threat to the political and ecological welfare of the nation. The former is mainly because of their involvement on both sides of the conflict in Laos during the "secret war." Some Hmong took the side of the Communist Party in Laos and some few hundred joined the Communist Party of Thailand. During the late 1960s and early 1970s, the Thai army led an anti-Communist campaign in the hills. This became known as the "Red Meo War." Villages were napalmed and many Hmong were moved out of the mountains into valley resettlement areas. However, as Hearn has shown, the extent of the Thai army's response to a few tribal insurgents was unnecessary and caused a great deal of pain for many [31]. The real problem was not the few insurgents but rather the Hmong wrath at the attempts made by Thai police to extort taxes for opium [32, 33]. This led to a Hmong revolt which triggered an even greater problem of increased Thai repression.

The Hmong have also been cited as a source of environmental degradation because of their slash-and-burn agriculture, and as the opium growers *par excellence* in the hills [34, 35]. This, along with the perceived security risk discussed above, has led to development projects aimed specifically at the Hmong. These projects, funded and directed mostly by international monies from Australia and the United States, among others, included crop replacement schemes, many of which have failed. In several villages one can see coffee bushes covered with berries which Hmong do not bother to harvest because the market price is not worth the effort. Coffee was seen as a good investment crop by funders when world market demands brought good prices. It began successfully, but changes in the global production of coffee negatively affected the price of local coffee and led to disaster. This is a good example of global connections which affect the livelihood of the Hmong and one which was beyond the control or forecast of the "global developers." I have seen baskets of tomatoes, also introduced as an alternative crop to opium, dumped along the highway as Hmong, as well as other hilltribes, have been unable to sell them in the valley. In the research village, cabbages and leeks are grown successfully and sold in the valley markets to Japanese traders. Nevertheless, it takes many more of these vegetables at the going rate of 7 baht (25 cents) per kilogram to make anywhere near the amount of money one can get from a kilogram of opium, which now fetches between 4-5,000 baht (160-200 U.S. dollars). In addition to being unprofitable, these crops take a great deal from the soil and require fertilizer and pesticides which are health threatening to the people. Moreover, much more land is used with little or no fallow time to improve the soil. Contributing further to land shortage, increasing numbers of northern Thai peasants have moved into the hill areas due to lack of valley land for their own use, thus changing the views of the uplands as only for "primitive hilltribes."

Incentive programs to stop the cultivation of the poppy crop were not completely successful and many Hmong still grew poppy. In the early 1980s the Thai government decided that they must be more forceful in their efforts at eradication. With funding from the United States, the northern area was mapped by satellite photography; local confirmation was provided by aerial photography; and helicopters were used to spot poppy fields and destroy the crops. Pressure to eradicate cultivation has led in the past decade to Hmong and other highlanders' involvement in the cross-border heroin trade as refiners, traders, and users.

As demonstrated by the problems caused by the development-related upheaval described previously, development itself is a moral issue. It must be conducted with ultimate care and attention to the disruption it can bring to the lives of the people it touches, especially with respect to the economic and cultural issues involved. Development projects among the Hmong may have been conducted with good intentions. As is often the case, however, they have had many unwarranted consequences. Hmong livelihood, and their sense of what it is to live a good life, has changed radically due to the enforcement of government policies and development programs. Government policies have reduced Hmong access to land due to their proclaimed interest in "saving the forests." Policies against voluntary movement of Hmong and other hilltribes have led to problems with the traditional methods of balancing local populations and land use and have resulted in the destruction of the traditional subsistence economies.

The Hmong cultural autonomy has been destroyed by the current political and cultural economy in which they live and work. As their farming livelihood dwindles, the Hmong are obliged to look at new ways of living. They are systematically pulled into the national, political-economic, and cultural orbits of the Thai. The highlands are no longer an autonomous cultural domain where the Hmong prestige economy of asking for blessing, feasting and the exchange of wealth leads to repute (*hwm*), the basis of cultural well-being. As Klein Hutheesing has so ably shown in her research on the Lisu tribal minority in Thailand, the decline of repute has led to loss of prestige and self-esteem, and engendered fears that blessings are withheld [36]. This social and cosmological loss has psychological ramifications—the center is not holding and things seem as though they are falling apart at the seams: Hmong ability to make sense of their world has changed. Village social structures are also breaking down as desires for material goods increase. The result is that luxury items like pick-up trucks to take produce to market, and motorcycles to visit other villages, change the views of prestige economy and lead to the start of a class structure within villages. Increasing involvement in wage labor and the market economy leads many Hmong men to valley towns where they often visit bars and drink alcohol. In the past, few Hmong drank alcohol outside of the ritual feasting contexts during which homemade rice liquor was consumed. In some cases, alcohol (especially beer or whiskey) has replaced the use of opium as a crucial substance for socializing and entertainment. Misuse of alcohol often leads to HIV risk behavior through visits to brothels and the use of commercial sex workers [37].

Exposure to the valley economy has also led to the introduction of biomedicine, albeit in limited form. This does not mean that Hmong have given up traditional forms of shamanism and herbal medicine, but it does mean that they are aware of and use new medical treatments, such as antibiotics, which are frequently misused. The most popular "modern" form of medicine for many mountain people is injections. As among rural ethnic Thai, treatment is often sought from itinerant "quack injection doctors" [38]. Needles are not sterilized and patients often report to the local health workers with abscesses at the injection site. Re-used needles might also of course transmit HIV, and there is an especially pronounced danger in the common re-use of infected needles in blood transfusions. One of the principal means of transmission, however, appears to be injection drug use.

ADDICTION, INJECTION DRUGS, AND HIV RISK

In the past, "white opium" or heroin was smoked. It was easier to use because it didn't require the lengthy pipe preparation raw opium requires. Cigarette paper was filled and rolled into a smoke and a person could get two "fixes" from each cigarette. It didn't have the sweet, sickly smell opium exuded and could be smoked in relative secrecy. It was also used as a "fumer." A small amount of heroin was placed on a piece of foil, heat was applied from beneath, and a drinking straw was used to breathe in the fumes [39]. This "white opium" was first brought into villages by "Haw" and other traders and given to opium addicts to try. It was also offered to young men, women, and sometimes children—both as medicine and as a pleasurable experience, creating new addictions. In one village, more than twenty boys and girls under ten years old were reported addicted in 1994 [40].[7] Addiction to heroin occurs faster than to raw opium; people are hooked quickly and need it more frequently.

Thai authorities have attempted to reduce heroin addiction in many villages with little or no success. This is partially because individual detoxification has been the most important mode of substance abuse treatment. Drug addiction has been seen as a physical problem requiring a biomedical approach [41].[8] Social and cultural issues are only now starting to be addressed. The problem is much more complex than individual addiction, and the increased vulnerability to HIV that injection of heroin brings to Hmong is becoming more obvious. In one village in Thailand visited during research in 1993-94 on HIV, I was told about a government team which was attempting to rehabilitate drug addicts. On the day the team visited to enroll addicts in a nearby clinic, heroin/opium traders hid in the nearby forest. Fearful that they would lose trade on account of the rehabilitation team, they offered the substances to anyone who would meet them in the forest. Many of the addicts took advantage of their offer. In this village of 1,234 people, 112 people were reported addicted to heroin through injection [40].

The Northern Drug Dependency Centre (DDC) in Chiang Mai in 1992 reported 173 Hmong male addicts treated and thirty females. To date, information is

---

[7] It must be noted that this statistic is taken from a newspaper report and caution must be used with this "soft data."

[8] A new study is being conducted by Khun Chupinit using a community approach to drug rehabilitation.

lacking on the total numbers of HIV positive Hmong addicts, but the DDC reports that of 152 hill tribe heroin addicts both smoking and injecting, ninety-one were HIV positive—and of 4,507 opium addicts both smoking and injecting, there were ninety HIV positives [42]. Many of the addicts who smoked opium and/or heroin now inject heroin; they get a quicker "fix" than they do from smoking. As with the opium pipe, heroin shooting is a social event as well as an individual need. The syringe is passed from one person to another, as is the pipe. This is also because there are not many syringes and needles available. In the village mentioned above, a man died in January 1994 from AIDS. His wife and child had not yet been tested for HIV. In Nan Province, where there are many relocated Hmong villages, a case study by Chupinit demonstrates the growing problems of addiction [41]. At the early stages of development in 1968, there were thirty opium addicts. In 1991, the same Hmong village had ninety-three addicts.

Hilltribe people have been afflicted by Thailand's HIV/AIDS epidemic since it began. A hilltribe infant infected perinatally was among the first twenty-five recorded AIDS deaths in the country. Although there is no systematic testing of the highlanders, in a 1993 survey of four villages in Mae Chan, Chiang Rai Province [43], a sample size of 463 persons (206 males, 257 females) revealed that .0 percent of males and 3.7 percent of females in the ten to eighteen age group tested HIV positive, 1.6 percent of males and 8.6 percent of females in the nineteen to thirty age group tested positive, and 5.8 percent of males and 2.3 percent of females in the thirty-one to forty-five age group were HIV seropositive.[9] These results indicate that seropositivity is already high in at least some hilltribe villages. Moreover, they reveal that young women are at greatest risk of infection and that young people, among whom seropositivity is still low, must be targeted if they are to avoid infection.

The combination of sexual activity and increasing levels of injected drug use, as discussed above, places hilltribe people in double jeopardy, especially as HIV seroprevalence increases. As the above rates continue to grow, there are no specific "groups at risk" to single out in hilltribe society. As Watney states, "With HIV it cannot be sufficiently emphasized that risk comes from what you do, not how you label yourself. There is no intrinsic relation between HIV and any individual or population group" [44]. Yet women are in an especially precarious position; as previous research has shown, many remain unaware of the facts about HIV and are therefore powerless in the face of the epidemic [5, 7]. Part of what makes them susceptible is their ignorance about how HIV is spread. In order to

[9] This particular study was conducted on two Akha and two Lahu villages—not Hmong. I use it merely as an example of the current state in some mountain villages. No antibody testing of the Hmong alone has been reported. During July and August 1994, saliva testing was conducted by a U.S. public health institute in four selected villages of each of the major tribal groups. Two of these villages have development projects and are close to roads leading to the valley. Two of the villages are more remote. Results of these tests are not yet available.

explicate the position of Hmong women and their special vulnerability to the HIV virus, an understanding of the social structure and cosmological beliefs of the Hmong is necessary.

HMONG SOCIAL STRUCTURE, HIV, AND WOMEN

The Hmong are organized into patrilineal exogamous clans. Marriage is not an individual act but reflects the strengthening of inter-clan ties. Upon marriage, silver bars (bride price) are exchanged for a woman and her fertility. The bride price received for a daughter provides the means by which a daughter-in-law, a wife for a son, can be brought into the family. The fertile couple will provide infant bodies, the receptacles into which the souls of dead clan members can be reborn and thus continue the patriline. Young Hmong women, then, are extremely valuable. Their sexuality is carefully controlled (through encouraged abstinence) until marriage, and for this reason one seldom sees unmarried Hmong women engaging in the active trading which is seen now on the streets of Chiang Mai, Chiang Rai, or Bangkok. It is almost always married Hmong women who participate in the sale of goods bought at the borders of Myanmar or Laos; goods for sale are most often handicrafts that Hmong women now sew mostly in order to obtain cash.

The Akha, another hill tribe group living in close proximity to the Hmong, with the same peripheralization problems, have no bride price to serve as a source of cash [8, 11]. In contrast to Hmong practice, young Akha girls are sometimes used in times of political-economic stress as a means of acquiring money: some Akha sell their daughters into the sex trade. We can see here how anthropological investigation can lead us to understand why young Akha girls are among the highest numbers of highlanders in Thailand's enormous illegal commercial sex industry, while the Hmong numbers are relatively low. For example, recent data collected in twenty-nine brothels in Chiang Rai, where some 10,217 Hmong live, revealed that in addition to 166 Thai prostitutes, there were twenty-nine Akha, twenty-one Lahu, two Karen, and two Lisu—all hilltribe women: no Hmong were found [46]. It is interesting to note that the ethnicity of the sex workers' clients was not reported. Hmong social structure, the use of bride price, and cosmo-logical beliefs are cultural protection for young Hmong women, as is the still important training and face-saving issue of raising physically strong and obedient young girls.

Within Hmong society, however, polygyny is practiced and men are expected to have more than one sex partner. This does not mean that all Hmong men have more than one wife, but it does mean that sex for procreation takes place with a wife or wives, while men's sex for adventure and enjoyment can take place outside of marriage. Hmong men, as described above, are becoming more involved with the lowland political economy. They sell goods in town; some work on construction sites; and still other young men go to towns for schooling. In the evenings, some of them visit brothels and in Hmong terms "buy bodies." Because of the Hmong minority status within Thai society, it is a psychological plum for a Hmong man to be able to "buy" a Thai woman. The dangers for HIV transmission are obvious, not only for commercial sex workers but also for Hmong men and their Hmong wives. Traditionally prohibited from extramarital relationships, Hmong women can contract HIV from their husbands, who are culturally permitted to experiment with sexuality for pleasure with other women. In contrast, a Hmong woman's sexuality is strictly and exclusively for the task of procreation. "Sex with a Hmong woman is for making children for the lineage, for the strength of the clan, and so that there are more workers to help with the fields," a young Hmong man stipulated. Charged with this responsibility, women are only recently engaging in protected sex for birth control purposes, and this is usually with Depo-Provera® or, more recently Norplant®, not protective condoms. In effect, the double standard of sexuality that restricts women from prostitution concurrently may expose women to HIV infection through their husbands. Because they are enjoined to marital fidelity, however, women's vulnerability may not be socially acknowledged. Moreover, many of these Hmong women cannot be reached for education in Thai language as they are monolingual in Hmong. But even with education they are powerless to instigate change. Although Hmong women have begun to use birth control, condom use is not the first choice. Both women and men say condoms are uncomfortable.

Because of their reputation as exotic and free sexual beings, many of the young tribal women have been recruited into the commercial sex trade. Many of the villages are visited by "Madames" who offer money to the young girls' parents for their daughters. Sometimes they are hired to work in hotels or in restaurants and end up in closed brothels. Although Hmong women seldom are involved in the sex industry, recruiters have begun to make inroads. In one Hmong village which I visited in Chiang Rai Province, a young Hmong woman committed suicide. She was HIV positive. At seventeen, she was the youngest of eight children in a poor household where both the mother and father were addicted to opium. Most of her siblings were married and only one older brother and she lived in the family home. She worked hard in the rice field nearby in order to support her parents. A man and woman came to the village and offered her and two of her friends money to go to Bangkok to work in a hotel. The recruiters told the parents of these girls that they could make a lot of money and then they could return home. There was a great deal of trouble in the village and the headman—employed by the government— threatened reprisals from the village upon the families of the girls. It was suspected by the headman that the girls would be hired as commercial sex workers. It was considered shameful (*txaj muag*) for all Hmong if young girls were involved. They left, however, and went off to Bangkok. When the three girls discovered that the work was indeed commercial sex, two of them fled and returned home to the village. Mae (a pseudonym) stayed. She sent money home each month for her parents, and her brother purchased a motorcycle which he planned to pay for in installments. In some brothels in Bangkok young prostitutes are now tested periodically for sexually transmitted diseases including HIV. Mae was told she must leave because she tested HIV positive. She returned home to the village but she and her parents had "lost face" in the community. Her brother had to return the motorcycle to the dealer and he, too, felt *txaj muag* (shamefaced) at his material loss. He was mean and cruel to his sister. The aim and responsibility of a Hmong woman is to marry. Unmarried women are looked down upon and not respected. Mae's brother reminded her constantly that no man would want her and that she had disgraced her family. One morning she went to the field and ingested rat poison.[10]

It must be noted that death is viewed differently by Hmong than it is in the West [11]. Souls are believed to be recycled from one body to another. When a man or woman dies there is a long and important ceremony conducted by able elders in the clan. This ritual and the words which accompany it guide the souls (*tus plig*) of the dead from the Land of Light to the Land of Darkness. There, in due time, they will be given a "certificate" which glosses as a "mandate for life" (*ntawv niaj ntawd xyoo*) to return for rebirth. Death is not the end of Hmong—it is in a cultural sense integral to being Hmong. I have been told by Hmong that if there is no cure for AIDS and one will surely die, it is better to do it quickly and be reborn into a new and "clean" body. It remains to be seen as more people test HIV positive if more Hmong will act upon this philosophy and what effects this will have upon the increasingly fragile social fabric.

CONCLUSION

In this chapter I have shown how the political economy of Thailand has changed the lives and affected the cultural logic of one of the hilltribes, the Hmong. I have attempted to show how these changes have made Hmong more vulnerable to HIV infection. To do so, I have described Hmong culture and history as they have been influenced by wider political and economic forces associated with capitalistic development and international politics. In the past Hmong lived their lives on the highest level of the mountain tops, subsisting on their own resources. One of the major factors in their predicament today is the active suppression of their political and cultural autonomy and associated agricultural practices by the Thai state. This and their incorporation in the Thai economic system has led uplanders to seek new ways of making a living, which makes some at high risk of HIV infection. Upland culture is also changing from an emphasis on blessing/repute to progress/ modernity along lowland Thai lines. It is now part of life for most upland men to wish to own a pick-up truck, and for some to visit bars and brothels in lowland

---

[10]Data for this story was provided by informants in the village.

towns and cities. It is also part of the lives of some men to participate in the drug trade because access to other resources is denied.

The critical relationship between societal discrimination and vulnerability to HIV is the central insight gained from over a decade of global work [47]. Anthropologists have shown that the spread of HIV in populations is strongly influenced by identifiable societal risk factors which include the scope, intensity, and nature of discrimination practices within a society [2-5]. Linkages between Thai and Hmong societies are complex and multi-stranded. As I have shown, the Hmong are influenced as a minority within the larger context of the Thai society as well as in a transnational context. They are also influenced by their own cultural factors which place them at particularly high risk of HIV/AIDS infection. Hmong sexuality has a double standard: women are required to be monogamous and childbearing, but men are free to experiment as they please. The conflict between the cultural uses and abuses of the opium poppy and the pressures of the political economy, including the cutting down of poppy fields by Thai authorities under pressure from outside (U.S.) authorities, forces Hmong to seek alternative methods of maintaining their livelihood. These pressures also contribute to the increased vulnerability of the Hmong to HIV/AIDS as they become involved in wage labor, selling alternative crops in the valley economic market and participating in the sexual norms of the valley, which today often means visiting brothels, which increases sexual transmission of the disease. Furthermore, because the Hmong no longer have a steady access to opium, some of them now resort to buying heroin, a dangerous substitute because it is most often taken by injection.

There is still inequality for Hmong in areas which include little access to information, education, and health care. However, it is not enough now to take information and education to these minority people, although this is still an important part of the prevention of transmission of HIV, if education programs are conducted in culturally specific ways. Changes in behavior may not be rapid, but are part of a gradual process which requires a combination of time and effort. Education and prevention are a start but gender equality and participation of highlanders, both men and women, in the political process must begin. In the end, empowerment is the critical issue in the vulnerability to HIV infection. The challenge is great, but increased attention to the culturally and historically specific vulnerability of the Hmong and other minorities in the hills is necessary if the HIV epidemic is to be contained.

ACKNOWLEDGMENTS

I would like to express my gratitude to the American Foundation for AIDS Research (AmFAR No. 001781-13-RG). I would also like to thank the Thai-Australia Northern AIDS Prevention and Care Program (NAPAC) for their insight, care, and continuing funding for the "Hmong Community HIV/AIDS Education Project. Thank you also to Cornelia A. Kammerer, Otome Klein

Hutheesing, and Ralana Maneeprasert for their collaboration on HIV/AIDS research in Thailand, and Mee Moua and May Kao Yang for their summer research assistance. Thanks to Hjorleifur Jonsson for discussions on the chapter and the use of his printer on the borders of the "Golden Triangle." Thanks also to Dr. Vichai Poshyachinda for his insight regarding drug use, for his friendship, and for his great kindness to myself and my Hmong field teams. My appreciation to Robert Carlson and Brooke G. Schoepf for their comments and suggestions and to Nancy Hill and Daniel Odess for their computer expertise.

For funding previous research that informs this chapter I would like to thank the Watson Institute for International Studies at Brown University. I am also grateful to the National Research Council of Thailand for permission to conduct fieldwork in their country and members of the Tribal Research Institute of Chiang Mai for their kind cooperation on my HIV/AIDS research.

Ua tsaug ntau to all Hmong who have assisted me in my previous research and my present HIV/AIDS project.

As always, special thanks to Alan E. Symonds for his patience, love, and support.

REFERENCES

1. P. Farmer and A. Kleinman, AIDS as Human Suffering, *Daedalus, 118*:2, pp. 135-162, 1989.
2. P. Farmer, *AIDS and Accusation: Haiti and the Geography of Blame*, University of California Press, 1992.
3. C. Bateson and R. Gatsby, *Thinking AIDS: The Social Response to the Biological Threat*, Addison-Wesley, Reading, Massachusetts, 1988.
4. B. G. Schoepf, Women, AIDS and Economic Crisis in Zaire, *Canadian Journal of African Studies*, 22:3, pp. 625-644, 1988.
5. B. G. Schoepf, Gender, Development and AIDS: A Political Economy and Culture Framework, in *Women and International Development Annual*, Vol. 3, R. Gallin, A. Ferguson, and G. Harper (eds.), Westview Press, Boulder, Colorado, pp. 53-85, 1993.
6. UN body forecasts huge rise in AIDS, *Bangkok Post*, p. 1, June 26, 1994.
7. M. A. Muecke, The AIDS Prevention Dilemma in Thailand, *Asian and Pacific Population Forum*, 4:4, pp. 1-8, 21-27, 1990.
8. C. A. Kammerer, O. Klein Hutheesing, R. Maneeprasert, and P. V. Symonds, Vulnerability to HIV Infection among Three Hilltribes in Northern Thailand, in *Culture and Sexual Risk: Anthropological Perspectives on AIDS*, H. ten Brummelhuis and G. Herdt (eds.), Gordon and Breach, Philadelphia, pp. 53-75, 1995.
9. H. H. Pyne, *AIDS and Prostitution in Thailand: A Case Study of Burmese Prostitutes in Ranong*, unpublished MA thesis in City Planning, MIT, 1992.
10. R. Bolton and M. Singer, Introduction, in *Rethinking AIDS Prevention: Cultural Approaches*, R. Bolton and M. Singer (eds.), Gordon and Breach, Montreux, p. 3, 1992.
11. P. V. Symonds, *Cosmology and the Cycle of Life: Birth, Death and Gender in a Village in Northern Thailand*, Ph.D. dissertation, Brown University, 1991.

12. B. G. Schoepf, E. Walu, C. Schoepf, and D. Russell, Women and Structural Adjustment in Zaire, in *Structural Adjustment and African Women Farmers*, C. Gladium (ed.), University of Florida Press, Gainesville, pp. 151-168, 1991.
13. Tribal Research Institute, *Tribal Population Summary in Thailand*, Chiang Mai University, Chiang Mai, Thailand, October 1992.
14. T. B. Grandstaff, The Hmong, Opium and the Haw: Speculation on the Origin of Their Association, *Journal of the Siam Society*, 67:2, pp. 70-79, 1979.
15. C. A. Kammerer, *Opium and Tribal People in the Golden Triangle*, paper presented at the American Anthropological Association Annual Meeting, Washington, D.C., 1989.
16. N. Tapp, The Hmong of Thailand: Opium People of the Golden Triangle, in *Indigenous People and Development Series No. 4*, Anti-Slavery Society, Cultural Survival, London and Cambridge, Massachusetts, 1986.
17. N. Tapp, The Hmong—Political Economy of an Illegal Crop, in *Ethnic Histories and Minority Identities*, J. G. Taylor and A. Turton (eds.), Monthly Review Press, New York, pp. 230-240, 1988.
18. A. W. McCoy, *The Politics of Heroin in Southeast Asia*, Harper and Row, New York, 1972.
19. G. Y. Lee, *Ethnicity and the State: Historical Overview of the Hmong in Lao Politics*, paper presented at the International Conference on Thai Studies, Australian National University, Canberra, July 3-6, 1987.
20. P. T. Cohen, Opium and the Karen: A Study of Indebtedness in Northern Thailand, *Journal of Southeast Asian Studies*, XV:1, pp. 150-165, 1984.
21. Dr. Ursula Lowenstein, personal communication, June 1994.
22. P. Kamnuansilp, P. Kunstadter, and N. Auamkul, *Hilltribe Health and Family Planning: Results of a Survey of the Hmong (Meo) and Karen Households in Northern Thailand*, Ministry of Public Health, Bangkok, 1986.
23. A. T. Kirsch, *Feasting and Social Oscillation: Religion and Society in Upland Southeast Asia*, Cornell University Southeast Asia Program Data Papers, 92, Ithaca, 1973.
24. J. Westermeyer, *Poppies, Pipes, and People: Opium and Its Use in Laos*, University of California Press, Berkeley, 1982.
25. J. Mottin, *A History of the Hmong*, Odeon Store Ltd., Bangkok, p. 55, 1980.
26. W. R. Geddes, Opium and the Miao: A Study in Ecological Adjustment, *Oceania*, 41:1, pp. 1-11, 1970.
27. H. Jonsson, Rhetorics and Relations: Tai States, Forests, and Upland Groups, in *State Power and Culture in Thailand: An Historical Perspective*, E. P. Durrenberger (ed.), Yale University South East Asian Studies Monograph 44, New Haven, pp. 166-192, 1996.
28. J. McKinnon, Structural Assimilation and the Consensus: Clearing Grounds on Which to Rearrange Our Thoughts, in *Hilltribes Today: Problems in Change*, J. McKinnon and B. Vienne (eds.), White Lotus-ORSTOM, Bangkok, pp. 303-359, 1989.
29. R. G. Cooper, The Tribal Minorities of Northern Thailand: Problems and Prospects, *Southeast Asian Affairs*, VI, pp. 323-332, 1979.
30. Office of the Narcotics Control Board (ONCB), *The Fifteenth Anniversary (1976-1991) of the ONCB: Third Annual Report 1991*, Amaniu Opium and Narcotics Printing Group, Bangkok, p. 63, November 1992.
31. R. Hearn, *Thai Government Programs in Refugee Relocation and Resettlement in Thailand*, Thailand Books, Auburn, New York, 1974.
32. G. Y. Lee, *Minority Politics in Thailand: A Hmong Perspective*, paper presented at the International Conference on Thai Studies, Canberra, July 3-6, 1987.

33. B. Gua, Opium, Bombs and Trees. The Future of the H'mong Tribesmen in Northern Thailand, *Journal of Contemporary Asia, 1,* pp. 70-80, 1975.
34. P. Kunstadter, Ethnic Group, Category, and Identity: Karen in Northern Thailand, in *Ethnic Adaptation and Identity: The Karen on the Thai Frontier with Burma,* C. F. Keyes (ed.), The Institute for the Study of Human Issues, Philadelphia, pp. 119-163, 1979.
35. C. F. Keyes, Introduction, in *Ethnic Adaptation and Identity: The Karen on the Thai Frontier with Burma,* C. F. Keyes (ed.), Institute for the Study on Human Issues, Philadelphia, pp. 1-23, 1979.
36. O. Klein Hutheesing, *Emerging Sexual Inequality among Lisu of Northern Thailand: The Waning of Dog and Elephant Repute,* Brill, Leiden, 1990.
37. G. Fordham, *Northern Thai Male Culture and the Assessment of HIV Risk,* presented to the IUSSP Working Group on AIDS, Seminar on AIDS Impact and Prevention in the Developing World: The Contribution of Demography and Social Sciences, Annecy, France, December 5-9,1993.
38. C. E. Cunningham, Thai Injection Doctors, *Social Science and Medicine, 4,* pp. 1-24, 1970.
39. Dr. Vichai Poshyachinda, personal communication, July 1994.
40. Heroin Plagues the Hilltribes, *Bangkok Post,* pp. 19, 24, June 26, 1994.
41. C. Kesmanee, *An Overview of the Drug Abuse Situation in the Northern Thai Highlands,* paper prepared for the workshop on Sociocultural Dimensions of HIV/AIDS Control and Care in Thailand, Chiang Mai, January 1994.
42. Dr. Jeroon, *Northern Drug Dependency Treatment Centre Statistical Report,* Chiang Mai, Thailand, 1992 (unpublished).
43. *Improving Hilltribe Village Health Status in Selected Villages of Mae Chan District, Chiang Rai Province, Thailand, Incorporating a Study of HIV/AIDS,* Australian International Development Assistance Bureau/Royal Thai Government Public Welfare Department, May 1993.
44. S. Watney, AIDS, Language, and the Third World, in *Taking Liberties: AIDS and Cultural Politics,* Serpent's Tail, London, p. 185, 1989.
45. C. A. Kammerer and P. V. Symonds, AIDS in Asia: Hill Tribes Endangered at Thailand's Periphery, *Cultural Survival Quarterly, 16*:3, pp. 23-25, 1992.
46. *The Ethnicity of Commercial Sex-Workers in Chiangrai,* Chinaware Province Monthly Report of the Sexually Transmitted Disease Division, January 1992.
47. J. Mann, *Towards a New Health Strategy for AIDS: A Report of the Global AIDS Policy Coalition,* Harvard School of Public Health, Cambridge, Massachusetts, 1993.

Conclusion

AIDS has emerged as a fundamental and enduring feature of the human health scene. While phrases like "stop AIDS" have a useful and important political function in motivating and organizing human resources in fighting the epidemic, the truth is the AIDS epidemic is not being stopped. In fact, AIDS continues to spread to new communities and populations around the world, in some cases at a highly accelerated rate. Why? While lab scientists have learned a great deal about the virus that causes AIDS, more probably than any other known virus, and social scientists and epidemiologists, in turn, have developed a considerable body of knowledge on the interpersonal contexts and behaviors that underlie person-to-person transmission, we still have not been successful in stopping AIDS in any community once it has begun to spread. Why? While AIDS is a global phenomenon, the disease is not spread equally, some populations have suffered far more than others. Why? It is the argument of this book that part of the answer to these questions lies in the failure to pay adequate attention to the political economic conditions and forces that constrain life choices and put individuals or groups at risk for infection, and, once infected, block their access to the health and social services that would enable them to stay healthy longer. While the human immunodeficiency virus is a biological entity that, like all viruses, lives to spread and spreads to live, our ability to interrupt this process and actually stop AIDS is hampered as much if not more so by social conditions of inequality than biological conditions of viral activity. The chapters in this volume have explored many of these social conditions, including ethnic or gender discrimination, insensitive government policies, actions of international development organizations, labor control policies, and related phenomena. What these factors have in common is that they all are directly or indirectly political or economic (or intertwined political-economic) forces designed to serve the interests of dominant groups at the expense of subordinate ones. In other words, we have not stopped AIDS because the conditions that contribute to its spread, like South Africa's labor migration policies or anti-Puerto Rican prejudice, serve the self-centered interests of powerful social groups. To stop AIDS, as Samuel Friedman and his co-workers argue in Chapter 5, we need not only one-on-one AIDS education, personal counseling, sterile needle exchange programs, bleach and condom distribution efforts, media education campaigns, or even vaccine trials, in addition, we also need social movements to challenge the various kinds of social inequality that produce and sustain the AIDS pandemic. The purpose of this volume is to call attention to this need because, like other topics having to do with the spread of AIDS, silence equals death.

Contributors

RICHARD CURTIS, Ph.D., is an Associate Professor of Anthropology at John Jay College of Criminal Justice, and an ethnographer at National Development and Research Institutes, Inc., New York. His major research interest is in the area of street-level drug markets and law enforcement.

DON C. DES JARLAIS, Ph.D., is director of Research for the Chemical Dependency Institute at Beth Israel Medical Center, a Research Fellow with the National Development and Research Institute, and Professor of Epidemiology and Social Medicine at Albert Einstein College of Medicine in New York City. As a leader in the fields of AIDS and intravenous drug use, Dr. Des Jarlais has published extensively on these topics. He serves as a consultant to various institutions, including the Centers for Disease Control, the National Institute on Drug Abuse, the National Academy of Sciences, and the World Health Organizations. He is a former commissioner of the National Commission on Acquired Immune Deficiency Syndrome (AIDS).

SAMUEL R. FRIEDMAN, Ph.D., is a Senior Research Fellow at National Development and Research Institutes, Inc., New York City. His current research projects include: (a) a study of social factors, social networks, and HIV risk among drug injectors; (b) multisite national and international studies of risk behaviors and HIV among drug injectors; (c) study of risk behaviors and parenterally- and sexually-transmitted infections among youth in high-risk neighborhoods; and a study of the networks, behaviors, and lives of women drug injectors who have sex with women. He is experienced in quantitative, qualitative, and historical research, and has authored or co-authored more than 200 scientific publications. His substantive areas of expertise include sociobehavioral science; social epidemiology; racial/ethnic variations in risk behaviors and in HIV/AIDS; risk factors for HIV among drug injectors; social and behavioral aspects of drug use; the study of social movements and of workplace organization and conflict; and research on methods of HIV prevention such as syringe exchange, drug users' organizations, and outreach.

MARJORIE GOLDSTEIN, Ph.D., is a Project Director at National Development and Research Institutes, Inc., New York.

CHARLENE HARRINGTON, Ph.D., R.N., F.A.A.N., is Associate Director of the Institute for Health and Aging and Professor of the Department of Social and Behavioral Sciences in the School of Nursing at the University of California, San Francisco.

DAVID HIMMELGREEN is Associate Director of Research at the Hispanic Health Council and Co-Director of the University of Connecticut Family Nutrition Program Needs Assessment documenting the community nutritional problems of inner-city Latino preschoolers living in Hartford. He received a Ph.D. in biological anthropology with a specialization in nutrition, growth and development from the State University of New York at Buffalo in 1994. He has conducted research on Gestational Diabetes Mellitus in Buffalo, New York, gender differences in nutritional status among children living in Kashmir, India, and maternal-child nutrition in Lesotho. In addition to his research on nutrition, he has participated in research on AIDS in Africa and the evaluation of various HIV/AIDS prevention programs including Project COPE (the Community Outreach Prevention Effort) and the Hartford Needle Exchange Program in Connecticut.

GILBERT ILDEFONSO, A.S., is an Assistant Project Director on the HIV Risk and Transitions from Non-Injecting Heroin Use study at National Development and Research Institutes, Inc. Since 1987 he has worked on a number of projects at NDRI in a variety of positions, including interviewer, recruiter, and database specialist. He has been co-author on several publications dealing with HIV risk among drug injectors and has also translated HIV risk assessment questionnaires for use with Spanish-speaking populations.

BENNY JOSE, Ph.D., is a Project Director at the Institute for AIDS Research National Development and Research Institutes, Inc., New York. He has published papers on risk factors for HIV and on HIV prevention among drug injectors. His dissertation studied racial/ethnic differences in HIV seroprevalence among drug injectors in the context of social and risk network factors. Current projects include studies of social and risk networks among drug injectors, and a study of risk behaviors and parenterally- and sexually-transmitted infections among youth in high-risk neighborhoods.

ANTHONY J. LEMELLE, JR., Ph.D., is Associate Professor of Sociology at the Department of Sociology and Anthropology, Purdue University, West Lafayette, Indiana. He teaches in the areas of race relations, black society and culture, health and aging policies, and cultural studies. Dr. Lemelle's research agenda focuses on theory and policy issues concerning urban black men and black male gender studies, AIDS and AIDS care health policy, and black community studies.

SHIRLEY LINDENBAUM, Professor of Anthropology at the Graduate Center, City University of New York, studied kuru in Papua New Guinea, cholera in Bangladesh, and AIDS in New York City. From 1987 to 1994 she was a member of the National Academy of Sciences Committee on AIDS Research (CBASSE), and has worked with various international agencies concerned with diarrheal disease and AIDS. Her publications include *Kuru Sorcery: Disease and Danger in the New Guinea Highlands* (1979), *The Time of AIDS* (1992) co-edited with Gilbert Herdt, and *Knowledge, Power and Practice: The Anthropology of Medicine and Everyday Life* (1993) co-edited with Margaret Lock. She also contributed segments to the National Academy of Sciences publications *AIDS, Sexual Behavior and Intravenous Drug Use* (1989), *AIDS, The Second Decade* (1990), and *The Social Impact of AIDS* (1993).

ALAN NEAIGUS, Ph.D., is a Principal Investigator at National Development and Research Institutes, Inc., in New York City, where he is conducting a longitudinal study of HIV risk and transitions to injecting among non-injecting heroin users. He is also a Co-Investigator on the Social Factors and HIV Risk project and the Drug Use and HIV Risk among Youth project. He has published papers on the social and risk networks of drug injectors and has conducted research on behavioral and network HIV risk factors among new injectors and on HIV risk reduction among drug injectors as a consequence of outreach interventions.

RUSSELL ROCKWELL, of National Development and Research Institutes, in New York City, has been involved in research among injecting drug users since 1988. He has focused on access to, and utilization of, HIV-related health and social services.

NANCY ROMERO-DAZA, a Colombian national, received her Ph.D. in medical anthropology in 1994 from SUNY, Buffalo. She works as a research scientist and co-coordinator of the AIDS Unit at the Hispanic Health Council in Hartford, Connecticut. She has been involved in various HIV/AIDS prevention projects as well as in program evaluation. Her interests include women's health (especially sex workers), AIDS in development countries and among ethnic minorities, health care decision making, and traditional medicine.

MERRILL SINGER, Ph.D., is the Associate Director and Chief of Research at the Hispanic Health Council and a member of the graduate faculty at the University of Connecticut Health Center. Dr. Singer is a member of the American Anthropological Association Commission on AIDS Research and Education and a Board Member of the Society for Medical Anthropology. He has published extensively in the social science literature on AIDS, drug and alcohol abuse, and ethnic and gender factors in health, and is the co-author or co-editor of *New Approaches in AIDS Prevention: Cultural Approaches* (Gordon and Breach Science Publishers, 1992), *Critical Medical Anthropology* (Baywood Publishing Co., 1995), *Syringe Exchange and the Prevention of AIDS* (Gordon and Breach Science Publishers, in press). *Medical Anthropology and the World System* (Greenwood Publishing Co.), and *African American Religion in the Twentieth Century* (University of Tennessee Press, 1992). Dr. Singer's current research includes a longitudinal study of drug use and AIDS risk in the inner city, an examination of the intersection of substance abuse, violence, and HIV risk in the Puerto Rican community, and an assessment of syringe exchange in AIDs prevention.

ELISA JANINE SOBO, Ph.D. (University of California at San Diego) carried out the work described in this volume while a postdoctoral fellow in medical anthropology at Case Western Reserve University in Cleveland, Ohio. The larger project that the work presented here is a part of is described in full in *Choosing Unsafe Sex: AIDS-Risk Denial among Disadvantaged Women* (University of Pennsylvania Press, 1995). In additional to pursuing HIV/AIDS research, Dr. Sobo is active in the field of Caribbean studies. Her book *One Blood: The Jamaican Body* (State University of New York Press, 1993) concerns traditional Jamaican ethnophysiological and ethnomedical beliefs and practices.

JO L. SOTHERAN, of National Development and Research Institutes, Inc., is a sociologist who has worked in HIV research for over twelve years, and is currently Project Director of a NIDA-funded study of injection practices, especially those known collectively as "indirect sharing," as well as Co-Investigator on another NIDA-funded study of risk factors for HIV. Her research centers on injection practices, syringe sources, and the influence of gender and domestic life on injection drug use.

BRUCE STEPHERSON, M.P.H., received his B.A. in the Social Sciences from Long Island University and his M.P.H. from the Hunter College Community Health Education program. He has been employed as the Director of the Center for AIDS Outreach and Prevention, at National Development and Research Institutes, Inc. in New York City, since 1992. He is a former heroin addict and helped found Bronx-Harlem Needle Exchange in New York City. He served as the first Board President of New York Harm Reduction Educators, Inc. which is the not-for-profit entity under which Bronx-Harlem Needle Exchange operates. He has written papers, made presentations, and advocates for the needs of drug injectors. He serves on the Boards of several community-based organizations that work with HIV-infected substance users, and he serves on several local and state HIV/AIDS advisory committees.

PATRICIA V. SYMONDS is an Adjunct Assistant Professor in the Anthropology Department at Brown University. Her main teaching interests are Medical Anthropology and Peoples and Cultures of Southeast Asia. She has done considerable research with the Hmong in northern Thailand. The most recent research project consisted of the anthropology of HIV/AIDS among the Hmong in Thailand. The result of this research has been an education and prevention program. The Hmong participants have been trained to go to villages in the mountains and teach other Hmong how to avoid the risks of HIV and how to care for people with AIDS. Symonds is now a consultant to the project.

MEREDETH TURSHEN is Associate Professor of Urban Studies and Community Health at Rutgers, the State University of New Jersey. She authored two books, *The Political Ecology of Disease in Tanzania* (1984) and *The Politics of Public Health* (1989), and edited two others, *Women and Health in Africa* (1991) and *Women's Lives and Public Policy: The International Experience* (1993). She serves as Political Co-Chair of the Association of Concerned Africa Scholars and as overseas editor of the *Review of African Political Economy*.

Name Index

Topic Index

For Product Safety Concerns and Information please contact our EU
representative GPSR@taylorandfrancis.com
Taylor & Francis Verlag GmbH, Kaufingerstraße 24, 80331 München, Germany

www.ingramcontent.com/pod-product-compliance
Ingram Content Group UK Ltd.
Pitfield, Milton Keynes, MK11 3LW, UK
UKHW021430080625
459435UK00011B/219